Praise for *A Wall of White*

"A triumph of storytelling, of capt[...]n the midst of a massive natural dis[...]e automatically compared to the wo[...] ...ungci ana jon Krakauer, but in this case the comparison is apt: Woodlief tells a true story that is compelling, dramatic, and haunting."

—*Booklist* (starred review)

"Woodlief does an admirable job of building the tension by recreating the lives of those affected by the avalanche."

—*The Washington Post*

"Weaves the complexities of snow science into a narrative that provides a unique psychological composition of those involved, those who died and those who survived."

—*Tahoe Daily Tribune*

"Woodlief uncovered fine details about how the mountains of Bear Creek Canyon defied expectations and roared."

—*San Francisco Chronicle*

"Whenever you are faced by something that seems impossible to conquer, remember *A Wall of White*. It's a mesmerizing tale of human courage and heroism. Having been buried by an avalanche, I can confirm that this story will be unforgettable to readers—adventurers and couch adventurers alike. Read it, be inspired, and keep on looking ahead!"

—Nando Parrado, bestselling author of *Miracle in the Andes*

"Fiercely compelling and at times heartbreaking, Jennifer Woodlief's *A Wall of White* builds with the power of an oncoming avalanche until the last, and final, redeeming moment. A powerhouse inside-look at mountain rescuers' lives. . . . Required reading for adventure fans."

—Wayne Johnson, author of *White Heat*

This title is also available as an eBook

A WALL OF WHITE

The True Story of Heroism and Survival
in the Face of a Deadly Avalanche

JENNIFER WOODLIEF

ATRIA PAPERBACK

New York   London   Toronto   Sydney

ATRIA PAPERBACK
A Division of Simon & Schuster, Inc.
1230 Avenue of the Americas
New York, New York 10020

First Atria Paperback edition February 2010

ATRIA PAPERBACK and colophon are trademarks of
Simon & Schuster, Inc.

For information about special discounts for bulk purchases,
please contact Simon & Schuster Special Sales at 1-866-506-1949
or business@simonandschuster.com.

The Simon & Schuster Speakers Bureau can bring authors to your live event.
For more information or to book an event contact the Simon & Schuster Speakers
Bureau at 1-866-248-3049 or visit our website at www.simonspeakers.com.

Designed by Nancy Singer

Manufactured in the United States of America

10   9   8   7   6   5   4   3   2

The Library of Congress has cataloged the hardcover edition as follows:

Woodlief, Jennifer.
  A wall of white / Jennifer Woodlief. — 1st Atria Books hardcover ed.
  p. cm
  1. Avalanches—Tahoe, Lake (Calif. and Nev.) Region—History—20th century. I.
Title.

  QC929.A8W655 2009
  979.4'38—dc22   2008033896

ISBN 978-1-4165-4692-4
ISBN 978-1-4165-4694-8 (pbk)
ISBN 978-1-4391-5658-2 (eBook)

To
Tess, Griffin, and Owen,
for adding to the challenge

Photo by Jack Unruh / *National Geographic* Image Collection

A
WALL
OF
WHITE

ONE

It was snowing as hard as it could possibly snow.

–

Larry Heywood, assistant patrol director at Alpine Meadows in 1982

It was around 5 a.m., just before daybreak, when Larry Heywood pulled into the Alpine Meadows parking lot on March 31, 1982. The multi-day snowstorm would finally force the ski area to shut down entirely that day, but open or not, as assistant patrol director at the resort, Larry was one of the few employees who still had to report to work.

The blizzard had hit the Sierra Nevada the previous Saturday evening, and it had been snowing steadily—and hard—for the past four days. With two to three feet of new snow falling daily, by that Wednesday morning the storm had dumped nearly seven and a half feet of new snow on top of an existing 89-inch base.

Most of the roads were impassable because snowplows were unable to keep ahead of the snowfall, and the tourists up for ski vacations were more or less trapped in their rental houses and condos. Larry's big old turquoise Jeep Wagoneer, nicknamed Gus because that's what the random letters in the license plate happened to spell, had made it, barely, from his home on Lake Tahoe's West Shore to Highway 89 and then down the three miles of Alpine Meadows Road that dead-ended at the ski area. Between the road conditions and the fury of the blizzard, Larry had been creeping along at maybe six mph. He spent much of the drive with his door open, craning around it to try to see where the road was and if anyone else was on it.

On his way to work Larry had picked up Thom Orsi, a member of the ski area's trail crew. Thom, who had spied crocus bulbs beginning to bloom in his yard the previous Saturday, trudged down to the street that morning on top of the snowdrifts in his driveway, with his car, unseen, buried somewhere beneath him. As they headed toward the ski resort, the drive was oppressive, almost claustrophobic. Maneuvering his Jeep in a virtual elevator shaft of snow, Larry asked Thom to keep an eye out for avalanche activity on the slopes above them. "You see anything moving," Larry told Thom, "you scream." Thom spent the remainder of the trip—in the dark, in a near whiteout—clearing off his foggy window and gaping up at the snow-drenched mountains.

Two days earlier, Alpine Meadows had closed the upper part of the ski area, and the previous day, it was running only the three lowest chairlifts for the benefit of a dozen or so skiers. The lifts high up on the mountain, leading to the advanced runs, were swaying too much in the shrieking winds to be operated—ironically, skiers who were hard-core enough to ski despite the storm had access to just the shortest, easiest slopes.

On the thirty-first, the intense snowfall—several new inches continued to fall every hour—combined with winds gusting up to 120 mph, made it too risky for the resort to operate at all. The acres of existing snow up on the ridges above the ski area remained poised and still, piling higher and building up ton by ton with new snow. As fresh snow fell, the violence of the southwesterly wind whipped it across and down, cross-loading the mountain and transporting more snow to the lower slopes. On top of that, the freakishness of the fluctuating temperature over the past few days helped add up to one unstable snowpack. The virtually unprecedented mix of these particular elements resulted in the U.S. Forest Service snow ranger station, as well as Alpine Meadows' own avalanche forecaster, issuing a warning that the level of avalanche hazard on March 31 was "extreme."

Covering approximately 2,000 acres, Alpine Meadows is located in Bear Valley on the east side of the Sierra Nevada, along the Sierra Crest ridgeline, five miles north of Lake Tahoe, California. It shares its northern ridge with Squaw Valley, located one valley over. The terrain was originally heavily glaciated, which produced a series of enormous cirques separated by steep ridges. The resort's high floor—almost 7,000 feet above sea level—guarantees an immense amount of snow, and the ski runs range from tame to some of the country's most challenging, nearly all of which showcase a postcard view of shimmering Lake Tahoe.

Alpine Meadows was established on land leased from the Southern Pacific Land Company and the U.S. Forest Service. Soon after it opened, on December 28, 1961, the intensity of the snowfall and the steep terrain in the area caused the Forest Service to label Alpine Meadows as one of the few Class A avalanche areas in the country, the highest possible hazard designation. As a result, the resort developed one of the most proficient, experienced, and intense avalanche forecasting and control programs in the country.

Larry had been at Alpine Meadows working ski patrol on and off for the past dozen years. In 1982 the patrol was made up almost solely of men (a lone woman had signed on just a few seasons prior) and an incredibly macho bunch at that—the type that couldn't wait to get to work in the morning and blow things up. In addition to saving lives, the main function of the Alpine Meadows ski patrol was to control avalanches, which meant throwing bombs and firing artillery into the slopes to set off small avalanches in an effort to prevent big ones. The guys on ski patrol were essentially made up of equal parts firefighter, cop, paramedic, explosives expert, mountain guide, and ski bum. Their reason for living was to make things safe, and although they took this role incredibly seriously, no one ever had more fun at their job.

The orientation alone seemed like it would have driven most

prospective patrollers out of the snow for good, but on the contrary, the challenge only seemed to strengthen their resolve for the work. Larry's initiation to the danger of avalanches during his rookie season was a terrifying, sickening experience, sort of like a hazing prank gone wild. Norm Wilson, the mountain manager at the time, took Larry out to Peril Ridge to become accustomed to the feel of the snow, to learn how sometimes merely adjusting his weight at the wrong place on an unstable slope could set off an avalanche. Norm's plan was to teach Larry not merely about the potential threat of the snowpack, but also the hazards of overconfidence. Larry saw the snow in front of him hump up, and then, like a tablecloth yanked off a set table, he was knocked completely back off his feet. It wasn't a big enough slide to bury him, but it was a huge moment in his life, teaching him more in those few seconds about power and respect than he had ever learned before. The experience did not, however, deter him from wanting to be on ski patrol.

Despite Larry's passion for the work, by age 34 he figured it was just about time for him to move on and start building houses for a living. There were two men above him—Bernie Kingery, the mountain manager, and Bob Blair, the patrol director—who loved their jobs just as much as he did and weren't going anywhere.

Already a few feet of new snow had filled the parking lot since the previous day. There was almost no place to park, not because the lot was full of cars, but because there were massive piles of snow everywhere. One of the spots closest to the resort happened to be shoveled out, and Larry pulled in right next to the ski lodge.

As he and Thom got out of the Jeep, movement near the ground caught Larry's eye. Through the dawning light and swirling snow, he made out an owl—definitely alive, but bouncing along the parking lot, tumbling with the wind and the blizzard. It was a small owl, maybe 8–10 inches tall, with yellow eyes and a white face outlined in brown and white. It had intricate off-white and light brown markings and no ears.

In all the time Larry had spent in the area, he had only seen an owl maybe once or twice before, at dusk, while camping deep in the forest. This particular type of owl, which he later realized was a Saw-whet owl, is secretive, strictly nocturnal, and almost never glimpsed by humans. Bird-watchers consider a sighting of this specific kind of owl to be a once-in-a-lifetime experience.

The mythology of owls throughout the world is connected to a general belief that the bird is an omen of evil, and that forest owls in particular are a portent of death. For many Native Americans (especially the Apaches and the Ojibwa) and the Aboriginal people of Australia, as well as several cultures in Africa, Asia, and South America, the perception of owls involves powerful taboos with deep roots. In West Africa, the pidgin English name for owl is "witchbird." In old Armenian tales, owls were associated with the devil, and in Russian folklore, owls, especially small ones, were believed to be harbingers of deaths and disasters. Even Shakespeare, in *Macbeth,* describes the owl as a messenger of death, calling it "the fatal bellman"—a night watchman who rings a bell at the door of a prisoner scheduled for execution in the morning.

Larry followed the owl that morning, trying to help it, save it, but eventually the storm blew it underneath a parked bus, and he could no longer see it. He gathered up his gear and headed in to work.

TWO

Mountaineers wanted for extremely hazardous
and dangerous mountain work in the winter
environment using explosives.

–

Magazine ad seeking applicants for Alpine Meadows' ski patrol

While in 1982 the neighboring Squaw Valley ski patrol had strict rules about maintaining a clean-cut appearance, including no beards and no hair below shoulder length, the Alpine Meadows crew looked more like a biker gang. With the excuse that facial hair helped to prevent frostbite in their frigid working conditions, most of the two dozen or so members of the patrol wore scruffy beards and ponytails. Well aware of their reputation as rebels, they were not above sneaking into the patrol shack at Squaw Valley and covering the chalkboard with sexually explicit drawings poking fun at the squeaky-cleanness of the rival crew.

There were relatively few rules at Alpine Meadows governing the ski patrol, but one strictly enforced policy held that the members of the patrol could not wear jeans. During that era, powder pants weren't necessarily a viable alternative. In the days before

Gore-Tex and other high-tech waterproof gear were available, the early '80s option, known as 60/40 pants, was made of a nylon blend of heavy pack material that tended to let as much water in as out. Most of the patrolmen flaunted their rebellion against this regulation by dressing in absurd outfits considerably less professional than jeans would have been—Larry Heywood had a penchant for corduroy knickers, and veteran patrolman Casey Jones could usually be found in tight, lime-green stretch pants.

The men on the Alpine Meadows patrol were tough and wild, and they partied at least as hard as they worked. They rigged the old-fashioned soda machine in their office to dispense, for 50 cents, only different types of beer. They blared Grateful Dead music wherever they went, including in the lift lines.

They hooted and hollered in the midst of crippling, no-visibility blizzards, feeling the power, experiencing what they referred to as "the magic." They were caught and swept up in so many avalanches they themselves had set off—an experience they quaintly referred to as "taking a ride"—that they couldn't recall them all. They were a rowdy team of total mavericks, doing whatever they wanted and avoiding their radios as much as possible so they couldn't be found.

Despite—or because of—all that, the men working patrol at Alpine Meadows were also extraordinarily successful at what they did, and primarily what they did was protect people and save lives. Some of it was hard, physical work—hauling injured skiers and lugging hundreds of pounds of rope and bamboo poles used to mark terrain and hazards. Their duties included such mundane tasks as posting and digging out signs, stringing rope lines, and wrapping sprained knees. Occasionally they coordinated lifesaving rescues and evacuated skiers after near fatal accidents. Mostly, however, the job of the ski patrol was to use heavy explosives and military artillery to stay one step ahead of an adversary that they knew could destroy them and everyone they loved. They waged war against an invisible enemy—one that both signaled its presence and masked its danger with falling snow.

The origin of ski patrol dates in the United States back to 1936, when the friend of a man named Charles Minot Dole hit a tree and died during a ski race in Pittsfield, Massachusetts. In response, Dole decided to help develop a group with organized standards to address ski safety and rescue. The National Ski Patrol system began in 1938, with a group of volunteers familiar with basic first-aid and evacuation procedures for injured skiers. They also did their best to enforce safety regulations and slow down skiers who were going too fast.

As the interest in skiing continued to grow, the National Ski Patrol (often referred to as NSP) expanded as well, to the point where well-trained volunteers now donate their time at over 600 North American ski areas. The bigger resorts, however, are staffed full-time by core teams of pro patrollers who handle safety issues as well as avalanche control duties. On a resort's professional ski patrol, there are no volunteers, no part-timers—you are either on it or you aren't.

While respected, in the early '80s the National Ski Patrol members were often looked upon as weekend warriors, skilled skiers who usually came in from out of town to handle wrecks and first-aid but were not permitted to participate in the dangerous explosives work. At Alpine Meadows, the National Ski Patrol members were viewed as Boy Scout-y. The pro patrollers, not so much.

Alpine Meadows, presumably by design, drew a particularly extreme type of individual for its ski patrol, the kind who responded to ads posted in outdoor magazines that read along the lines of adventurous bordering on suicidal. The sort of men who found that job description appealing were hard-core climbers from Yosemite Valley, the Grand Tetons—cool, rugged, real-life action heroes who spent their summers scaling walls and rescuing people and their winters restlessly seeking the same intense high.

In '82, there were about 22 guys on Alpine Meadows' ski patrol, depending on how many were out on injured reserve with some body part or other broken or torn. They were overwhelmingly male, white, young (all under age 40 except for one), and single. Most patrollers were motivated by a true desire to help others; others found that the job fed a deep yearning to be needed. Every one of them seemed to thrive on doing hazardous work for subsistence pay simply for the right to the adrenaline rush that came with saving lives.

None of them, certainly, did it for the money. In the '81–'82 season, patrollers risked their lives for somewhere in the range of $6 to $7.50 an hour. As the assistant patrol director, Larry Heywood's salary was $768 for two weeks, an income that would have put him under $20,000 for the year, assuming the work was year-round. The other aspect of the financial package was that the work was strictly seasonal—the patrollers worked the ski season, usually only November to May.

Still, some members of the ski patrol couldn't believe they were getting paid at all to wake up every day to do what they loved, to hold a job whose duties included skiing powder, watching the sunrise over the mountain peaks, hanging out on the ridge on sunny spring days. And there were perks, experiences that they wouldn't necessarily have had the access or opportunity to do, like having the summit to themselves before dawn, or laying down the first, solitary tracks on a backcountry slope glistening with fresh, untouched powder up to their noses. For some of these guys, that they *got* to do these things at all was what mattered, and to get paid on top of it was just a bonus.

There were a few novices who left patrolling after a season or two, but for the most part, once these guys started the job, they were in it for keeps. Virtually every member of Alpine Meadows' ski patrol, however, began his career by thinking of it as something to do for a season while he postponed having to grow up and get a real job. Then they were hooked, and the rest of their lives ended up more or less revolving around their commitment to patrolling. Many of them were thrilled to disprove their parents' argument that they would get bored skiing every day. For a patrolman, each day was an adventure.

In many cases the patrollers' education didn't extend beyond high school, although several members of the crew had college degrees or even PhDs. But it wasn't like these guys could get jobs in a bank, even had they been willing to. Once they pledged to ski patrol, they had to find temporary, seasonal jobs that would allow them to feed themselves and their patrolling habit. In the off-season, many patrollers took jobs in construction, and several took on the summer equivalent of extreme public service and fought fires, some as members of elite, first-strike tactical teams. They weren't thinking career so much as a job that would pay enough to cover rent, gas, and six-packs. One veteran member of the patrol used to pump gas at a Shell station in Tahoe City in the off-season—a position that paid a dollar more an hour than his job keeping the mountains safe for skiers.

It was an eclectic, outrageous group in an especially unique time and place, a culture brimming over with mountain spirit and alternative lifestyle. To a large extent, the 1960s were still alive and well at Alpine Meadows in 1982. The resort was a party destination for aging hippies looking for jobs, some who had served in the war in Vietnam and some who had gone to the ski area to evade it. There were lost souls desperate to check out of reality and party on, and lots of young American kids just out of college who loved to ski. Most everyone was living paycheck to paycheck, and no one had a reliable car. But there were jazz and rock and roll bands at the resort and skiing parties in the moonlight just for the employees. There was dancing and drinking and pot and cocaine. At the annual Groomers' Ball, usually held at the local Elks lodge or a nearby restaurant, the raffle always billed first prize as a trip to Hawaii: a shot of LSD while someone shook a picture of Hawaii in front of the winner's face.

It was, for these people, at that moment, truly the best of times. They had all chosen passion over other, straighter paths. They were mountain people, skiers, climbers, fishermen, outdoorsmen. The employees of Alpine Meadows were their own community, the tightest of families, where the members genuinely took care of each other. Even on ski patrol, which had a bit of a gang mentality and tended to knock rookies out if they were soft, the established crew all had each other's backs.

The patrol was headed up by Bernie Kingery, age 49, an avalanche hunter with 20 years' experience. The beloved mountain manager was pitch-perfect in the role, down to the bushy, mountain-man beard and the sweetness beneath the gruff exterior. As patrol director, Bob Blair was below Bernie in the chain of command. Bob, with his long, thick, dark hair and self-possessed smile, was a frequent crush of the girls working the ski lifts and ticket sales. He came to Alpine Meadows from his hometown of Sacramento when he was 20 years old, first working as a lift operator. That was in 1968, back in the days when his ponytail-length hair was forbidden and he tried to get around the restriction with lots of hats that never came off.

What had started out as a short-time gig for Bob soon became more permanent. He got a job as a lifeguard at the Lake Tahoe beaches in the summer, found friends in the community, began to fit in. In '72 he threw away his poles and learned to ski with a shovel as a member of the ski patrol, taking a cut in pay for the opportunity to do so. On his two days off a week he plowed snow off roofs, easily making as much money in those two days as he did in two weeks of patrolling.

Bernie offered Bob the position of patrol director in the fall of '76, to which Bob responded, "I'm gonna need a hand on my shoulder, but I'd like to do it." That promotion moved him from an hourly to a salaried employee, although given how many hours he worked as director, financially it was clearly a demotion. He was more like one of the guys than a stern authority figure, although from time to time he was known to hurl their backgammon set over the ridge when he caught his patrolmen congregating on an over-long break in one of the mountaintop lift shacks. He had a quick, occasionally volatile temper and he was willing to tell management what he thought, the combination of which backfired on him from a professional standpoint more than once. It was no secret that he didn't get along with Howard Carnell, the resort's general manager—a burly, brisk guy who wore the collar on his ski jacket up and punctuated every word he said with a period—but Bernie was always there to act as a buffer between them. Soft-spoken and emotional, Bob was a good organizer of people. He listened to the patrollers and protected them whenever possible.

Larry Heywood, as assistant patrol director, was just beneath Bob, and took over Bob's responsibilities on his days off. He theoretically reported to Bob, but he would frequently take issues to Bernie or even straight to Howard. In direct contrast to Bob, Larry knew how to talk to management and was savvy enough to tell his superiors what they wanted to hear. His critics claimed that he was positioning, calling him an opportunist, a "climbing guy." The fact was, he was driven in an occupation where ambition wasn't necessarily the norm and it was therefore viewed with suspicion. He might have been self-absorbed, maybe a little haughty, but he was also a born leader.

Even though he certainly partied as hard or harder than the rest of the crew, in relation to some of the guys he supervised Larry was viewed as a straight arrow, almost a goody two-shoes. He wasn't the only married member of the ski patrol—although the majority of them were single—but it wasn't just his wife and 12-year-old son that set him apart a bit from the rest of the patrollers. For starters, his appearance was more clean-cut than most of the other patrolmen: sun-bleached blond hair cut well above shoulder length and no facial hair. He somehow simply looked the part—tall, lanky, fit, and tan, dressed in a cotton turtleneck and one of his ubiquitous gray wool sweaters. His face was good-looking in a boyish sort of way, with hazel eyes masked by ever-present Vuarnets and a ruddy, peeling nose from too much sun exposure and too little sunscreen. And beyond that, he had the whole package in terms of the image management wanted in a representative of the resort. He was not just smart, articulate, and responsible, he also came with built-in stability: a house, a family, a wife who worked as the registrar at North Tahoe High School.

Larry was raised in San Jose, California, the oldest of four children, all with names that began with "L." His parents and three other couples often got together for poker and cocktails, a tradition that soon expanded to frequent joint family ski vacations in Tahoe. As a result, Larry became fairly fluid on skis by age five.

Larry met his wife, Kathy, at Abraham Lincoln High School, although they weren't a couple during school. He graduated in '65 and married Kathy a year later, when they were both 18. At the time, he was attending classes at San Jose State as well as working nearly full-time hanging drapes for his dad's business. Larry's maternal grandmother had been a seamstress, and during World

War II her shop, Custom Made Draperies, did a brisk business making blackout drapes. Larry's dad went into that business as well, running Heywood Drapery in Santa Clara, California, where Larry learned the unique and specialized trade of hanging fancy drapes.

Larry and Kathy had a baby boy, Shawn, in 1970. With the mounting pressure of making a living and being a dad, Larry ended up flunking out of college. For a change of pace from the grind of the previous few years, he moved his family to Lake Tahoe, renting a tiny house on the West Shore for $130 a month. The winter of '70–'71 was an especially big one in terms of snowfall, so Larry was quickly hired onto the ski patrol at Alpine Meadows. He started at $2.50 an hour, although he got a raise in the spring, with Bernie bursting into the ski patrol office and triumphantly announcing, "I got you a nickel!"

The irony of Larry coming to the mountains for a break was that he ended up working every day of the week. He couldn't support his family on his patrolman's pay, so on his days off he was back to hanging drapes again, this time at a place called Mary's Drapery on the South Shore of Lake Tahoe. The following year he headed back to San Jose with his family so he could finish school. He ultimately graduated with a special double major in natural science and photography, then spent the next few years in the antique furniture business with Kathy's dad, who owned an antiques store in Indiana. Larry and Kathy bought a truck and toured the country coast to coast hauling American oak furniture, buying low and selling high. They wholesaled to auctions, kept a booth in a store in Los Gatos, California, and sold to Bay Area stores.

Larry had long wanted to return to patrolling, realizing that the taste of it he had experienced earlier only made him crave it more. One day in 1976 he shared a moment with Kathy, the two of them stuck in traffic in San Francisco, when they decided they simply had to get out and go back. They sold the truck and the furniture and put a down payment on a house in Homewood, back on Lake Tahoe's West Shore. Larry returned to Alpine Meadows the year Bob Blair became patrol director, and at that point his real ski patrol career began. His third winter back, Bob asked Larry to be the assistant patrol director.

A self-described control freak, Larry reveled in being in charge. The new, younger patrolmen tended to look up to him, even though he was perhaps brusquer than necessary in training them. He had a huge ego, but so did everyone else on the ski patrol. There was something the slightest bit slick, almost ruthless, about him. His nickname was Cujo, from his habit of flying into a rage and foaming at the mouth to get his point across. He was initially more than a little sexist about the idea of female patrollers, which set the tone for the rest of the patrol. But despite his flaws, he was organized and efficient and also exceptionally successful. As time went on, even his detractors came to respect him for knowing his stuff.

While not quite an adversary, perhaps Larry's biggest, albeit quietest, rival on the patrol was an introverted, analytical snow hippie named Jim Plehn. A perfect foil to Larry's leadership style, Jim was equally effective in his approach, methodically revolutionizing avalanche forecasting at the resort. And unlike Larry, once Jim found his place at Alpine Meadows, he wasn't tempted to leave in the slightest, not by the lure of an advanced degree or a bigger paycheck or frankly, by anything city-related.

In 1982 the resort was packed full of quirky characters who wore the trademark ski patrol royal blue jacket with one yellow cross on the back and one on the front: Casey Jones, a fearless, steady, overgrown puppy of a man; Tom Kimbrough, a world-class mountain climber who was working through trauma in his personal life by essentially volunteering to relinquish his own safety to protect the team; Igor Goulaevsky, a gregarious Russian who hosted elaborate dinner and vodka parties for the crew; and Lanny Johnson, a talented and sensitive photographer who worked as a Himalayan mountain guide in the off-season.

Almost by definition, a collection of men who welcomed the idea of slinging 40 pounds of bombs over their shoulders to go set off avalanches was bound to result in strong and divergent personalities, many of which did not easily mesh. Some of the patrollers were high-strung, many were loners, but all of them were independent thinkers. Off the mountain, clashes were common. But while they were doing their jobs, their reliance on each other was the only way to stay alive.

They had all been caught, to varying degrees, in slides over the years, and their partners were the first, and sometimes only, ones there to help them get out. They may have hated each other personally—and some of them certainly did—but that didn't affect their willingness to risk their lives for each other on the job. They trusted and respected each other as members of a team, but it was more than that—on the mountain they were completely dedicated to each other. Their bond went beyond camaraderie inherent in a dangerous, high-stress occupation—it was wartime deep. No doubt that heightened level of dependence on another person added to the addictive nature of the job, making it so hard to walk away from in the end. They were comrades, a band of brothers, and they would have done anything for each other.

Whatever their differences, every one of the patrollers shared a case of hubris, some of them openly admitting to taunting the elements. They acted in defiance of the gods of nature, in disregard of their fate. The very name for the work they did flaunted their audacity, their arrogance. Some other ski resorts referred to the job with milder terminology such as "snow safety" or "avalanche mitigation." At Alpine Meadows, the patrolmen's declaration that they could control avalanches, essentially tame nature, confine and overpower mountains of snow, was the epitome of excessive conceit that inevitably led, at least in classic Greek tragedies, to the downfall of the hero.

These men lived to fight back, to best an unseen adversary. Possibly they were fooling themselves, or maybe they were self-aware enough to understand that they were battling more than the accumulation of snow. Either way, no matter what demons they were confronting, and whatever may have been coming undone in their personal lives, during the big storms they could come alive. The men on the Alpine Meadows ski patrol in 1982 were young and invincible, and, until March 31, they still believed that there was a part of their world that they could control.

THREE

New-fallen snow is one of the most unstable
natural substances on earth.

—

U.S. Forest Service, *Avalanche Handbook*

The members of the '82 Alpine Meadows ski patrol knew as well
as anyone that avalanche snow is not made up of puffy, light snowflakes. It is not some romanticized ideal of snow-angel snow, and
the experience of being caught in it is not like leaping and tumbling
into winter's equivalent of a pile of leaves. It is a thick, dense mix-
ture that has been wind-pounded and ground-up and pulverized by
the turbulence of the slide. Inside the churning mass, the heat of
friction—the energy generated by the collision of billions of snow
particles—melts the snow enough so that when it's moving, an avalanche takes on the properties of fluid, like a thick white river.

When this wet snow finally grinds to a stop in the runout zone,
the heat dissipates and the individual snow grains sinter and bond
together, almost instantly causing the snow to fuse into the consistency of concrete. The snow pins a victim in place, not letting him
breathe or move, much less struggle to get free. Avalanche snow

is like stone-solid, bulletproof ice, and extricating a person from it usually means chipping away at it with steel shovels.

The icy grip of an avalanche entombs people so quickly that even shallowly buried victims can rarely save themselves. People trapped only ankle-deep have felt the snow pulling on them like quicksand and have had to rip their boots off to survive. Firefighters searching the site of an avalanche in Cordova, Alaska, in 1999 escaped a second slide only by tearing their feet out of their boots and racing across the churning snow in their socks.

Jimmy Mott, who ran the Squaw Valley ski patrol (and who is infamous for his decision, during a tram accident at that resort in 1978, to scale the cable to the gondola swaying 80 feet above a knife-edge ridge to help rescue the passengers), was partially buried in an avalanche near a lift tower in early '82. He was ultimately able to call for help on his radio, but the snow had hardened around him so completely that it took him almost 40 minutes just to get his hands to the radio strapped around his chest.

The forces generated within the largest avalanches are among the most powerful on earth, and they all—volume, speed, densities of mass, hydraulic imbalances, air pressure, heat, friction, and gravity—fluctuate wildly as millions of tons of snow race down a mountain. There is perhaps no more volatile, erratic, and potentially deadly natural disaster. An avalanche moving at top speed resembles a Category 5 hurricane, except that an avalanche's density makes its immediate path a lot more destructive.

Unlike any other natural material, snow exists within a degree of its melting point, exquisitely fragile, perpetually on the edge of shifting between liquid, solid, and vapor. Sometimes snow can even achieve the incredibly rare state of existing near its triple point, meaning in all three forms at the same time. It is known as viscoplastic, meaning it has the ability to flow, like some liquids, and to stretch or compress without losing its structure, like some solids. Its strength and structure—from ice to water and back again—are constantly in flux. This state of instability enables its molecules to transform extremely quickly in response to the slightest change in external conditions. Temperature, wind speed, water content, and even the angle of incline of the slope can cause snow to oscillate between the soft, flimsy consistency of feathers and the brutally crushing density of lead. In practical terms, that means that snow is a complicated—and extremely excitable—substance.

When snow crystals fall throughout a season, they don't coat the ground and the mountains in a single blanket, but in distinct layers of varying thickness and strength. While snow appears solid, it is really more like lace, a delicate network of frozen water linked with airspaces filled with water vapor molecules. True to what is taught in childhood, no two snow crystals are ever identical. (Snowflakes, formed when microscopic snow crystals bash into each other in random flight and cling together, are obviously unique as well.) They fall in a myriad of shapes and sizes—stars, plates, columns, needles, pellets, fragments—but the classic form, the six-pointed star little kids aim for when they fold and cut paper, is known as a stellar crystal.

Even old snow densely packed on a sidewalk contains more than half air, but gorgeous, intricate stellar crystals create newly fallen powder that is almost completely air, with only 5–10 percent frozen water. Floating down lazily from the sky, usually when the weather is relatively warm, these are the snowflakes of dreamy paperweight globes, the ones schoolchildren can't resist trying to catch on their tongues. Yet despite their beauty, pure stellar snow crystals can be devastatingly dangerous, creating a fluffy, unstable base for heavier layers above or even enabling an avalanche to soar airborne over a mountain, flying on a sheet of velvet.

The snow cover is never in a state of rest. It is constantly being pushed, pulled, warmed, chilled, ventilated, shaken. Individual grains of snow bond to each other within each layer, between layers, and between the snow and the ground. Over time, some layers become stronger, while others progressively weaken. Temperature fluctuations during a storm also contribute to the instability by creating snow layers with significantly different characteristics of strength, density, and cohesion. The process in which snow crystals constantly change throughout the winter is known as snow metamorphism, and an avalanche forecaster's job revolves around the meticulous monitoring of this progression.

At the most basic level, if there is too much snow on a steep-enough slope, it will slide off. Avalanches also occur when the snow changes internally and loosens its grip with a layer underneath. Avalanches happen on a roof, on a windshield, even. The extraordinary aspect of snow is not that it avalanches, but that it usually stays on the mountains so well.

A slide can occur on a slope with an angle as shallow as 15–25 degrees (an average staircase is about 30 degrees). On the very steepest slopes, from 45 degrees to vertical, snow slides off continually during storms, hardly able to accumulate at all. Avalanches are most common, and most devastating, on slopes with angles of 35–45 degrees, the steepness of expert runs at a ski resort.

There is a direct relationship between snow intensity and avalanches, especially when combined with severe winds that create turmoil and wind-load the slopes with additional snow. The quicker new snow piles up (one inch per hour is usually a red flag) the more weight and stress is applied to the snowpack. No snowpack can tolerate an infinite amount of stress. The faster pressure is applied, the sooner the snow reaches its breaking point and sets catastrophe on a hair trigger.

The biggest and most destructive type of avalanche is known as a slab avalanche. A slab is a cohesive plate of snow, often several feet thick, that tears loose from the slope as one large block and slides en masse on the snow beneath it—picture a desk tipped at enough of an angle so that a book glides straight off it. It is the cohesiveness of the slab—one or more layers that are more unified than the layer below it—that makes the snow capable of instantaneously breaking on a wide front. It is the characteristic of total release that makes it so treacherous, as compared to a loose snow avalanche that begins at a point and expands on the way down. The slab avalanche is the dramatic kind, the one that looks like a clean break, as if the mountain has been sliced like a knife through frosting.

From the starting zone, the fracture in a slab avalanche instantly spreads out horizontally across the mountainside, then seems to freeze in time for a split second before all the snow beneath it falls straight downslope and ruptures into smaller blocks. As it picks up speed down its track, the avalanche creates a white plume of icy, crystallized snow dust that churns upward, crashing like a tidal wave, sometimes hundreds of feet in the air.

Since they primarily occur during storm cycles, avalanches (except those deliberately set off by avalanche control crews) are rarely seen or heard. The movie version of avalanches usually shows them sliding in silence—and slow motion—but that's not exactly the case. Before the actual sharp crack of the fracture, there is often a deafening whoomp, like dynamite exploding, of the slab collapsing as air is pushed out of the snowpack. Witnesses at the base of huge avalanches have also reported hearing a rumble, quickly followed by a roar that grows more and more intense until it drowns out all other sound.

In the biggest avalanches, the snow is preceded by a massive air blast, a shock wave caused by the force of the avalanche slamming faster and faster against nothing more than the air in front of it. The buffeting effect is analogous to, but much more powerful than, riding in a convertible on the highway when an 18-wheeler whizzes by in the opposite direction. Displacing enormous quantities of air, creating winds of hurricane force around it, the air blast can be destructive beyond its boundaries. Anything in its way—buildings, vehicles, trees—is blown apart rather than crushed.

The air blast is immediately followed by the screeching of the wind—wind vicious enough to toss trucks, implode buildings, and obliterate anything in its path. Then there is the sound of the snow mass itself, a noise that, as described by the few people who have been that close to an avalanche and survived to talk about it, sounds like a freight train passing inches away from their ears. The train sound is indeed the sound of snow moving, but it is also the noise of whatever that snow has destroyed and carried along with it as it travels down the mountain—trees and rocks, certainly, but in some cases, also buildings, power lines, and people.

And that movement down the mountain is fast, faster than anyone expects, faster than any human could outrun, or, except in the rarest of instances, even outski. That movement, in a massive slab avalanche, can reach speeds of more than 200 mph. At high enough speeds, the snow is basically sucked ahead into a powerful vacuum, and the resulting pressure imbalance can actually cause the snow to accelerate more quickly than gravity is moving it.

In 1964 one of the fastest skiers in the world tried—and failed—to outski an avalanche. American downhill racer Buddy Werner, 28, was in St. Moritz, Switzerland, being filmed for a promotional movie on slopes clearly marked with avalanche warning signs. As he and some other skiers, including Barbi Henniberger, an Olympic ski racer from Germany, set off down the mountain, an avalanche fractured across the slope above them. Buddy immediately dropped into a tuck and raced straight down the hill, the wall of snow flowing immediately behind him and gaining speed. His friends (those that survived) say he almost made it, but about 15 feet before safety, the avalanche caught and buried him. Rescuers dug out his body—as well as Henniberger's—about four hours later.

Worldwide, avalanches have killed hundreds, even thousands, of people at a time. The two deadliest avalanches in history both occurred in Peru, just eight years apart. At the north end of the Andes mountain range, the Cordillera Blanca (White Range) is dominated by the 22,205-foot summit of Mount Huascarán. On January 10, 1962, a fragment of Huascarán's ice cap broke off and fell over a half mile onto the lower glacier. When it started, the avalanche was made up of about three million cubic yards of boiling glacier ice and snow. On its way down, it gorged out so much shattered ice, snow, rubble, and mud that it multiplied its mass to about 13 million cubic yards. A churning wave 175 feet high and a mile wide, the avalanche fell 13,000 vertical feet and traveled a distance of ten miles. It destroyed whole villages. It dammed, then flooded, the Santa River, taking out all the bridges and carrying bodies 100 miles out to sea. In the end, the avalanche killed over 4,000 people and 10,000 animals.

In 1970, triggered by an earthquake, Huascarán avalanched again. This time, the avalanche took over 20,000 lives.

Nothing anywhere near that type of death toll has ever occurred in the United States. The worst avalanche disaster in U.S. history (in terms of loss of life) occurred in 1910 on the Great Northern transcontinental railroad line in the Cascade Range of Washington. On March 1 of that year, along Stevens Pass in the little railroad town of Wellington, a loaded passenger train was stranded in a blizzard. The storm had been raging for days, and with the snow piling up too deeply and too rapidly, the railroad line was blocked in both directions. The train was parked on the sidings along with a mail train and a collection of locomotives, snowplows, and boxcars. Around midnight, a warm wind blew in. At 1:20 a.m. an enormous snow slab, a quarter mile wide by a half mile long and 20 feet deep, sheared off the mountain above the tracks and fell on the passengers sleeping in the train. Everything—and everyone—was swept into the canyon below the tracks. The last of the bodies, at least 96 of them, were discovered after the spring thaw.

The vast majority of fatal avalanches in the United States have only involved one or two victims and have been inadvertently started by those victims themselves. Their mere presence—on skis, for example—in an avalanche area can disrupt the snow enough to set off a disaster. When someone dies in an avalanche in America, it is invariably the result of an extreme skier, snowboarder, or snowmobiler who, despite the obvious risk, can't resist playing in the backcountry and ends up disturbing an unstable slope or cornice (a wave-shaped drift that can weigh twenty tons). In a rare turn of events, that would not be the cause of the avalanche at Alpine Meadows. The deadliest slide ever at a ski resort in North America would be triggered by an act of nature, not an act of man.

On the theory that a starfish is harder to bury than a pebble, avalanche safety courses teach the concept of trying to "stay big" in an avalanche, meaning a victim should stick out his arms and legs and furiously claw at anything and everything to get to what he believes is the top. But unless he is somehow able to frantically swim and fight his way to the surface, and stay there while the snow is still flowing, he will become encased in a casket of ice, unable to move even a finger. If a victim's eyes are open when the snow stops moving, they will remain open, and if they are closed, they will stay that way. The effect of the snow-hardening is so extreme that someone confined in a slide cannot even flutter his eyelids.

Being swept up in the violence of an avalanche is not unlike experiencing a plane crash; the person is ripped away from anyone or anything he was holding on to. The pure force of an avalanche may strip off clothes—not just hats and gloves and goggles, but often boots and jackets as well. A victim's wind is completely crushed out of him, and then he is trapped in a thick, white, liquid prison with the walls closing in on him—tumbling, beyond disoriented, with no ability or opportunity to react. His instinct is to open his mouth wide to fight for additional air, but the avalanche will just respond by stuffing it with more snow. Every breath he takes sucks in a mix of snow and air, creating an ice plug in his throat.

A person caught in an avalanche is not floating in a wave but pounded in relentless surf, shaken like prey in the teeth of the mountain. Akin to being wrestled in the jaws of a massive alligator in the churning darkness, if he sees the sky at all, it is in frantic snatches.

The best chance for survival is to gauge when the snow begins slowing down and starts compressing, and then immediately protect the nose and mouth with one or both hands and push as much snow away from the face as possible. The bigger the airspace, the more time someone can stay alive under the snow. The other option is to throw one arm up so it has a chance of breaking the surface of the snow, but since a victim is unable to tell up from down, the best he can do is fling one arm out, away from himself, and hope it is aiming skyward. A person obviously has a much greater likelihood of being rescued if some part of his body or a piece of his gear—a piece that is still attached to him—is protruding from the snow.

While someone is somersaulting inside an avalanche, in a small percentage of cases he might be killed instantly from a broken neck or head trauma—by being swept over a cliff, for example, or by bashing into a tree or slamming into debris swirling within the slide. The fury of the avalanche itself can also dismember, or potentially even decapitate, a person ensnared in its frenzied whirl.

A victim might also be literally crushed, as is the case with deep burials. It is rare for someone to survive being buried deeper than six feet under the snow, not only because it takes longer to find him and dig him out, but also because of the compressive burden upon him. Snow cover can weigh over 200 pounds per square foot, and when several tons of it is piled on top of someone, with his first exhalation he is gone, unable to expand his chest again.

Most avalanche deaths, however, are caused by suffocation. It is not a fast or merciful or pretty death. There is a tiny amount of air in even the densest avalanche debris, but that doesn't matter if mouths and noses are plugged with snow. If a victim's face is clear and he can gasp for breath, his time is still dwindling with every breath he takes. The act of breathing itself will use up the airspace he has: When he exhales, his breath will initially melt the snow but then it will freeze, coating the snow around his mouth with ice and sealing off any possible source of air.

Avalanche victims are often found with their faces completely covered by an ice mask, heartbreaking evidence that they survived the slide and were fighting for life under the snow afterward. Thick ice masks, meaning that the person struggled while enduring his burial for at least several excruciating minutes, haunt rescuers who know that if the victim could have been located—and dug out—sooner, he could have been saved.

Unless a victim is rescued in a very short time—and the odds aren't good—his air supply will simply get shorter and shorter. Since snow provides powerful insulation, with an air pocket a person could survive as long as 90–120 minutes under the snow without freezing to death (and be resuscitated as if he were a cold-water drowning victim). It is therefore rare for an avalanche death to result from hypothermia, the third prong of the so-called triple H syndrome. Technically, the most common cause of death from an avalanche is asphyxiation, caused by a combination of the other two H's: hypoxia (a lack of oxygen) and hypercapnia (an excess of carbon dioxide from rebreathing air in a tight space).

With too little oxygen and too much carbon dioxide, a victim spends agonizing minutes feeling the life being squeezed out of him, gasping for air and knowing that he is slowly smothering to death. Even if he could somehow move his lungs enough to scream, like a scene out of an especially gruesome horror film, no one could hear his cries. Snow is an extraordinarily efficient insulator against sound, and in a torturous enigma, sound essentially travels only down through snow, not up. Conscious but helpless to move, a person is able to hear his rescuers, but they cannot hear him.

After being enfolded in avalanche snow for about four minutes or so, a victim will begin to fade into sleep. Not only does that mean an end to the frantic, desperate feeling of being buried alive, but losing consciousness also means that he will use air at a slower rate. That is a crucial factor, because after about eight minutes, brain damage may set in.

In an avalanche rescue the searchers are often racing the weather—a continuing blizzard, the danger of another avalanche—but most of all they are competing against time. Every minute, every second, is critical. Even if a search team quickly pinpoints someone's location under the snow, he can easily suffocate in the time it takes rescuers to dig him out. They must dig down at a 45-degree angle so as not to destroy any air pocket the victim may have. Even if a victim is only buried a few feet down, at minimum, the rescuers have to dig a hole about the size of a refrigerator to extricate him. The weight of that much avalanche snow is about a ton and a half. Best case, it takes two men with shovels at least twelve minutes to carve away an area of snow that size. It takes five times as long without a shovel.

Overall, 35 minutes after an avalanche, the chances of a victim's being found alive are only 30 percent. After that, the survival rate drops precipitously. After two hours, the odds of someone being rescued from under the snow are merely around 3 percent. The few recoveries worldwide that have occurred after a few hours—in which victims had, or made, some sort of air pocket—are considered miraculous.

In the spring of 1982, all of Alpine Meadows was hoping for such a miracle.

FOUR

Holiday greetings from the redwood country
of northern California, where the Christmas trees
grow 300 feet tall!

–

From the Nelsons' Noel News

Far removed from the world of avalanches and snow and cold, Katy and Bud Nelson were in the New Orleans airport on January 26, 1982, in a total panic. The flight from New Orleans to Eureka, California, was experiencing some sort of weather delay, and the chances of making it back home for their daughter's eleventh birthday were looking increasingly bleak. They had left Laura and her six-year-old brother, Eric, in the care of a friend for the previous few days while they traveled to New Orleans to see Bud, at just age 39, inducted into the American Academy of Orthopaedic Surgeons.

It was a tradition in the family for Katy to make a special dinner at home for each of the children on their birthdays. That year Laura had chosen a menu with the same favorites her mom might have picked—steak, scalloped potatoes, and artichokes—with the addition of fruit cocktail and Jell-O salad. While Bud was pleading with airline officials to put them on another plane, Katy called the babysitter and asked her if she could pick up the cake Katy had ordered for Laura at Jan's Cake Box bakery. It was a pink champagne, nine-inch layer cake with whipped cream frosting, decorated with a rainbow and 11 candles on top. Laura had a special connection to rainbows at the time, initiated by the release of the "The Rainbow Connection," sung by Kermit the Frog in *The Muppet Movie*. She had them just about everywhere—her bedspread had a rainbow on it, her sneakers had rainbow laces.

In the end, the Nelsons were able to talk their way onto a flight that arrived in time for Katy to prepare Laura's birthday dinner. An adorable freckle-faced little girl with delicate, classic features that hinted at the effortless beauty she could become, Laura was just beginning an age when she was excited to receive clothes as a present. She was also starting to experiment with new styles on her hair, a shade of light brown naturally highlighted with sun-streaks of blond. For her fifth-grade class photo, she had jettisoned pigtails for a few backswept curls created with her new curling iron. Laura's birthday gifts from her parents that year included a kid-size pink bathrobe and a deep blue Gunne Sax–style dress with small pink flowers and white voile sleeves that Katy had made for her. They also gave her some new music for her record player—the *Xanadu* movie sound track and *Mickey Mouse Disco*—and brought her a mini license plate from New Orleans with a street lamp and her name on it. A few days later Laura had another birthday party with a slew of little girls, but what mattered most to her about turning 11 was that her mom and dad had been there with her to celebrate her day.

The weekend trip to New Orleans was a relatively small outing for Bud and Katy, both voracious travelers who had visited, and lived in, some of the world's most exotic locations. They had attended Purdue University at the same time, but they didn't meet until after they graduated. As a textile technology major, Katy's classes didn't overlap with Bud's, who graduated with a degree in chemical engineering, just like his dad, Leroy.

Bud's real name was also Leroy (Leroy Carl named his firstborn Leroy John), but he was born while his dad was in WWII on the island of Adak in the Aleutian Islands, and Leroy's letters home asking after his little buddy resulted in a lifelong nickname. Bud was born in 1942 in Akron, Ohio, the oldest of four brothers. He was an absolute force of energy as a child, a circumstance to which his parents responded by putting him on a leash whenever he was outside. His grandfather erected a corral in the backyard to try to fence him in, but Bud managed to find a way to crawl over it.

Growing up, Bud excelled at track, especially middle distances, winning the Missouri state championship in the half mile. His talent was such that he nearly made the 1964 Olympic team, and at one point he competed overseas on a team sponsored by the U.S. State Department. While Bud's parents were proud of their eldest son's athletic accomplishments, Leroy made it clear that he believed sports were secondary to academics. Leroy's father had been a blacksmith, and his family had grown up poor in a southwestern Iowa farm town. Leroy felt that his own scholarship to college was his way of escaping poverty, and he wanted his sons to have the same chance at success. As a result, Bud turned down several track scholarships at other colleges to attend Purdue.

Much as Bud appreciated the mental challenge of chemical engineering, he knew he wanted to be a doctor, and since he related to sports, orthopedics seemed like a natural fit. It was in February of his final year of medical school at Jefferson Medical College in Philadelphia that he met Katy. Although her signature reflects her full name, Carolyn, since childhood she had always gone by Katy. When someone telephoned the house asking for either Leroy or Carolyn, the couple could tell it was someone who didn't actually know them.

At the time they met, Katy was living in Philadelphia and reverse-commuting to her job outside the city as a technical writer for a textile company. Her roommate, a nurse at Jefferson, knew Bud from the hospital and invited him over to meet Katy. They became serious immediately, but Katy had already booked a one-way ticket to Europe, where she planned to stay as long as her money lasted. Not wanting to resent Bud if she gave up the trip to stay with him, Katy left for Europe in May as planned. At a prearranged mail drop in Copenhagen, she received a sweet letter from Bud that, to the extent she could make out his handwriting, urged her to enjoy her trip but announced that when she got back, he wanted to marry her. When she arrived in Greece, Katy reserved a phone booth at an American Express office to call Bud and accept his proposal.

Katy didn't return home from Europe immediately after she got engaged, but once she did come back, in September 1969, she didn't want to wait any longer than absolutely necessary to marry Bud. She planned a small wedding in her hometown of Indianapolis for family and friends for October 18 of that year. With no time to wait for them to be engraved, she hand-wrote the invitations. The only wrinkle in the wedding plans was that Bud was a practicing Catholic and Katy was Presbyterian. This caused Katy's mother serious doubts about the union, which she expressed up to and including the morning of the wedding. Katy and Bud managed to assuage most of the controversy by getting married both by a Catholic priest and a Presbyterian minister in two churches a block apart.

After their honeymoon—two days in a cabin in an Ohio state park—they lived in Pittsburgh while Bud completed his internship, then returned to Philadelphia for Bud to do his residency back at Jefferson. There Bud and Katy rented a tiny apartment on Locust Street near the hospital, and on January 26, 1971, Katy gave birth to a baby girl. After their daughter spent three days as "no-name Nelson," they named her Laura Michelle.

Katy sewed a christening dress for Laura, the first of many outfits she would make for her over the years. As a baby Laura was as easy as she was cute, except for a stubborn insistence on wearing a tiny pink jacket that, as a result, frequently appeared in many of her earliest photographs. Her most cherished possession was a seemingly indestructible doll named Honey that she took everywhere she went, including the beach.

Throughout Bud's manic residency schedule and simultaneus PhD studies, Katy maximized their family time by packing up Laura and meeting him at the hospital for lunch or dinner. His residency focused on synovial fluid in finger joints, for which he was conducting NIH-funded research with a full-grown chimpanzee. He would periodically put the chimp to sleep and do research on his hands, after which the chimp, in rebellion, would put his fingers between the bars and break his casts. Bud was constantly trying new things in an attempt to make the chimp happier, including buying him a TV.

During this period, the one extravagance the family always carved out time and money for was travel. When Laura was a year and a half old, they took a six-week trip to the North Cape in Europe, traveling to northern Norway, Sweden, and Finland, mimicking a trip Katy's dad had taken in the 1920s. The family camped well north of the Arctic Circle, with Bud blowing up an inflatable wading pool every night as a makeshift crib for Laura.

Bud and Katy's love of far-flung places was obvious in the so-called dream sheet they filled out for the navy. Bud had a two-year obligation to the navy to fulfill, having joined the military on the Berry Plan (under which physicians were deferred from the draft to complete their residencies before entering active duty) following his graduation from Purdue. Since the navy was paying to relocate the family, Katy and Bud were in agreement that they would choose the most exotic, interesting places possible. They picked Japan first, then a few other bases in Asia. One Saturday morning Bud picked up the mail and Katy heard him opening a letter as he was walking into the apartment. "Oh, shit," he said. "Where in the hell is Guam, anyway?"

They hadn't listed it as a choice, but apparently the navy felt that if the Nelsons were willing to travel to a distant locale, they might like Guam. The navy was right. Bud and Katy's time on the tropical island was an idyllic adventure.

They arrived in the summer of '75, when Laura was four and a half years old and Katy was pregnant with their second child. They lived at the naval air station, in an airy, three-bedroom cinder-block house on a cliff overlooking the Philippine Sea. The temperature was always 78–83 degrees, a warm, humid climate that the family took advantage of by swimming almost every day.

As a lieutenant commander in the navy, Bud was receiving decent pay for the first time in his career, and in comparison to the tight budget of residency, this was the high life as far as he and Katy were concerned. In addition, since the navy stationed two orthopedic surgeons on Guam and there was only enough work for about one and a half, Bud had lots of time for his family.

Bud and Katy became fast friends with the other doctor, Larry Guinney, and his family. Larry had gone to medical school at USC but completed his orthopedic training at UCLA, allowing him to cheer for either football team unless they were playing each other, in which case his Trojan colors came out. Larry's wife, Barbara, and Katy also hit it off, and Laura got along well with the young Guinney boys. The two families were often together, swimming at the beach, playing in the sand, sharing picnics and dinners. Bud and Larry went scuba diving in the clear sea several times a week, hoping no one needed an orthopedic surgeon while they were both underwater. Bud bought a 15-foot Zodiac dive boat that made it easier to go out over the reef, and they went on some spectacular night dives, spotting eels, sharks, and barracuda.

Laura attended nursery school at the naval station, where she showed an early proficiency for art work and printing, and it wasn't long before she could write words more legibly than her dad. After school she rode her bike along palm and coconut tree-lined streets to nearby parks. The only downside to this utopia for Bud and Katy was its remoteness, but they soon got around that with more and more travel. They were off the island frequently, sometimes just by themselves but often with Laura as well. They went back to the States to see family, but mostly they went on trips to that part of the world—Japan, Hong Kong, Thailand, Singapore, Saipan, and the islands of Yap, Palau, and Truk in Micronesia.

As a couple the Nelsons were high energy, but it was mostly Bud driving the fast, almost frenetic pace of their lives. Never willing to sit still, he was perpetually in motion, physically and mentally, always wondering what was happening next. He was an aggressive, hard-charging idea man who thrived on change and wanted to be on the next plane going anywhere. He was vibrant verging on distracted, constantly looking for the next exciting thing to happen. Raised by his family with nearly insurmountable expectations, Bud likely would have been happy just being an adventurer.

In contrast to her husband, Katy was calmer, stalwart, almost a little formal. Petite and compact, she wore her dark hair short. Unlike Bud, she was occasionally content to sit still and gaze out a window. Yet she was also a whirl of efficiency who maintained relationships around the world, planned visits to extended family, sent lengthy Christmas letters every year, and kept a calendar with dozens of birthdays marked on it to be sure everyone received a card. In the relationship, there sometimes seemed to be a bit more focus on what Bud wanted, while Katy implemented the groundwork for plans that he came up with. She was the one who booked the airlines, made the reservations, got things done. Bud couldn't have managed without her.

Katy was the perfect balance for Bud—a steadying influence to be sure, but she was certainly no long-suffering wife. She more than kept up with him, and she loved traveling, for example, at least as much as he did. Their marriage was hectic, a little frenzied even, but it was an equal partnership, and undeniably solid.

With four and a half years before their second child was born, Bud and Katy had spent a lot of undivided time with Laura, but they needn't have worried about her being jealous of a new baby. From the day Laura's little brother came home from the hospital—Laura wearing a new dress Bud bought her for the occasion—she loved him deeply. She was such a good little mother to him, always fussing over him and comforting him. The kids shared a bedroom in the house in Guam, and when Eric would cry in the night as an infant, Laura was always the first one up to talk to him and pat him on the back. She also took him right out of his crib sometimes, to play with him and read him stories.

By the time Laura was six, she had traveled extensively throughout southeast Asia and experienced tropical storms, an earthquake, and several typhoons. Typhoon Pamela, with winds of 190 mph, forced Laura and Eric to hide in the typhoon closet with Katy for 20 hours while Bud dodged exploding windows at the hospital and performed operations by flashlight. The family lost power for ten days, their phones for six weeks. And still, the whole venture was a glorious, dreamy time for the Nelsons.

Upon returning from Guam, the family settled in Marion, Ohio, where Bud joined a multi-specialty medical clinic. The kids liked the snow and went sledding on a little hill near their house, and Bud, who had a bit of a fear of heights, conquered it enough to ride the chairlifts and ski a bit on local slopes. Still, it didn't feel like home to anyone, and after living in the tropics Bud and Katy wanted out of the cold.

Larry Guinney, their friend from Guam, had ended up in private practice in Santa Rosa, California, and Bud began asking him what it was like to live in northern California. Within a couple of years, Bud found an opportunity to share office space with another surgeon in Eureka, California, a secluded seacoast town nestled in the redwood forest about 250 miles north of San Francisco. Katy and the kids approved the house Bud found for the family—a big, rambling 95-year-old Victorian on a corner lot with lots of hidden nooks and crannies and a claw-foot bathtub.

The spring the family moved to California, Bud woke up one morning and couldn't use his right arm. He had ruptured a cervical disk and faced the loss of use of his right hand, a situation that couldn't have been scarier for a right-handed surgeon. Normally clean-shaven with a flat-top hair cut, Bud, unable to lift his arm high enough to shave, sported a bushy beard that summer. By the fall he had gained back full use of his arm, and to get back into shape began running again, competing in several local races in their new community.

Initially fearing that Eureka might be too isolated, their first year there Bud and Katy rented an apartment in San Francisco to use for weekend visits. Long before the end of the lease, they realized that they didn't miss a big city. The family did, however, continue to engage in a phenomenally busy travel schedule, taking trips all around the country as well as abroad. They also began to see a lot of the Guinneys again, including going on a three-week medical conference/vacation to Europe together where the couples skied in Davos, Switzerland. Laura and Eric didn't go on that trip, instead skiing for the first time on a visit to Bend, Oregon, but they did go on many, many others. Aside from one incident when Katy had to help a crying Laura out of the bathroom on a plane—she wouldn't leave because every time she opened the door the light went out—the children loved traveling as much as their parents.

The family chose to live in Eureka, giving up certain things to do so—higher income, fancier shopping—but in exchange, they received a extraordinary quality of life. Bud was secure in the role of small-town doctor, and he participated, both in the family and the community. He was active in his church, Sacred Heart, where he took Laura and Eric every Sunday morning after a breakfast of jelly doughnuts. Bud was the doctor on call at race events in town, and he helped found the Vector Hand Clinic, a rehabilitation center that centered on injuries among local residents in the lumber and fishing industries. Although he was a successful surgeon, providing for his family meant more to him than just making sure they were taken care of financially. He was entirely committed to them, their protector in every way.

Bud always had time for the kids, taking them out for hot dogs or milkshakes, or to his office, where he let them play on the typewriters. He didn't miss a single one of their various practices, games, recitals, and talent shows, and Laura and Eric counted on his being there. He often picked Eric up after nursery school, reviewed his new papers and projects with him, and brought him home for lunch (a bit of a mixed blessing for Katy, who then felt compelled to fix a meal for everyone). He helped Eric with models and trains, and even gave piano-playing a shot, game to try to figure it out together with his son.

Holidays were a big deal in the Nelson family, and Bud played a huge role. At Easter, he was the bunny. On Halloween, he helped the kids walk all over town for candy and then confiscated their Milky Ways. And at Christmastime, it was a tradition for just Bud to take Laura and Eric to get the tree, Katy having been disinvited since she only picked the scrawny ones.

At work Bud dressed in suits and ties that he had had made for him in Hong Kong, but at home he wore torn jeans, plaid shirts, and often dirt from the garden. He and Eric liked to muck about planting vegetables, while Katy and Laura planted flowers together every spring, Laura particularly delighting in the delicate forget-me-nots that flourished among all the other blooms.

Laura had developed a little bit of her dad's restlessness, his desire to stay busy and engaged. She liked *Mr. Rogers*, for example, but could barely sit still to watch an entire episode. As a fifth grader at Marshall Elementary School, she was not just a straight-A student, but also a class leader, a library assistant, and an active Girl Scout. She took piano lessons, practicing every day before school for 20–30 minutes with Katy. She was crazy for the pet ducks that lived in their backyard and always made plenty of time for them. Laura and Eric shared the ducks and worked out a schedule for their care, with Laura feeding them in the morning before school, Eric feeding them in the afternoon after school, and both of them changing the water on weekends.

Laura liked lots of typical little-girl activities: playing dress-up, collecting dolls from other countries, baking cookies, roller-skating, doing gymnastics (even after breaking her arm). She was also especially creative, designing block print cards and making her own barrettes. Her tiny dolls lived in elaborate houses she constructed for them, papering the walls and building furniture, using buttons for stove burners and scraps of fabric for rugs. She was joyful and energetic, and extraordinarily nurturing for such a young girl. She got twenty cents for washing the dishes, and with her allowance she bought arts and crafts supplies, penny candy, and often, small gifts for Eric.

Laura loved her baby brother above all else, and as time went on, the bond between them only got stronger. She was the one he went to when he was scared or cold at night. If Eric woke up with a bad dream, knowing his dad was on call and needed his sleep, he would go to Laura's bedroom on the other side of the house and crawl into her bed with her.

Laura was forever trying to teach Eric things. Her favorite role was playing teacher, and she aimed 99 percent of her efforts toward Eric. She had a chalkboard in her room and she would set up school there for him. Usually he was a willing pupil, although occasionally she would have to hold the doors shut so he couldn't get out of the room.

Laura's lessons for Eric extended beyond merely academics. She taught him how to make toast. She showed him how to tie his shoelaces, make a gingerbread house, roller-skate, dance to *Mickey Mouse Disco*. Every so often she would get annoyed with her brother if he messed up something in her room, but even so, her love for him was unconditional. She gave him constant love and attention, and in return he was her faithful companion, always following her around, wanting to be with his big sister. When Laura went door-to-door selling Girl Scout cookies, Eric was in the wagon guarding the stash.

Eric was a bit of a daredevil, always pushing limits, but Laura looked out for him, protected him as best she could. She went down slides holding on to him, played leapfrog with him, helped him find shells and dig big holes in the sand at the beach. She organized Super Ball games with him on the sidewalk in front of their house, at least until the ball went in the street and Bud took it away from them.

Life in the Nelson family was absolutely packed, with every member continually on the go. It was almost as if they lived their lives in dog years, loading seven years' worth of experiences into every one. Bud occasionally expressed a belief that he might not live a long life, that he wouldn't necessarily survive to be an old man. It was that feeling, perhaps, that contributed to his desire to live such a full one.

Katy threw a surprise birthday party for Bud in December 1981, with a family cake in the kitchen turning into a huge celebration when friend after friend rang the doorbell and piled into the house. The event caught him completely off guard, since it was a relatively insignificant birthday to celebrate—his thirty-ninth. Shortly thereafter, the family planned a spring vacation trip to the mountains with the Guinneys. Both families were unfamiliar with Lake Tahoe and none of them had ever been to Alpine Meadows before, but Barbara Guinney saw an ad for a condo there in the magazine section of the *San Francisco Chronicle*. It was spacious enough for both families and located within walking distance of the resort, so Barbara reserved it for all of them for a long weekend at the end of March.

In preparation for the trip, Katy made Laura a green ski jacket and pants with a lining of pink and red flowers for her to wear in the snow.

The Nelsons left home in their old blue Honda Civic mid-afternoon on Thursday, March 25, 1982, and drove to Santa Rosa. They rented some ski equipment there, then spent the night at Larry and Barbara's house. On Friday morning both families got up early and began caravanning to Alpine Meadows. About eleven o'clock, the burnt orange Dodge Mini Ram van Larry was driving broke down below the summit and had to be towed to Nyack to be repaired. The Nelsons followed the tow truck so they could all stay together.

The families hadn't yet crested Donner Summit at that point, but even so they were close to being enveloped by that distinctly Tahoe smell—the sweet, pungent aroma of fir, pine, cedar, and giant sequoia mixed with manzanita and mountain air and, seemingly, the scent of pure lake water. The weather was crisp but sunny, and while it was still a little early for the infamous Sierra spring skiing of shorts and bikini tops, it was the kind of day made for hitting the slopes in just jeans and a T-shirt.

It turned out that an electrical wire had fallen onto the Guinneys' engine block, where it had burned and shut down the ignition system. It was a relatively simple repair. They were all on the road again by three o'clock and headed up Highway 80 toward Alpine Meadows.

FIVE

A stack of marbles ready to go.

—

Bernie Kingery, mountain manager
at Alpine Meadows in 1982,
describing an avalanche

It made complete sense that the Nelson and Guinney families had picked Alpine Meadows for their spring vacation. Despite the myriad eccentrics on staff, in the early '80s the resort was widely known as a kid-friendly, family ski resort. In those days, a pre-snowboard era, an extreme skier would likely not have come there, probably choosing Squaw Valley instead. The resort always promoted its spring season, with skiers consistently relying on an abundance of lifts and smooth grooming deep into May. For many years Alpine Meadows had built up a reputation as the last ski resort in the area to close for the year, usually on Memorial Day. At the end of March 1982, however, there had been so little snowfall for the past two months that it looked as if the operation would be winding down early, and Larry and the ski patrol crew reported to work without knowing when their seasons, and their paychecks, would come to an end.

While the patrolmen didn't necessarily discourage their image as ultimate ski bums—or as beer-drinking, pot-smoking, jolly good old boys—the fact was, no one ever really saw them when they were doing their job. The bulk of their work, the complicated, pressure-filled part, was done from about 6 a.m. to 9 a.m., out of the public eye. Despite how cavalier or unruffled they appeared on the outside, work was a profound affair for them. The crew knew that on a weekend day, approximately 5,000 people were depending on the patrol to protect them from unstable slopes and get them off the mountain if they hurt themselves. Up on the ridge, handling explosives, throwing bombs, keeping the area safe, the patrollers were consummate professionals.

Depending how strenuous their day had been, Larry and the other patrolmen often went home after work rather than out for beers together. They were beat at the end of their shift, and if they went to bed at two in the morning, they still had to be up at 5 a.m. They couldn't easily cover up a night of drinking, and they couldn't come in drunk and expect to live very long.

That was not to say it never happened, that drinking and drugs never overlapped with the job. Patrollers did, on occasion, report to work hungover, and now and then one of them would stow some pot in his pack and linger at the top of the ridge to smoke a joint before throwing dynamite. It was a challenge on many levels, because they knew it was all over if they got caught. The policy of the resort across all departments—ski patrol, trail crew, lift operations, vehicle maintenance, grooming—was that if anyone was high or caught with drugs at work, he was gone. If their boss didn't directly know about it, however, it didn't happen.

Bernie Kingery, the resort's mountain manager, was less willing than other supervisors to look the other way. As a result, the employees tracked him. It was hard to keep up with Bernie's location—he presided over the whole ski area and he liked to be hands-on, roaming the mountain, sometimes even joining in the avalanche control, frequently checking back at his office to oversee more administrative chores like making sure buses were running, then rotating through the various departments. Calls would regularly come in over the radio warning everyone in a particular vicinity that Bernie was on his way.

Bernie was constantly walking up to employees and sniffing them, then pulling their immediate supervisor over to do the same and demanding to know their opinion of a certain odor. "Come here," Bernie would say. "Go to that lift shack and tell me what you smell."

The managers, in an effort to protect a good employee dumb enough to get high at work, would generally maintain that they didn't smell anything. "Go smell again," Bernie would insist, at which point the supervisor would offer an opinion that the smell was probably burning straw or a propane heater or some other improbable source. Bernie would be beside himself.

Bernie had served in the army and studied civil engineering and geology at the University of Delaware before heading west and starting his career as one of the country's foremost experts on avalanche safety precautions. He began at Squaw Valley loading ski lifts, then worked his way up to the avalanche control team in time to help keep the area safe for the 1960 Olympics. He came to Alpine Meadows in '64, where he occupied the positions of patroller, avalanche technician, patrol director, and finally mountain manager. As manager of the mountain, he was in charge of ski patrol, lifts, grooming, ticket checking, and all other on-the-hill operations.

Bernie replaced Norm Wilson, a legend in the avalanche field who had trained with Monty Atwater, widely regarded as the father of avalanche research and control in the United States. Norm was clean-cut and businesslike, whereas Bernie was, quite literally, the man of the mountain—a rugged, old-school kind of guy. It was Bernie who changed the policy to allow patrolmen to wear ponytails and facial hair (allegedly the reason he left Squaw Valley was because he wouldn't shave his beard). It was Bernie who could be found skiing down Peril Ridge with 50 feet of climbing rope trailing behind him as he went, an old-time avalanche safety measure from the days when he first started out.

Bernie was identified, even in the international ski community, with a particular item of headgear that he frequently wore, especially during storms—a funny little pointed dunce cap, reminiscent of the type of hat a garden gnome might wear. Made of sheepskin, it came down around his head like an alpine flower. When he needed to get up the mountain quickly, he would requisition a snowmobile to tow him to the top and ride off with his cap pointing up in the air, having the time of his life. The ski patrolmen would steal and hide the hat every opportunity they got.

Bernie helped establish the Tahoe Nordic Search and Rescue Team, an organization that participated in myriad backcountry and avalanche rescues. He also educated National Ski Patrol searchers, and in 1981 the NSP named him the outstanding patroller of the year for his dedication to ski safety and avalanche prevention. He trained all levels of staff at Alpine Meadows on avalanche safety, even those positions that theoretically shouldn't have expected any interactions with sliding snow. During every employee orientation, to illustrate the power of a mountain sliding as a whole, Bernie held a slightly tilted pile of books and, as he talked, added more books one by one until the whole stack tumbled.

With the ski patrol, Bernie's training was a little less theoretical. Early on in Larry's first season patrolling, Bernie took him up as his partner on the High Yellow route. In those days that route controlled all the paths from the Summit lift south to Shuttle Cornice and required more than 40 hand charges. Bernie and Larry left the top of the Summit chair and began hiking the ridge above Alpine Bowl in the midst of a snowstorm with visibility barely beyond their ski tips. It was the kind of raging blizzard that people, even advanced skiers, headed indoors to avoid. As members of the ski patrol, they headed out into it. Within the first few minutes, Larry, balancing 40 pounds of dynamite on his back, thrashed around in the high powder snow, lost Bernie in the gloom, got lost himself, threw his first bomb, and became totally addicted. Throughout the entire episode, Bernie was screaming with glee.

Bernie never confused his passion for avalanches with a disrespect for them, however, and he was not shy about scolding even upper management on avalanche awareness. The lectures he gave, while informative, were usually delivered at top volume and didn't pull any punches in forcing someone to confront the immense risk they had taken by, for example, sneaking off into a closed area to hunt down powder. Some of these lectures were almost punishing, but always in a way that stressed safety and education.

The same, or worse, treatment was given to a skier foolish enough to think he could talk his way out of trouble with Bernie. Every so often guests felt that their lift tickets entitled them to do anything they wanted at the ski area, and in rare cases, a patroller had to toss them out of the resort for skiing too fast, or out of bounds, or engaging in other reckless behavior. If skiers protested by asking to speak to someone in charge, the patrolman warned them that they didn't want to talk to his boss. If they insisted, the patroller merrily handed them over to the mountain manager. Bernie, five foot six inches of fury, would first spit out a lengthy safety lecture and then typically eject the skiers from the resort for more than just the remainder of the day.

While some employees could be caught derisively referring to members of the public as "cods" (as in mindless codfish), Bernie sincerely wanted to keep the guests safe and also assure that they had fun at Alpine Meadows. Much to the embarrassment of some of his staff, he often went out to the lift lines in mid-morning and very seriously made an announcement to the general public that if they would just stagger their lunchtimes to not all take a break at noon, everyone would have shorter lines and a more enjoyable skiing experience. He was right, of course, but the skiers tended not to heed that particular advice—at noon the cafeteria in the lodge remained jammed and the lift lines stayed remarkably skier-free.

Bernie's idiosyncrasies were also on full display to the employees at Alpine Meadows. He insisted that everyone use code on the radio to an almost ridiculous extreme, one time losing patience with a switchboard operator who didn't know what he wanted when he kept radioing his request for a camera only by means of an obscure call number. Fearing contagion, he ran around behind sick employees once they returned to work, cleaning with alcohol scrubs. He was an obsessive pack rat who kept his office a mess. He was also a big-time phone slammer, although by no means the only offender among Alpine Meadows' staff. At one point his assistant had to replace so many phones that had been thrown through walls or smashed into pieces in the ski patrol office that the phone company just brought a case of phones and left them.

Bernie had an actual office in the ski lodge, but he was just as likely to work out of the ski patrol office in the Summit Terminal Building. The resort had completed renovation on the ski lodge at the end of 1981, remodeling the existing one and doubling its size, and it was open to the public just before Christmas that season. Larry saw his first dead body in the midst of the employee party celebrating the opening of that new lodge, when he was called out to rescue a skier who had crashed over the backside of the mountain. It was a tricky operation, requiring him to be lowered on ropes to reach the immobile young man—all in a futile effort once he couldn't find a pulse and it became clear that the would-be rescue had degenerated into merely retrieving a broken body. Larry eventually returned to the celebration shaken up and pissed off.

The new lodge was built across from the Summit Terminal Building, which was located closer to the base of the mountains. The Summit Terminal Building was the nerve center of the resort—the headquarters for ski patrol, lift operations, trail crew, and the ski school. A three-story, 100-foot-long modified A-frame built in 1972 with steel girder construction, the building also housed the drive for Summit, the resort's major lift. The chairlift, including the massive 22-ton concrete counterweight that kept the cable secure, ran right through the building. The ski patrol room, an oversize area with tables and benches, was on the second floor, along with the patrol director's office, referred to on the radio as Base 4. The employee rooms and offices for running lift operations (for 80 or so lift operators) were also on the second floor, along with a large employee locker room with banks of close to 200 wooden lockers. The ticket checkers and trail crew had offices on the third floor. The first floor had restrooms, more lockers, offices for the ski school (about 120 instructors), and half a flight up, a small room that served as a kennel for the rescue dogs.

Bernie stocked the Summit Terminal Building with an extensive cache of avalanche rescue equipment, including beacons and hundreds of probe poles. Backup avalanche rescue gear—as well as sleds to evacuate injured skiers, oxygen, snow anchors, carabiners, slings, ropes, and medical supplies—was also stored at the top of the mountain in the three patrol stand-by stations. On their downtime, or to warm up, the patrolmen hung out in these shacks, the largest of which was at the top of the Summit lift. During storm cycles, as many as three patrollers often stayed overnight in the Summit station to de-rime the chairlifts (by climbing the towers and knocking the ice off) and do avalanche control in case the storm prevented access to the ridgetop the following day.

The patrollers usually stashed their personal backpacks—stocked out of the first-aid room with supplies like gauze, bandages, and tongue depressors to use for bite sticks—in the lift shacks. In addition to basic medical provisions, Larry's pack also contained search-and-rescue headlamps and probes, a flashlight, something for him to read, extra gloves, and lunch. None of the patrollers ever had much money, so their lunches were simple, usually peanut butter and jelly or cheese sandwiches. Larry used the little propane heaters in the shacks to cook modified grilled cheese sandwiches, toasting the bread somewhat and melting, or at least softening, the cheese on aluminum foil over the small flame. He and the other patrolmen built makeshift racks above the heaters in an attempt to dry out the hats and gloves they could never keep dry enough. Bernie, and also Bob Blair, habitually dropped by the lift stations to see what the patrolmen were up to in there.

Bernie was gruff and opinionated, steadfast in his beliefs, but also sensitive. He once marched into *Tahoe World* to tell the editor his newspaper was "a goddamn sensationalist rag," then called afterward to apologize for getting so upset. Once he started talking on a topic, he seemingly never stopped, a trait that was mostly endearing. Sometimes, however, he would make everyone crazy in a meeting by going on and on, analyzing minutiae and subtle nuances. One such meeting culminated in patrolman Casey Jones screaming at him in frustration, "I don't care how the damn clock works, I just want to know what time it is!"

He was a father figure to many members of his staff, and also that rare manager who actually tried to learn the name of every one of his employees. If need be, he also went out of his way to comfort and support them when they had a tough day. One time he sought out a first-year lift operator who was distraught after responding to an incident involving a child's safety. Bernie slid in next to her on the locker room bench, deliberately bumping her, then dried her tears and praised her for doing her job correctly.

Above all, Bernie was in love with that mountain and supremely dedicated to his job. Yet to some of the people around him, it seemed like he was letting the work consume him. Occasionally he had a tough time compartmentalizing his position and balancing it with a life outside Alpine Meadows.

In 1982 the ski resort was owned by Nick Badami, a dynamic, all-powerful figure who also owned Park City Mountain Resort in Utah. The general manager of the resort was Howard Carnell, a forceful, loyal, and demanding boss whose previous jobs included marine (in Korea), police officer, and heavy equipment operator. As a kid growing up in Tahoe City, Howard used to attach a rope to cars after storms and tow himself behind them on Highway 89, an activity of questionable safety known as skijoring or hooky-bobbing. He had worked his way up through the ranks at Alpine Meadows, beginning with snow removal, eventually becoming what some of his staff referred to as "an indoor boss." Howard was a back-in-the-office kind of guy who didn't often laugh or socialize with the employees. He generally distanced himself from people, yet he was the kind of man who could repeatedly call a woman working for him a "dummy" and still maintain her allegiance. Certainly no one ever questioned his commitment to the resort. Howard reported to Nick, and Bernie reported to Howard.

To be sure, Bernie was pulled in different directions, straddling the line between convincing himself that the resort was absolutely safe for the public and fielding incessant, if understandable, pressure from management to open the resort as soon as possible. Some mornings when avalanche control went longer than usual, Howard would be quick to give Bernie a hard time and demand answers as to why the resort was opening late. Bernie was forced to walk a tight-rope of stress, balancing protection against economic realities. If he lobbied to close the resort, or even some of the runs, every time he thought there was even the slightest risk, he would lose credibility along with his job. And rather than getting easier over time, the stakes just seem to be raised—the odds were against him making the tough decisions over and over and never getting one wrong.

Once Bernie was home from work, his wife, Julie, a ski instruc-tor at the resort, envied his ability to instantly relax and just be in the moment. Still, his perfectionist work ethic extended to his home life in that he often challenged his teenage daughter, Kris, to try harder at her various pursuits. As much as he might have pushed her privately, however, he did nothing but brag endlessly about her accomplishments in school and gymnastics to the patrolmen.

Despite what a busy time the holidays were at the ski resort, Christmas at the Kingery house was always especially magical. Bernie made sure to carve out time to shop for presents for Julie and Kris, and every year he brought home a tree that the family decorated on Christmas Eve until the wee hours of the night. On Christmas Day, they all sang carols at the local Christmas service, Bernie's clear tenor a striking contrast to Julie's soprano and Kris's young alto-soprano. Dancing was also a big deal in the Kingery fam-ily, with Bernie and Kris, at age 14, the top father-daughter team in the area in swing dance, often dancing at the local jazz band's "40s night." At Alpine Meadows events, Bernie and his wife would sway together as one, lost in their own trance on the floor.

It was away from his office that Bernie seemed happiest, which did not mean that he didn't love his job, but away from work he was a different man—lighthearted, looser. While he considered mari-juana use at work a fireable offense, after-hours he could relax with the ski patrol guys—put his glasses on backward, have a few too many drinks. He was wild about music, especially jazz, and he was a riot at parties, hopping up on little round bar tables and dancing until he fell off.

Perhaps the need to fuel that part of his personality was what caused Bernie to forge a seemingly unlikely relationship with Jake

Smith, a young, extraordinarily happy-go-lucky member of the trail crew. When Jake first started out at Alpine Meadows in the mid-'70s, he and Bernie clashed a bit, but over the years Bernie came to realize that with Jake, carefree didn't equate to lazy. Jake wasn't afraid to poke fun at the mountain manager, and for whatever reason, by the '82 season Bernie more or less let him get away with it. At one employee party Jake came right up into Bernie's face and, in an exaggerated imitation of him, sniffed dramatically. "Is that heroin I smell?" Jake asked. They ended up in a good-natured, if vicious, wrestling match on the floor.

And so it went with Jake. There wasn't a person at the resort who didn't adore him.

SIX

As a child, Jeffrey James Smith was the kind of boy who, upon reading the warning "Do not put near flame" on a bottle, would have to throw it in a fire to see what would happen. The type who, if told baking soda could be used to make a bomb, would need to see for himself. The sort of boy an exasperated pediatrician would compare to "a bag full of springs."

As an adult, he was pretty much the same.

He was always Jeff to his mom, but growing up in Lafayette, a Bay Area town east of San Francisco, he was mistakenly dubbed Jake by a Colombian housekeeper and the name pretty much stuck. It was an affectionate nickname, however, and it usually took him a while to get to know someone, to become close to them, before he told them to call him Jake. In March of '82 at Alpine Meadows, he was Jake to everyone.

The youngest of three children, Jake was a constant and

tremendous challenge for his mom, Bettigene, though she claims she was always entertained. He was curious and full of questions, a free spirit perpetually seeking adventure. He was also flat-out fearless, and as a result often crazy-reckless, but he mixed his danger with a high level of resourcefulness. When he was eight, he climbed 40 feet up to the top of a eucalyptus tree at a family picnic just to see if he could, causing everyone to panic over how they would get him down. Jake got himself down.

At age fifteen he hopped freight trains across the country, traveling to Nebraska, Colorado, the East Coast, usually with less than $5 in his pocket. On the Rio Grande line to Denver the train passed through the Continental Divide, and in the Moffat Tunnel at Winter Park, 6.2 miles long, the fumes were overpowering. Planning ahead for the possibility of carbon monoxide poisoning, Jake had brought along a box of big lawn and leaf bags and filled them with fresh air—enough to breathe into and survive through 20 minutes of tunnel on a freight train.

Jake was never particularly competitive growing up, but he did have an early and strong pull toward nature and the outdoors. His father, Russell, exposed him to fishing, and it became a lifelong pursuit. He and his siblings spent summers around Lake Tahoe, where he and his brother developed a call to the mountains at a young age.

Jake had exceptional chemistry with his older sister, Kathe, who he called Cake so their names would rhyme. He also had a strong relationship with his mom, frequently presenting her with a single red rose, his favorite flower based on the Grateful Dead association. Jake's parents separated when he was 13, and afterward he kept an eye on his mother's prospective love interests, setting them up to look bad in small ways that wouldn't come back to him. One time he disconnected the light switches in the living room before graciously showing a suitor in, then left him alone while his mom finished getting ready. As Jake predicted, she came in questioning why her hapless date was sitting in the dark.

Jake's brother, Dennis, just a year older, moved up to Tahoe in '73 and got a job with Alpine Meadows doing lift maintenance. Soon after graduating from Del Valle High School in Walnut Creek, Jake ditched his warehouse job in the Bay Area and joined him. Their mom thought they would each get the lifestyle out of their systems after a summer or so and go on to college, but her boys never got it out of their systems, never lived outside the mountains again. Bettigene used to joke that for children she got one yuppie and two hippies.

Jake flourished in the long Sierra winters, and he was always inventing new ways to play in the snow—diving off huge rocks into piles of it, skiing on the longest, fastest skis imaginable, fashioning a rudimentary snowboard out of old water skis. He signed on with Alpine Meadows soon after arriving in the area, initially working in lodge maintenance, moving briefly to lift operations, then to a mechanical position fixing and maintaining propane heaters, and ultimately to the trail crew. The trail crew, usually composed of only about half a dozen guys, entailed a diverse set of duties: grooming cleanup, brush and tree cutting, removing debris from trails, setting lines, shoveling, knocking down berms. Trail crew members were basically the handymen of the ski area.

The crew was created in part at the urging of Billy Davis, head of lift operations, because the ski patrol was always poaching lift operators to assist them with various jobs. With the emergence of the trail crew, patrolmen had a new place to grab a few extra guys to help out with avalanche control. As a result, the trail crew was viewed as more or less an entry into the ski patrol. Jake liked the autonomy of the trail crew, but playing with danger by blasting cornices of snow loose before daybreak excited him more.

Even when he was young, Jake was incredibly witty, taking a word or a name and giving it his own meaning or pronunciation, turning anything into a quip or a pun and keeping everyone laughing. He was a practical joker as well, always playing tricks and hiding things. Once when a patrolman got married on the top of the mountain, Jake scattered everyone's skis so they had to search for them before they could ski down after the ceremony. He celebrated the bicentennial by diving off a bridge in Tahoe City in front of hundreds of spectators, right into the middle of fish-filled, frigid river water. He carried, and frequently flashed, a Three Stooges official Knucklehead card. He was a hilarious, fun-loving, life-loving clown, a complete and total goofball.

Jake was obsessed with the symbol of a lightning bolt, and he designed a little sketch of a cloud with a bolt of lightning coming out of it and his initials, JJS, alternately in or near it. He carried a Swiss Army knife around with him everywhere, and he loved to carve that lightning bolt all around the resort—on the lift shacks, on rafters. When he fixed heaters at the resort before his position on the trail crew, several of the lift operators would call him Heater Man, joking when he came by to make repairs that it was "Heater Man to the rescue again." Consequently, he was responsible for at least one "HMTTRA" carved on the wall in the lift operators' room. There were always signs of Jake around Alpine Meadows.

In the summers, at different points Jake worked as a carpenter, a mason, and a cement worker. Having started out with black widow spiders as pets (he had to keep them one at a time, as they wouldn't tolerate each other), he traded up to a black Lab he named Zachariah Ukiah Jedediah Smith, Zach for short. Jake and Zach were completely inseparable, including at Jake's various places of employment. Jake brought him to the cement job, and having taught him how to dig on command, he simply said, "Squirrel, Zach," and the dog would start the pier holes.

Zach came to work with Jake so frequently in the winter that Jake had an Alpine Meadows ID tag made for him. The connection between man and dog was such that one day when Zach got in the driver's seat, knocked the clutch, and rolled away in Jake's truck, Jake simply waved away the resulting body damage to the vehicle with the explanation "Zach drove."

In his off hours, Jake spent a lot of time hiking or climbing, particularly in the trails above Emerald Bay. He was especially invested in fishing for rainbows out in the lake. He would come walking back over the ridge with a huge string of trout and new jokes about "Sid Vicious," the mysterious fish he claimed to be hunting. When he moved into a house in Tahoe City, he decorated the front door frame with "head mounts," trout heads with the gills pulled open and sprayed with Varathane.

Jake was somewhat of a militant environmentalist who didn't tolerate littering, and he made it his responsibility to police the area. When he was fishing, he gathered up other people's trash—lines, hooks, picnic debris—and packed it out. Aside from some righteous indignation from time to time, people seldom saw Jake angry. He was sentimental and surprisingly insightful, and he legitimately cared about other people's feelings. He was deeply sincere and willing to help someone in need, more than once stopping to help a stranger broken down on the road. Jake always pulled his share and then tried to do a little more. He was forever talking about what a good life it was.

Jake was particularly close to Billy Davis, the guy who ran lift operations at the resort and helped establish the trail crew. Originally from Southern California, Billy went to Sierra College for a degree in law enforcement, and then, on a whim, accepted a job as a lift operator in '72 when a cousin called and offered it to him. He hung up the phone wondering what a lift operator was.

Jake called him Snow Mo Bill, for snowmobile, because he drove one. Jake was constantly renaming people, once dubbing a childhood friend also named Jeff with the nickname Nick, allegedly to avoid confusion. Jake thought up other names for himself as well— when he worked for Billy, Jake's radio number was Alpine 29, and after moving to another position with a different call number, Jake began referring to himself as "Formerly 29."

Jake's stint working for Billy in lift ops didn't work out so well, culminating in Billy getting a call that Jake was at the top of the Subway run about to come to blows with a ski instructor who had been rude to a female lift operator. Jake was frequently getting into trouble at the resort, although he managed to evade detection just as often. Once while he was on duty and skiing way too fast, deliberately catching big air, he realized mid-flight that there was a children's ski school class beneath him. He couldn't stop, so he landed among them while the group scattered, unhurt. He had a pretty distinctive look—tall and rangy, with vivid green eyes and an extra-full, dark brown beard that he was constantly twisting ice out of in the winter—but he thought he'd try a disguise nonetheless. He headed

straight for the Summit Terminal Building, where he changed out
of his uniform, successfully camouflaged himself in a pink jacket he
found, and headed back out.

Most of Jake's escapades involved the best of intentions. Once
he and Billy were having drinks in the Compactor Bar in the Alpine
Meadows lodge with some ski patrollers, and one of the patrolmen
had an avalanche rescue dog at his feet. The bar supervisor came
over to ask them to remove the dog, a position he maintained even
after being informed it was a rescue dog. Someone mumbled the
word "asshole" under his breath, and the manager demanded to
know who said it. "I did," Jake said. He hadn't actually been the one
to verbalize what everyone was thinking, but he was willing to take
the blame, even though it resulted in his being thrown out of the
bar. It became a joke around the resort that he had been tossed out,
seeing as his call number at that point was Alpine 86.

Another time, Bernie replaced a broken intercom between the
patrol office and Billy's lift operations office with a big metal plug-in
unit. It had an open microphone that allowed the main base to hear
anything that was said in lift ops. Billy had it out with Bernie over the
invasion of privacy, but Bernie wasn't budging, so Billy asked Jake to
get rid of it for him. Always willing to help out a friend, Jake took it
to the locker room, drop-kicked it with his ski boot on, then kicked
it behind some wooden lockers. Later, Bernie was looking around
for the missing intercom, and he asked Jake if he had seen it.

"I think I've seen that thing kicking around here somewhere,"
Jake said.

Billy eventually developed neurofibromatosis, a rare, debilitat-
ing disease that increasingly affected his mobility. Jake responded
to the situation with his distinctive style of compassion, driving
his friend to the Bay Area to consult with specialists and staying by
him throughout various surgeries. In the summer of '81, Billy had
to undergo further surgery to remove tumors from his throat, and
his head had been shaved for the procedure. He woke up to a nurse
telling him that his brother had been to visit, a comment that didn't
make sense to Billy until he realized Jake had needed to imperson-
ate a family member to get access to him. Jake had left him a plain

white bag with a note that said, "Thought you could use this. Use it in good health. Love, your brother Jake." Inside was a hairbrush.

Billy's (platonic) roommate that summer was a beautiful blond, blue-eyed girl named Pam DeRyke who worked for Billy as a lift operator. She thought Jake was funny, but she already had a boyfriend when she first met him. Within a couple nights of Pam mentioning to Jake that she and her boyfriend had broken up, Jake showed up at her place unexpectedly, with a thin, lame story about how he'd just been out driving and thought he'd stop in to see Billy.

Their first kiss was that night. Up to that point Jake had been a big smoker, and he told Pam that he was embarrassed to kiss her with smoker's breath. When Pam admitted that she hated it, as a commitment to her, Jake quit that night and never smoked again.

Pam already shared Jake's love of the mountains, and he exposed her to another one of his passions, turning her into a Deadhead. They went to concerts together, and spent time skiing, hiking, exploring caves, bike riding. He covered every back street in town on his dirt bike and took it to Alpine Meadows in the off-season, once tipping over backward on it in an effort to impress his new girl.

Jake had long been a serious collector of all things he found outside, natural and otherwise. His pockets were always filled with rocks, shells (especially the empty spiral ones shaped like a straw), and wood, particularly pieces shaped like his initials—Jake was inordinately proud of his initials. He scavenged for stuff that Pam couldn't believe he would stop to pick up, digging around by the railroad tracks for bottles, horseshoes, coins, crystals, a rusty bolt. He filled crates with the items he discovered. At a time when they were both broke and joked that they were going to end up eating nothing but wild blackberries all summer, Jake gave many of his treasures to Pam. He also frequently presented her with flowers, including occasional splurges on his long-time favorite, red roses.

In February of '82, Jake, at age 27, and Pam, 25, moved in together and set up a home in a place called the Willow Cabin in Tahoma, on Lake Tahoe's West Shore. Jake's decorating tastes ran to hanging crystals in the windows and displaying old skis and ski boots about, but Pam worked out a compromise with him. He hadn't yet asked her to marry him, but he told a friend that was his intention.

That month they went up to Emerald Bay to look at the scene of an avalanche that had killed a hiker during a big storm a few weeks before. They viewed the destructive force of an avalanche together, saw firsthand what it could do—a steel building wrapped around a tree, massive old trees uprooted. Jake was moved by the experience.

A few weeks later, Pam and Jake were in Jake's truck, along with the ever-present Zach, when a Kinks song came on the radio. It was "The Last Assembly," with poignant lyrics about friends gathering together for a final farewell. Out of nowhere Jake mentioned to Pam that he would like the song played at his funeral, and added that he wanted red roses there as well. No one who knew Jake well, including Pam and his sister, Kathe, took this comment as any kind of premonition. On the contrary, they didn't believe that Jake thought he was ever going to die.

In early '82, Jake's family was still trying to coordinate the timing for a get-together to celebrate the previous Christmas. Schedules being what they were, it didn't end up happening until the end of March, but it was worth the wait. On Saturday, March 27, they all got together at a restaurant called Clementine's, a couple miles down Lake Tahoe's West Shore. The whole family was in the same place at the same time, including both Jake's mom, up from the Bay Area, and his dad, who had rarely gotten together since their divorce.

It was a gorgeous day, beautiful spring weather, when Jake's family and close friends—he had invited Pam and Billy—met up at the restaurant. Everyone got along, and they all had a wonderful meal together. Jake mentioned that he had gone to Emerald Bay to see the devastation caused by the January avalanche. As he talked about his fascination with the power of the slide, his mom expressed concern about her daredevil son helping to bring down avalanches. Dennis assured her that Jake was growing up, and stressed how much his brother loved his job.

Jake's sister, Kathe, in town from Lafayette for the occasion, had her children with her, a four-year-old daughter and an eleven-month-old baby named Jeff, after her brother. Jake was determined to have his little namesake skiing even before he could walk. At one point Jake's nephew got restless at the table, and after asking Kathe to "please pass the baby," Jake took him away from the table. After a while, Kathe went to check on them and found them both in the bar, hanging out together watching TV. Jake had requested a tea towel from the bartender and used it to secure little Jeff to the bar stool next to him.

After dinner, Jake took his nephew outside. While they were eating, snow had silently begun to fall. Jake carried Jeff in his arms, showing him the snow, looking in the windows with him to see their reflection surrounded by the softly drifting flakes. By the time they all said good-bye to each other outside the restaurant, the snow was starting to come down more steadily. The first few wisps trailed off the crests of the ridges, giving notice that the wind was beginning to stir, warning of the gathering storm.

"Take a bearing on the telephone pole," Jake said, "because it's going to dump like a big dog."

SEVEN

By the next morning, Sunday, March 28, the storm Jake had seen the first inklings of the night before had hit in full force. When Dave and Jeanne Hahn, up from Los Altos Hills, California, for a few days of skiing, arrived at their Alpine Meadows condo on Monday the twenty-ninth, they found themselves driving into the blizzard while most people were trying to get out.

In the 1940s, William Hahn worked for Canada Dry in a district covering Teaneck, New Jersey. He was married with two kids—a nine-year-old son named Dave that he was especially close to and a daughter just out of diapers. One day while William was riding in the company's delivery truck, it crashed and flipped over, crushing his head into the curb. He was pronounced dead at the scene and sent to the morgue. He was ultimately resuscitated, but he was never quite right after the accident. The resulting brain damage changed him into a different person than the one his family had known.

The Christmas Eve that Dave was 12 and his younger sister was seven, William walked out the door and never came back. He was simply out of contact and gone from his children's lives forever. There were a few rumors through the years—he was living in Texas, he had suffered a stroke—but mostly just a bunch of unanswered questions that no one in the family ever wanted to talk about.

At age 12, Dave took over the role of emotional support to his mom, Dorothea, as well as father figure to his younger sister. He kept his resentment toward his dad—first for changing, then for deserting them—to himself and stepped up, responsible, steady, to take care of his family. Knowing what an overwhelming burden she was forcing on him, Dorothea still relied on Dave to take over all the decision-making for the family and handle every crisis that arose.

Dave left home after high school to study math and physics at Wagner College on Staten Island. He attended college on a football scholarship, which paid his tuition but not his room and board. With no money for a place to live, he alternately roomed with a friend and slept in his car. He was a great running back, a fast, gifted athlete in general, but he was a bit short at five foot eleven and he was always getting injured—a dislocated shoulder, a broken jaw. Just about the time he got all the hardware off his mouth, in the fall of his junior year, he met a stunning freshman named Jeanne at the post office.

Born in Nyack, New York, Jeanne had long, thick, dark hair and enormous, kind eyes. She checked Dave out the first time they met, taking in his strong, kind face and muscular build beneath a brown-and-beige plaid shirt. Although Jeanne was majoring in elementary education in college, her focus at that point was on defying her mom. She wanted to be with Dave, and so a year after she met him, at age 18, she secretly married him.

Dave and Jeanne couldn't live at school as a married couple—in that era they would have been kicked out if they were discovered—and they also couldn't risk telling friends. They kept their union covert, and for the rest of his senior year Dave pumped gas at a station in Hasbrouck Heights to afford a room in the men's dorm, while Jeanne lived in the girls' dorm.

After Dave's graduation, he took a job with Sperry Gyroscope as a field engineer, and the married couple finally lived together. Their first place was in Elmont, Long Island, followed by Fort Worth, Texas, and then they were back in New Jersey in 1959 for the arrival of their first daughter, Linda. Three years later Jeanne gave birth to Stephanie, a name that resulted in Dave coming back into the hospital room three times to check with Jeanne to make sure he was spelling it correctly on the various forms.

When Dave accepted a position as an engineer in the aerospace division of Lytton Industries, the family moved across the country to Canoga Park, near Los Angeles. Despite all his technical expertise and experience, Dave preferred spending his time outdoors. He and Jeanne took their daughters camping a lot, sometimes on the beach in Ensenada, Mexico. Dave caught lobsters and cooked them on the beach while he told stories to his girls. He had the limitless energy of a toddler—returning home from an extended camping trip, for example, he would immediately begin mowing the lawn. He was athletic—a scuba diver, a fisherman, a skier—and always in great shape. He played tennis with his daughters and also competed against them in foot races. He never bought into the let-them-win philosophy of parenting—even when they were very young, he always tried to beat them.

Skiing was a major part of the Hahns' lives, and as members of the family the girls had no choice but to like it. For several winters in a row they loaded up their station wagon and headed up to Mammoth almost every Friday, back when lift tickets were only $8. They stayed by Crowley Lake at tiny little cabins known as Wally and Joe's, where they put their ski gear on in the morning and didn't return until the end of the day.

While they usually skied as a family, the ones most committed to the sport were Dave and Linda. Stephanie got a bloody nose her first time on skis, and between that and a broken leg a few years later, she never took to it as much as her older sister. Jeanne, who had grown from a teenage bride into a classy, elegant woman with a sort of pervasive sereneness, learned to ski as an adult and broke her leg her first time out. Undaunted, she stayed with it, albeit as a bit of a cautious skier, the perfect complement to Dave's daring style. Dave purposefully learned to ski without taking any lessons—he simply decided that he knew how to ski and then proved himself right.

Dave's belief that he could always figure things out, that whatever he wanted to do he simply could, and would, do, dominated not just skiing but every aspect of his life. Living that philosophy had never failed him. As a result, he was self-driven beyond reason. He basically did not acknowledge boundaries, a quality that made him a brilliant inventor. He spent an incredible amount of time working, including most Saturdays and business trips that took him to Europe for weeks at a time—a committed workaholic long before that word became popular. Dave wasn't always around for his family, but he balanced it more than most, so much so that when his daughters played volleyball in high school, he dropped everything to watch them play and, along with Jeanne, was proud to accept a trophy for the parents who appeared at the most games.

The family moved around a bit following Dave's career: to Roy Rogers Ranch in Chatsworth, California, and then briefly to New York. In '72, they moved back to California and settled in Los Altos Hills, a beautiful, upscale neighborhood in what would become Silicon Valley. The house they decided on was essentially Dave's choice. Jeanne flew out to look at ten houses a day for ten days and sent Dave back to look at her favorites. She knew right away which place Dave was going to like best—the one that needed the most work. He loved the project aspect of the house; he had a vision, saw things no one else could see. And he was right—he knocked down walls, landscaped, crafted precision stonework, and overall made the house bigger and better. He did it all himself, with the help of Jeanne and their then-adolescent daughters. The family joke was that when they first started the renovation project, Linda and Stephanie spent more time underneath the house than in it.

It was important to Dave that his daughters be self-sufficient, and he was constantly teaching them practical life lessons like car maintenance. One time he gave them each a gift of an air tire gauge. He was strict with them, and quite the disciplinarian. He expected a lot from other people, including his family—he was hard on himself and, to an extent, tough on them as well. Dave's family attributed some of his sternness to his German heritage. When he wanted something, he wanted it immediately and he wanted it done correctly. If he asked one of his young daughters for a crescent wrench, for example, they knew they had better produce the right tool and quickly. But rather than push back against his authority, the girls seemed to flourish under it, growing up athletic and capable and secure.

As they became teenagers and then young women, Linda and Stephanie believed they were more interesting to their dad as adults, and they began to see glimpses of what their relationships with him could grow into. Dave took a walk virtually every day, usually joined by Jeanne or the girls, and the conversations between Dave and his daughters during the course of those strolls became increasingly substantive, especially when they revolved around their shared interest in technology.

Throughout the mid and late '70s Dave determined that he didn't want to work for anybody else, and he began branching out in his career, first going into an entrepreneurial business setting up subscription television. He had always been interested in high-end stereos, frequently building his own equipment, including speakers with tiny parts that caused strife whenever Jeanne tried to vacuum in the vicinity. At one point he came up with an idea to build and program a sort of music player that would allow people to select their own musical playlist—a particular genre of music or a specific artist. As this was cutting-edge stuff at the time, there was a calculated gamble in committing to the venture, but Dave meticulously planned out every detail of the process. Security was important to him, and he never took risks that could hurt his family.

By the end of March, 1982, it was all coming together for Dave. His patents had come through for his music invention, he had moved into his own office, and major funding was coming in from a group in Taiwan the following week. In preparation, he was going through old boxes, cleaning out his home office, sorting out his life. He knew that if he was going to get away for a few days he needed to do it straightaway, on the spur of the moment, because starting in April he expected to be working nonstop.

The obvious choice was to escape to the mountains for a few days of spring skiing. While living in Los Altos Hills, the family still went skiing a couple times a month throughout the winters to resorts near Lake Tahoe—Heavenly, Northstar, Alpine Meadows. Dave preferred Alpine Meadows, since it often wasn't as crowded as some of the other ski areas, and he liked the challenge of the steep slopes there. Jeanne called Andy Wertheim, a Realtor in Alpine Meadows who had rented a condo to her a few times before, and arranged to rent a unit for the following Monday. They figured that waiting until Monday would allow them to beat the traffic and also get in a quick visit with Stephanie, who was coming home from UC San Diego for the weekend.

The Friday before the trip, Dave, a man of science and technology not given to mystic beliefs in spirits or visions in the slightest, came home from work shaken. He told Jeanne, who had been married to him almost 25 years at that point, about an experience unlike anything she had ever heard him describe.

"While I was driving home," Dave said, "I saw my father's face pass across the windshield."

Dave, at age 46, hadn't seen his dad since he had walked out on him and his family 34 years before. He didn't even know whether William Hahn was alive or dead. Dave rarely talked about his dad, but Jeanne knew he thought about him a lot, at one point contemplating tracking him down and forcing answers that had never come when he was a child. In the end, he decided not to look for his dad because he was too afraid of who he would find. Seeing his dad's face flash before him so many years later was very real to Dave and baffled him completely. It was a fleeting moment, but one he could not explain.

Jeanne and Dave took Stephanie to the airport that Sunday, March 28, and finished packing so they could get an early start to Alpine Meadows the following day. Linda, enrolled in college at San Jose State, planned to drive up separately two days later and join her parents for some skiing. She arranged to meet them at their condo on Wednesday, March 31.

Despite leaving very early in the morning, Jeanne and Dave didn't arrive at the Alpine Place 2 condos until late afternoon on

Monday—the weather conditions had almost tripled their driving time. When they got there, they saw kids making tunnels and snow caves in the parking lot, and they met the Nelson family as they unloaded their bags in the midst of the blizzard. The Nelsons confirmed what the Hahns had suspected—that rather than providing a few feet of fresh powder and some incredible skiing, the storm was so severe that it had rendered the skiing virtually nonexistent. Jeanne commented that after all the hassle they had experienced driving up, she wasn't even sure why they had bothered coming.

For quite a while, Jeanne and Dave tromped around unable to find their unit, in the building across the parking lot from the Nelsons, because someone had flipped the number on the door upside down. Although it was partially backward, on a quick glance it looked like a 31, rather than the number they were looking for—condo #13.

EIGHT

There's something sleeping under the snow.

–

Lanny Johnson, Alpine Meadows ski patrol, March 30, 1982

In response to the spring storm, Larry Heywood and the rest of the ski patrol had begun avalanche control on Sunday, March 28, throwing about 500 pounds of hand charges. By Monday morning, the day Dave and Jeanne Hahn arrived in Alpine Meadows, the blizzard had dropped another 18 inches of snow and persisted without a break. The patrol not only increased the number of bombs they threw, but also fired 26 rounds from a recoilless rifle in the morning, putting extra shots high and low in the target zones. By the afternoon, there was yet another 13 inches of snowfall. In an extraordinary measure, the patrol closed the lifts down early to fire another 14 shots from the rifle in the afternoon.

As one of only a handful of Class A avalanche areas in the country, Alpine Meadows was required to report weather and avalanche data to the U.S. Forest Service, and it routinely recorded more avalanches annually than any other ski resort in the country, mostly small slides deliberately caused by the control teams. The theory behind avalanche control was simple: knock down avalanches on purpose before they come down on their own. When the patrol threw explosives or fired artillery at designated places on the mountain, the explosion artificially jolted the snow, triggering small (and sometimes not so small) avalanches that were designed to spill harmlessly into closed areas. By setting off controlled slides, the patrolmen prevented the slopes from becoming overloaded with snow and releasing more massive avalanches.

In practice, the process was more complicated than it sounded. It wasn't just flinging bombs at the mountain and hoping for the best. The control program involved the intricate choreography of routes and shot placements, the meticulous discipline of calculating expectations and analyzing results.

The situation became more complex when patrollers pounded a slope with explosives and it did not slide. Perhaps they hadn't put the shot in exactly the right spot, or the force wasn't sufficient, or the assault was made too early or too late. As a general rule, however, avalanche control wasn't necessarily designed just to create avalanches, but rather to assess the stability of the slope, to check its propensity to move. Every shot was meant to test the potential hazard. If the snow did not release in response to explosives, there was reason to believe that the slope was stable at that time.

At Alpine Meadows in 1982, there were 15 distinct control routes covering over 300 diverse avalanche paths to be controlled by a staff of at most 20 patrollers on any given day. During and just after a storm, the ski patrol conducted avalanche control at least once and sometimes twice a day. Depending on the amount of snowfall, that usually worked out to about a third of the days the resort was open, or around 50 days a season. On an avalanche control day the crew could throw as many as 300 bombs, which was 600 pounds of dynamite. In contrast, patrollers at Vail may have thrown 40 charges in an entire season.

Patrolling in avalanche terrain meant that Larry and everyone else on the crew put themselves out there, exposed to tremendous peril, every time it snowed. Virtually all of the patrolmen had been caught in at least a few of the avalanches they or one of their colleagues set off. While they weren't completely nonchalant about the prospect, it was, quite literally, an occupational hazard. As much as they could reduce the risk with training and experience, over time they were subjecting themselves to Russian roulette odds. Every one of the patrolmen trusted his instincts unswervingly, knowing that at any time one of his judgment calls—such as believing a slope was safe or having an adequate exit plan if it wasn't—might prove to be his final decision.

The patrollers were forever tracking each other—eyes duty, they called it—whenever one of them went tumbling down a slope in a torrent of snow. They skied in teams of two, and if one of them got caught, the other one tried as best he could to get a fix on where his partner ended up in case he had to dig for him. The bomb packs they carried when they did control work always contained an avalanche probe and a shovel. When they were out patrolling, each member of the crew also wore a radio harness that strapped over his back with a pouch for a two-way radio about the size of a brick in front. In addition, the patrolmen had a Skadi avalanche beacon on them at all times. The beacons had a cord so patrollers could wear them around their necks, but most of them zipped the beacon into a pocket so it was less likely to get separated from them if they got caught in an avalanche.

Larry certainly wasn't immune to avalanches, but he sometimes seemed to lead a more charmed life on the slopes than many of the other patrolmen. Jim Plehn, the avalanche hazard forecaster, had been caught in more than a few slides going back to the late '60s, including one slab he set off himself just by traversing new fast snow on the razor-edge of Peril Ridge. One time another patroller, Tom Kimbrough, felt the snow give way beneath him and got sucked right off a ridge, dropping down ten feet just in time to see an enormous avalanche go past him down the mountain. Gary Murphy, a Vietnam veteran from Santa Clara, California, once set off an explosive charge that broke a five-foot crown face right beneath him, splitting his skis. He lunged for a tree and hung on to it, one ski dangling in midair, and watched the slide tear out trees as it raced down the slope.

Casey Jones, a bit of an avalanche magnet, experienced some pretty spectacular near misses over the years. Casey lived at 320 Kimberly Drive in Tahoe City, a party headquarters known, according to a large sign he posted outside, as the Kimberly Hotel. Casey came to Alpine Meadows in '70 from Martinez, California, when he was 19, first working as a ski instructor. Due to an early fascination with trains, he hadn't gone by his real first name of Robert since he was a toddler. Ruggedly handsome with a thick blond beard and an especially sarcastic sense of humor, Casey saw the resort as a target-rich environment for picking up girls. He was a part-time student, hitchhiking up and back to the Bay Area Tuesday through Thursday to take architecture classes at Diablo Valley College in Pleasant Hill. His first place was a rental with four other guys for $150 a month, pro-rated based on how many days a month any of them were there. It was only 600 square feet, but they managed to jam in a lot of visitors and, one winter, a motorcycle that one of his roommates brought up and had to park inside.

By the late '70s, Casey was working trail crew when one day Bob Blair handed him a ski patrol jacket. "Here's your new coat," Bob said, "and by the way, you get paid less." Casey hadn't applied for the position and he had to take 50 cents less an hour to do it, at a time when he was only in the $5-an-hour range to begin with. He decided to roll with it.

One morning early in his patrol career, Casey threw five bombs from a rocky notch called Keyhole, but the slope still hadn't released. He was just about to throw one more down low to see if it knocked anything loose when the ground beneath him opened like a table being spread apart to insert a leaf in the middle. With two feet of his skis extending out over the drop-off of an 11-foot fracture, he was somehow able to instantaneously levitate himself backward and escape being caught.

Another time, while shooting up on Scott in the midst of a storm, Casey wasn't as lucky. He and Gary Murphy were six shots into their route, moving carefully from anchor point to anchor point to stay safe. Gary had just crossed the slope and Casey started over in his tracks after him, traveling across one at a time to ease the weight on the snowpack and, in case of a slide, to prevent them from getting buried at the same time. As he skied, Casey felt the snow release beneath him about two feet deep. He attempted to ski out of the avalanche, but his skis became tangled in the roiling snow and came off. Gary yelled to Casey, asking him if he was all right. Casey, a front-line Forest Service firefighter in the off-season and an ultimately poised individual even in life-threatening situations, replied "No, I'm going for a ride." Just as he felt what seemed like a rug being pulled out from under him, he heard Gary radioing for backup. After tumbling about 400 feet down the mountain inside the avalanche, Casey sensed the snow starting to settle a little and he punched out with his right hand. When the avalanche came to a stop, only his head and his right arm protruded above the snow. Once he was dug out, he had to tramp all over the mountain trying to find his lost skis, poles, hat, and goggles. Every now and then in those situations, one of the patrolmen would suffer the inconvenience—and indignity—of permanently losing a ski up on the mountain.

In addition to the obvious and immense risk of the job, the patrolmen often suffered various levels of hearing loss from all of the explosions. Many of them also developed excruciating powder headaches from the nitroglycerin in the dynamite getting onto their hands and into their bloodstreams.

In exchange for all this, the patrolmen got to flex their testosterone by throwing bombs and firing artillery. They had the opportunity to play war games and fight the enemy with explosives, but the sides were man versus faceless nature. Not only were they not trying to kill anyone, they were actually trying to keep people safe. In their minds it was a total win-win.

In 1982 the patrolmen used ski cutting (traversing across a slope one at a time and trying to set off a slide with just their skis) as a frequent and viable method of avalanche control. The other three types of avalanche control all involved explosives: hand charges, a recoilless rifle, and a pack howitzer. The most common technique was for patrollers to throw individual two-pound hand charges filled with gelatin dynamite at predetermined placements on the routes.

The charges came in 50-pound boxes, 25 shots to a box. They looked like fat, waxy, cardboard-colored salamis, 12 inches long and about two inches around. On a big morning, between them the ski patrol might throw hundreds of bombs, making a well-developed throwing arm a side benefit of the job. The cap and fuse assemblies were usually prepared during non-storm periods and stored for later use. The fuse was a thin orange cord with a black powder core and a plastic textile skin. The patrolman setting up the assemblies cut 18-inch lengths of fuse from a 1,000-foot roll. He then crimped each cap, which came 100 to a small box, to each fuse with a bench crimper. The burn time was approximately 40 seconds a foot, and since the fuses burned slower in high elevations, 18 inches of fuse was generally considered to give the patrollers 70 seconds before the charge exploded. As might be expected, burn time was tested regularly.

To keep supplies ready throughout a blizzard, one of the patrollers was assigned to stay late the night before or come in early in the morning, around 4:30 a.m., to arm the charges with cap and fuse assemblies. He used a non-sparking punch to poke a hole in the side of each of their hard shells, then inserted the metal blasting cap, with the fuse already attached to it, into the stick of dynamite. The patroller would then use duct tape to secure the fuse to the bomb.

On Tuesday, March 30, 1982, Larry and the other patrolmen rode up the lifts throughout the storm with the heavy, cumbersome bomb packs already on their backs, then skied and/or hiked over to the locations where they planned to deliver the explosives. The big brownish-beige rucksacks were one of the few pieces of equipment supplied and kept by the resort, since once dynamite had been in them, they couldn't be used for anything else.

For the previous several days the wind had been blowing and gusting erratically, anywhere from 40 mph to 60 mph at the base of the resort and up to 90 mph on the summit. Due to both wind and elevation, the amount of snow accumulation up on mountain ridges was often as much as double or triple the amount of snow in the valley. The ski patrol was fond of saying that wind was the architect of avalanches because of the way the wind swept the snow from the ridgetops and whipped it across slopes as well as down to lower ones. Cross-loading or direct loading of snow from above were the fastest ways for a slope to become weighted down, a situation that didn't necessarily give the snowpack enough time to adjust to its load and process the stress of so much snow so fast.

As Larry got into position with 40 pounds of explosives slung over his shoulders, he had his partner retrieve a bomb out of his pack for him so he could keep it on his back. He obviously always threw the charges from what he believed to be a safe place, although he and the rest of the patrollers were wrong on occasion. Bob Blair used to say that the avalanches were way more dangerous than the dynamite, because the bombs were predictable. There were usually no more than two patrolmen doing a route together, so as to expose the fewest people to the hazard at a time. Another Bob Blair expression was that avalanche control was not a social event.

Up on the wind-whipped ridgeline Larry couldn't light the fuse with a traditional match, so he, as well as the other patrollers, carried a bunch of pull wire igniters in their chest pockets. About six inches long, an igniter—known as an igi—looked like a little cardboard pen with a wire sticking out of it. When Larry was ready to set the bomb off, he placed it between his knees and hunched over it, pushing the igi onto the fuse, which clipped the igi's tiny teeth onto the end of the fuse. As soon as he tugged the igniter, the match striker inside it ignited the black powder core in the fuse. When the hot spark of the fuse reached the cap, it set off a rapid chain reaction with the three internal types of explosives in the cap, which then detonated the charge. In the late '70s at Mammoth Mountain, within a short period of time one patrolman was injured and another one was killed using the pull wire igniters. As a result, the Alpine Meadows crew couldn't get them for awhile. In the interim, they were forced to use much more dangerous windproof matches that burned like sparklers.

As soon as Larry pulled the igniter, the charge became a live bomb. It wasn't actually ticking, but it might as well have been. Before he threw it, however, he had to confirm that it was lit, and he accomplished this by holding it close to his face and inspecting it. It wasn't a situation where, if in doubt, he could just throw it anyway, because he couldn't leave an unexploded charge on the slope for a skier to find. If the visibility was good, which was almost never the case, he would have seen a little smoke and been able to watch the fuse melting and bubbling. If it was not windy, which was never the case, he would have heard it hissing and smelled sulfur, like fireworks. If all else failed, he could have held the fuse to the snow to see if it burned it the color of charcoal.

After a couple of seasons, the patrollers seemed to get a feel for whether the fuse was lit or not. Larry, like most veteran patrolmen, had the bomb out of his hands within a second or two of lighting it. Seventy seconds after he pulled the igniter, the dynamite exploded with a muffled boom and almost simultaneously a chunk of the slope slid away. There were basically two outcomes the moment after a bomb exploded: Either the snow didn't move at all or (except in the rare circumstance of a delayed release) the result was instantaneous—when the charge went off, the avalanche ran.

Throughout March 30 Larry and the crew of patrolmen maintained their avalanche control efforts at a constant, wearing pace, throwing hand charges into the relentless torrent as well as blindly firing the rifle into slopes saturated with new snowfall. The Alpine Meadows patrol conducted intensive avalanche safety precautions— measures that years later, long after all the bodies had been found and the snow cleared away, would cause a jury to hold the men on the patrol blameless, to say they had tried as hard as they could to control the uncontrollable.

The patrol's first indication of unusual avalanche activity that day was late in the afternoon on the west route above the road. Around 4:30 p.m. two patrolmen threw hand charges onto a path on that route but weren't able to set off a slide. Casey was acting as a guard to keep people off the road, and Jim Plehn came down on a snowmobile to evaluate why the slide path hadn't released. A thousand yards away, Larry and his partner threw a double charge at the east route, an action that inexplicably triggered not just an avalanche on the east route, but also one on the west route, which released sympathetically.

The patrolmen heard the rumbling before they saw it coming, like being in a forest fire and listening to it burn toward them, and they took off running. The avalanche knocked Casey around and partially buried Jim; they survived only because they were on the very flank of it. Normally the patrollers are able to calculate how much snowfall it takes to reach the road and they attempt to do control work frequently enough so that avalanches won't reach it. This time, the slide buried the road and beyond.

All of the patrolmen had been getting fairly spectacular results from avalanche control throughout that day. Earlier, Casey and patrolman Lanny Johnson had triggered a deep slab avalanche with a four-foot crown on North Peril that went off huge, taking out trees and creating a gigantic amount of debris. Named Lansworth after his grandfather, Lanny, age 25, moved from Alberta, Canada, to the Bay Area in California in mid-high school. The transition was pretty extreme, and he found his salvation in the mountains. He scaled El Capitan in Yosemite at age 16, and by 19, he had taken his first Himalayan expedition and summited Makalu, the world's fifth-highest mountain. While on patrol at Alpine Meadows he took international guide exams in preparation for leading heli-ski expeditions, and in the off-season he worked as a guide in the Himalayas. All of his possessions fit easily into his Toyota truck.

Despite treacherous, 90-mph winds, Lanny and Casey taped four charges together and threw quad bombs all along the lift line on North Peril as they worked their way down the mountain. They could barely see each other, much less get their bearings, and at one point Lanny slipped over the edge of a cornice and fell about six feet. They could tell that the wind was distributing the snow lower down on the slopes, and they trained their explosives accordingly.

Afterward, Lanny and Tom Kimbrough, both serious mountain climbers, determined that to protect the lodge, they should try to control Beaver Bowl. The wind had moved beyond howling and was now roaring. A lift operator slowly bumped the chairs on the lift for them so they could access the ridge. At the top of the mountain, visibility was almost nonexistent. Their normal visual cues, particular rock formations and green iron bars pounded into the ridgetop, were useless to them. Between the wind and the concentration of the snowfall all around them, they had the disorienting sensation of being on an enormous white wave.

The ridgeline Lanny and Tom were standing on was indistinguishable from safe terrain. One of them would move completely out of the other's view but only be a few feet away. Even though it was a snowstorm, there were flashes of white lightning and tremendous amounts of static electricity in the atmosphere. The air was actually snapping—if they put their poles out, it would arc. They had a concern about the effect of static electricity on the 40 pounds of explosives on their backs, but they didn't turn back. The conditions were intolerable, and yet they remained.

Slowly they made their way along, Tom on cross-country skis, Lanny on mountaineering skis, protecting themselves with shots as they went. The snow was up to their armpits. Finally arriving at the mouth of Beaver Bowl, they tied charges together and threw quadruple-sized bombs over. Their mission was theoretically complete, although without the benefit of being able to see or hear anything through the storm, they had no way of knowing if they had been successful. Tom then announced that he was going to go to the edge of Beaver Bowl and check for avalanche debris, a nearly suicidal undertaking in those conditions. Tom wasn't under any illusions about the danger, telling Lanny, "This is as good a day as any to get the chop."

At the time, Tom was going through a lot of emotional trauma, primarily centering on a painful separation from his wife. While his resulting depression didn't exactly make him reckless, it did seem to bring out grandiose notions of sacrificing himself to save everyone else. Tom took a step forward, almost immediately moving out of Lanny's view. After what seemed to Lanny like an interminable wait, Tom returned to report that he was almost sure he had seen some fracture lines and large debris blocks on the slope.

At that point Lanny and Tom thought about trying to make it over to the Buttress. They tried to break trail toward that direction, but the snow in that area was as high as their chins. After doing avalanche control for a few seasons, ski patrolmen had a sense of when they were not in the right place at the right time. Lanny and Tom felt something immense brewing in the snow, and at that moment they knew they were not in, as they called it, a safe island. Lanny turned to Tom to assess the best way down the mountain.

"The forces here are so different," he said. "I feel like we're standing on top of a monster."

NINE

Dancin' on the edge of time
No one here that knows my mind
Flyin' high into the night
Not another soul in sight
Cruisin' low, the mountain tops
Pray to God it never stops

—

Beth Morrow, written on the top of Roundhouse lift, March 7, 1982

That Tuesday night, March 30, the violence and sheer remorselessness of the storm prevented Beth Morrow from making it home from the ski resort to her place on the other side of town. She had spent the day at Alpine Meadows tracking the patrolmen's avalanche control results with Bernie, and since she was scheduled to work again the next morning, she ended up crashing with her fellow lift operators Sandy Harris and Anna Conrad. Sandy and Anna were renting an old cabin halfway down Alpine Meadows Road, just a mile and a half from the ski resort, right by a sign warning drivers that they were entering an avalanche area.

Sandy and Anna had been roommates at UC Davis. Sandy came

up to Alpine Meadows the previous fall, and Anna moved up to join her in December after she finished her degree in wildlife biology. Anna intended to return to Davis to attend her graduation ceremony in June, but in the meantime the plan was for the two of them to live together and work at the ski resort for the season.

The house was a steep, modified A-frame, with little or no insulation. The women tried to burn wood in the fireplace, but it didn't give off much heat unless they stood right next to it. When they were in the house they mostly lived in their bedrooms under electric blankets. Anna and Sandy were each only making $4.35 an hour as first-year lift operators, so there wasn't much left of their paychecks for luxuries like heat—an average bill was $230 per month—after they covered the $800 per month rent. The place had two bedrooms and a loft, which functioned as enough space to squeeze in tenants from time to time to help them with expenses.

The cabin creaked like an old ship when it was windy, and an ice dam had flooded the kitchen and then frozen in the indoor/outdoor carpet, so the women had to wear boots as they crunched over the floor to make breakfast. The house did have a window with a peak view of the mountains, but its primary advantage was its convenience to the resort. Anna and Sandy could walk to work or, since all the employees had to pass by their house, easily wave someone down for a ride rather than shovel their own cars out of the driveway.

With its proximity to the ski area and a location right off the main road, the cabin became known as a bit of a party house. They had a big New Year's Eve party there to bring in 1982, with one guest dominating the lone bathroom by passing out in the bathtub. Anna simply closed the shower curtain on him and deemed the bathroom operable. So many guests stayed over that night that the sheriff stopped by in the morning to inform Anna and Sandy that the plow operator couldn't clear the main road with all the cars parked on it.

Sandy had been friends with Beth since their first day of training the previous November when they came back to the cabin together for a lunch of grilled peanut butter and jelly sandwiches. At that time, the primary choices of seasonal jobs for women at the resort were checking tickets or running the ski lifts. Ticket checkers in that era had a reputation for being cute but not especially bright, so Beth, Sandy, and Anna had all applied to be lift operators. Jake's friend Billy Davis was in charge of lift ops, and he received a considerable amount of pressure from the ski patrolmen to hire attractive women. It was a time and a place with loose standards regarding sexual harassment—the female lift operators were constantly being bounced on the laps of the men who worked at the resort.

Although all three of these women would have been strong candidates based on the ski patrol's criteria alone—Anna had straight, shoulder-length blond hair and a wholesome face with cornflower-blue eyes; Beth had long blond hair, pronounced eyebrows, and big brown eyes with enormous lashes; and Sandy was tall with a luxuriant mop of curly auburn hair—they all had plenty of other hiring qualifications going for them. Responsible employees were sometimes hard to find for seasonal work, but these women, despite the fact they were all essentially up at Alpine Meadows for a fun, temporary winter/spring adventure, were also conscientious, reliable workers.

Beth joined in the socializing and attended the parties, but she wasn't necessarily as loose as some of the other employees. She more or less stumbled upon the job—during her interview Billy got the sense that she didn't quite know what she was getting into in terms of the lift operators' duties. In most cases, the interviewees were asking Billy for the job, but with Beth, who seemed particularly dependable, Billy turned the interview into a sales pitch to convince her to take the position.

Beth had finished three years of college at the University of Nevada, Reno, and she was up at Alpine Meadows during a year off from school before going back to finish her degree. At work her colleagues were exposed to different, almost incongruous aspects of her personality, some seeing her as shy and introspective, others viewing her as bubbly and outspoken. Her true character seemed faithful to a little of both, mixed with a lot of innocent enthusiasm. She was a natural beauty who could look glamorous when she wanted to, but she didn't feel like she quite fit in among sorority sisters who devoted so much time to their hair and makeup. That environment seemed phony to her, and although she was committed to graduating from college, she first wanted to take a break and live a more unspoiled existence in the mountains, ideally at a ski resort. Alpine Meadows, where she had skied in the past, happened to be where she found a job.

Beth's dad, John, was an inspector for the air force, and she had spent much of her early childhood moving around the country—Texas, Massachusetts, Nevada, Oregon, Arizona. As a result, Beth and her younger sister and brother all learned to make friends quickly. In high school in Austin, Texas, Beth was on pep squad but also spent a lot of time volunteering on a crisis line for people who had overdosed on drugs, taking shifts as soon as she could drive. Beth and her sister Carol, who was just a year and a half younger, were longtime confidantes, a bond that in Beth's mind included unfettered access to Carol's closet. They shared a room together until they were teenagers and forever kept each other up late, talking into the night.

The family vacations in those years often involved camping in a big Travelall that looked like an old school bus and going out on the water in an open-hulled boat. During trips to Oregon and Colorado, Beth, a huge John Denver fan, filled her diary with passages about the beauty of the outdoors and her desire to see the world and live in the mountains.

The Morrow family moved to Sparks, Nevada, outside Reno, in the summer of '77. The move was hard on Beth, who was just entering her senior year of high school and missed her friends in Texas, but Nevada did offer proximity to skiing. Proficient on water skis, she picked up snow skiing right away.

After Beth graduated from Reed High School, she lived at home while she went to college at UNR, focusing on classes in ecology and earth science. She lived on her own for the first time in the summer of '81, when she took a job as a surveyor for the Bureau of Land Management. She moved from site to site, lugging stakes and tromping around in the wilds of Nevada. The oversize pillows her mom, Del, made for her provided some comfort, but the job was pretty rough. Beth, at five foot four and 115 pounds, increased her physical strength that summer and also grew up quite a bit. The job overlapped into the start of her fall semester at college, which was perhaps a convenient reason for her to take the year off school. She was worried about telling her dad, who had both a law degree and an MBA, of her decision to delay her graduation, but he was supportive. Her plan was to make enough money to go to Alaska the following summer to visit her dad's sister and travel around the state.

Beth was never without friends, but she was also comfortable being alone and often sought out solitude. A lot of her interests—playing flute, learning guitar, writing, reading, learning languages—were fairly solitary pursuits. At other times, she loved being social, which at Alpine Meadows meant going out for beers with the patrolmen or cheap margaritas at Hacienda in Tahoe City with Sandy and Anna. That winter she had dated a ski instructor a couple of times and had periodic crushes on other employees, but she wasn't seeing anyone seriously.

Beth and Sandy used to light up the extensions on the switchboard at their respective lifts, planning breaks together and comparing their impressions of various hot guys on the slopes. Within the subculture of the employee pool, ski patrolmen were the strong, dashing young men of the mountain, as opposed to the ski instructors, viewed by some in that era as pretty boys. Many of the female employees were up at Alpine Meadows for experiences they could only find in the mountains—and they could always find ski instructors in the city.

While Beth usually adapted fairly easily to new situations, she was particularly tuned in to injustices, and if she perceived an issue as unfair, she wasn't afraid to argue her point. She didn't always temper her thoughts, but neither did she seek to offend or respond just for shock value. She was straighter than many of the people she worked with, always wanting things to be right, and yet she had some unconventional ideas as well. With her reflective, artistic soul and occasional mood swings, Beth simply wasn't a round peg.

Often alone at the top of Roundhouse lift, during slow times or on breaks, Beth wrote poetry almost as if she were keeping a journal, chronicling the layers of her personal exploration through insightful poems that spanned an array of emotions. Some of her poems were dark, almost fatalistic, and many of them were dreamy and wistful. One of them contained an especially sincere expression of some of the yearnings she was feeling at that time:

> Oh Lord, carry me away to forever in a sunshine
>   kaleidoscope carriage
> Where orange blossoms carry the scent of memories
>   of a different age
> And today with her troubles can be forgotten
>   with the closing of my eyes
> The truth is so painful and I've heard so many lies
> I search for myself, my flight in the sky.

Bernie Kingery took notice of Beth's desire to be involved, to be part of the mountain beyond simply operating a lift. He needed someone to scribe for him, a job that entailed sitting next to him in the patrol office, known as Base 4, and taking notes, including writing down everything that was said over the radio. Beth volunteered for the position, and Billy Davis, her lift ops supervisor, seeing that it was important for her to be needed in a professional sense, let her do it. She scribed for avalanche control in the mornings before the lifts opened, then headed up to her shift at the ski lift. If she was needed to continue scribing, someone opened her lift for her and covered her duties until she could get there. It was an important function keeping accurate logs and records, and Beth was excited to be among the first to hear what was happening on the mountain, learning which slopes were sliding and which weren't. By the end of the season she scribed every day she was assigned to work. Bernie was comfortable with Beth, and as she became familiar with his lingo, she kept track of the radio traffic with ease. The specialized position set her apart and gave her an identity at the resort.

To her coworkers Beth seemed to be living for the moment, but much as she valued her time at Alpine Meadows, she wrote in her journal and talked to her family about wanting other experiences in her life. By that March, Beth, age 22, was planning ahead, ready to leave the resort at the end of the season and come back to what she referred to as "the real world."

Throughout the winter Beth had been commuting back to Reno, about an hour away, to take an evening math class at UN Reno until a rotary snowplow wrecked her car and she no longer had transportation. When she was home for the weekend in late March visiting with a friend from Austin, her dad had to give her a ride back. She stayed a little longer in Sparks because she was having so much fun, filling up on her mom's cooking and resting after trashing her body skiing the week before, an incident in which she split her skis across a stream and lost her good sunglasses. Her dad drove her back in the storm to the place she was renting in Alpine Meadows on Monday night, March 29, then walked behind his truck to kiss her good-bye. "See ya, Dad," she said, before bouncing away over the drifts.

The next night, Tuesday the thirtieth, was a full house at Sandy and Anna's cabin, with Beth staying over and also Anna's boyfriend, Frank Yeatman, in town for a visit. Unlike Beth, Sandy and Anna were more committed to the Alpine Meadows lifestyle, kicking back with parties at their house and doing their laundry in town over a few Lucky Lagers, the cheapest beer they could find. Food was sometimes hard to come by—although they could usually be counted on to have a 39-cent can of soup hanging around for guests, and maybe some bread to go with it—but there seemed to be enough cash to keep the margaritas, if not flowing, at least within reach now and then.

Once Anna had been at Alpine Meadows for a month, she was already contemplating the idea of making the seasonal adventure a two-year stint. Everyone at the ski area knew that Anna, who had just turned 22, had a boyfriend she was faithful to, but she still enjoyed the social scene at the resort. Her steady, even demeanor was blended with an affability that made her the ideal operator for Meadow chair, a lift that led to beginner runs and therefore required lots of interaction with novice skiers.

Since infancy Anna had displayed a tendency to be almost alarmingly well grounded. When she was a baby in Corvallis, Oregon, her parents, Gene and Joan, noticed some stiffness in her legs when she started to grab the sides of her playpen to pull herself up. She was diagnosed with hip dysplasia, a condition affecting the development of her hip joints. To keep her knees apart and her hips in the proper position so they could heal, Anna was required to wear a splint that resembled a saddle for the next year and a half, including when she was sleeping. It wasn't long before she was up on her feet, learning to walk with the harness, shoving one leg and hip forward and then the other. Although her mom and dad tried to carry her up and around various barriers, she wouldn't even let stairs stop her, quickly learning to manipulate them with the splint on and without any help.

Perhaps because she taught herself so very early in life that giving up was not an option, Anna grew up overcoming obstacles as a matter of course. The youngest of three children, she constantly tried to keep up with her two older brothers and managed to hold her own much of the time. She took swim lessons along with her brothers, for example, despite being several years younger. When school administrators in Richmond, California, determined that there were too many students in her fifth-grade class, she simply skipped fifth grade and enrolled in sixth without missing a beat. Anna had so much confidence in her abilities that the only flaw her parents saw was the possibility that her self-assurance might exceed her actual skills.

She was a respectful, considerate child, the type who instinctively knew right from wrong. One of her brothers had a speech problem, and Anna always offered to help out, sitting with him in the corner and engaging in long conversations that she then interpreted for her parents. Gene and Joan felt that their daughter could easily have been spoiled, but it never went that way.

Anna was a serious student, especially interested in science and always involved in gifted programs. In high school in Glendora, California, about 30 miles east of Los Angeles, she swam on the school team and played clarinet in the band, balancing those activities with a part-time job at a local veterinary office that required her to wake up at 4 a.m. most mornings before school. Her first exposure to the mountains was through frequent hikes and backpacking trips with her dad and her brothers, but she didn't ski much until she got to college at UC Davis. Unconcerned that fellow students had been skiing for a decade or more, Anna found the sport came so naturally to her that she ended up joining the intramural ski team.

It was in the spring of her junior year of college that Anna met Frank Yeatman—tall and thin, with gripping brown eyes and curly brown hair—in a science class. They began dating that summer, were close by September, and devoted to each other after that. Since Anna had left the campus in December, they took turns visiting each other every weekend—either Anna would drive the two hours back to school to see Frank, or he would drop into her life at Alpine Meadows.

Frank, also 22, was still enrolled at UC Davis and on schedule to graduate the following June. He was majoring in wildlife and fisheries biology as well as completing a minor in environmental toxicology. After graduation, his plan was to work for the Forest Service for a year while he applied to graduate school in wildlife biology. He knew that he wanted to work outdoors, not behind a desk, and he felt that a master's degree would expand his career options as a research scientist. Extremely intelligent and a focused, dedicated student, Frank, when he wasn't studying, was attracted to active, outdoor activities.

The youngest of three boys, Frank grew up in various parts of northern California, including Sebastopol and Petaluma. When he was in fourth grade, his parents, Marie and Hoyt, settled the family in Ben Lomond, California, near Santa Cruz. Frank had always been an easy kid and an honor student, but once he hit eighth grade, his focus on schoolwork coincided with the development of a passionate interest in nature.

Frank became an accomplished hiker and camper, taking trips with his family for several weeks at a time along the John Muir Trail, setting up caches of food to recover along the way. He brought home every kind of creature he could find to keep as a pet, particularly ducks and birds. He also became a registered falconer, hooking up with an organization where he took care of sick hawks. It was only a matter of time before he brought one home, and Kimo, a red-tailed hawk, soon became his best friend. He flew her and doted on her, and the two of them were virtually inseparable until he left for college.

Frank's mom took care of Kimo in his absence, and by the Thanksgiving break of his first year, Marie was forced to break the news to Frank that she thought his hawk was ill. Frank came home and spent the entire holiday at her side. At one point he took some books outside in the backyard, sitting at a redwood table with Kimo resting on his arm. Marie was concerned about the proximity of Kimo's beak mere inches from her son's eyes as he studied, but Kimo never hurt him.

At the time Frank met Anna he already had a girlfriend that he had been dating for several years. There was some drama as he eased out of his existing relationship, but once he was with Anna, they fell very much in love. They talked of a future together, not in specifics, but definitely in terms of permanence.

Anna may have appealed to Frank's studious side, but she also seemed to bring out the more fun-loving aspects of his nature. A lot of their time together centered on their shared allegiance with the outdoors—they hiked Crater Lake, took long runs, and cross-country skied. Frank gave Anna a pair of cross-country skis for Christmas, and during his weekends at Alpine Meadows, they began exploring the Lake Tahoe region on skis together.

The last week of March was spring break at UC Davis, and Frank had spent the first part of it at home visiting his parents before heading up to visit Anna. On Tuesday, March 30, the two of them had cross-country skied over by Squaw Valley. Frank planned to leave Alpine Meadows on Wednesday night, March 31, to get ready for his last quarter of classes at Davis.

On Wednesday morning, the entire household awoke to yet more snowfall. Anna, Sandy, and Beth trudged down the driveway to catch a ride to work, submerged up to their waists in soft, new snow.

There weren't many vehicles on the road that morning, but the women did run into a truck with two young Alpine Meadows employees, Randy Buck and Tad DeFelice, heading to work at the resort.

When the men told them the resort was closed due to the storm, Anna and Sandy gratefully headed back inside, while Beth, yelling out to her friends, "I need the hours," swung up into the truck.

It wasn't a sure thing that Beth would be allowed to work that day, but even though the resort was closed, there was still a need for employees to shovel out some of the ski lifts and bump the chairs up so the assemblies didn't freeze. In any event, Beth figured that she would likely be able to scribe for Bernie at Base 4 at least in the morning. Despite her comment, Beth's friends knew that she was motivated by the opportunity to be a central part of the operations at least as much as the paycheck.

Sandy, who was recovering from a particularly nasty head cold, returned to the cabin and slept for awhile, waking up in time to have pancakes with Anna and Frank. Sandy snuggled up under a blanket to watch TV while Anna and Frank discussed what to do that day given the unexpected benefit of Anna not having to work. Frank felt confined in the small house and he didn't want to sit around all day. He at least wanted to go outside to shovel out his car—buried in the driveway under several feet of snow—so he could leave that night, but Anna didn't have the right clothes at the cabin to help him. The women didn't have a lot of money for cold-weather gear to begin with, and certainly not for extra sets. There were no Alpine Meadows uniforms for the lift operators and Anna generally needed ski clothes at the resort more than at home, so she kept her snow pants in her locker in the Summit Terminal Building.

Since Anna and Frank both wanted to get out of the house and do something anyway, the idea of retrieving her powder pants from Alpine Meadows was motivation enough. Anna had never cross-country skied to the resort before, but since that was the obvious choice of transportation, they decided to ski the mile and a half there together. She called up to the ski area to confirm that there was no avalanche control going on and that the road was open.

Both Anna and Frank dressed in long underwear tops and bottoms for the trip, and Frank put on two pairs of socks and some light blue bib overalls over his Levi's. Anna tugged on a wool sweater but decided against a jacket, since she knew she would work up a sweat skiing. They walked outside, balancing on top of Frank's car as they worked their way down the driveway. At one point Anna slipped off to the side, falling into a well filled with six feet of soft and extremely wet snow. The snow was packed in all around her, above her in some places and up to her armpits in others, and as she tried to swim her way out, she just sank deeper into the gully. Even with Frank's exceptionally patient help it still took Anna over an hour to get out, and by then she was mad, hot, and soaking wet.

At that point it was after 2:30 and Frank offered to go back inside, even though neither of them wanted to. The driveway turmoil behind them, Anna and Frank strapped on their skis and glided away down Alpine Meadows Road.

TEN

I just like blowin' shit up and making things move.

—

Casey Jones, Alpine Meadows ski patrol, 1978–present

Right from the start, it was no secret that Alpine Meadows, surrounded on three sides by high, steep mountains, was located in dangerous avalanche terrain. When the area was first contemplated as a possible ski resort back in the 1950s, Monty Atwater, the country's pioneer of avalanche forecasting and control, wrote a memo essentially describing the area as beautiful ski terrain that had the potential of avalanching like crazy. He also identified an ideal location for a gun mount from which to fire on the slopes, a placement that the Alpine Meadows patrol later dubbed Gunner's Knob. By the early '80s, the use of a rifle platform on that site was an integral part of a highly developed avalanche control program.

Historically, the practice of shooting artillery into the mountains to set off avalanches wasn't employed only as a safety precaution. During the mountain campaigns of World War I, when the Austrian and Italian armies were fighting for control of the Tyrol, they used avalanches as a weapon of war. From 1915 to 1918, conservative estimates put the death toll by avalanche during that combat at around 40,000 men (an estimated 18,000 of whom died in one two-day battle in December 1916). Some of the slides occurred naturally, but most were triggered when troops (from both sides) fired shells into snow-laden ridges, deliberately releasing avalanches to crash down onto the soldiers below.

The birth of avalanche control as a modern technology in the United States took place at Alta, Utah, shortly after WWII. Atwater came to Alta, an abandoned silver-mining camp nine miles up Little Cottonwood Canyon in the Wasatch Mountains, in 1946. An MIT graduate, he was fresh from the U.S. Army's Tenth Mountain Division, where he had seen explosives successfully set off slides in the Alps. At Alta he became a U.S. Forest Service snow ranger and founded the first avalanche research center in the Western Hemisphere.

When Atwater started out, all he had in the way of equipment was a set of thermometers, a stake for measuring snow depth, and a bundle of signs that read Closed Area, Avalanche Danger. His only available methods of avalanche control were to shut down the resort, a risk in that skiers tended to ignore the signs, or to ski the slopes himself, figuring that if they didn't slide with him, presumably they wouldn't with anyone else either. As a alternative to those drastic (and potentially deadly) options, Atwater began experimenting with drilling holes in cornices and tamping them with dynamite. He also suspended charges just above the snow surface and lowered large bombs over the edge of ridges. His first real success was in 1948, when he took a bunch of solid, bricklike tetratol explosive to the top of a run called Rustler's Face and threw it over the ridge. It triggered a massive avalanche that not only rendered the slope safe for skiing, but opened up terrain that had never before been skied. The art of patrolling with hand charges was born.

Atwater's advances in avalanche control, with explosives as well as weapons, paved the way for the development of Alpine Meadows. As soon as it opened in '61, Alpine Meadows became one of the top few ski areas in the country for avalanche action, and perhaps the toughest to control in terms of the layout of the resort.

Neighboring Squaw Valley, for example, was a bigger resort, but unlike Alpine Meadows, its access road was not located in a potential avalanche runout zone.

Located right off Highway 89, Alpine Meadows Road ends at the ski resort, then, to ease traffic flow, curves to the left and makes a complete loop to Ginzton Road, which intersects back with Alpine Meadows Road. This huge circle at the end of the road encloses several acres of parking lot. The creation of a three-mile-long access road leading to the resort made avalanche control particularly complicated, since the ski patrol had the responsibility of controlling not just the ski runs but the slopes above the road as well. In addition, as the road was the sole artery to the resort, there were always considerable demands on the patrol to complete the control quickly and allow the public to reach the ski area.

The avalanche control program at Alpine Meadows was finally formalized in 1976–77. Up to that point, it seemed as if the place learned the hard way, all the way along.

The first trouble occurred back in March of '74, when the mountain was coated in ice from a rainstorm, then covered with lots of loose sugar snow and topped with a sort of layer-cake assemblage of new snow. Jim Plehn and another patrolman threw six bombs into the High Yellow area, including one high into the shady, exposed peak, without triggering an avalanche. They called down on their radio to Base 1, saying that they had finished shooting but were still evaluating the situation. The hill groomers only heard the first part of that transmission. When the patrolmen threw another charge, they heard not just the boom of the explosive going off, but also the grinding V-8 engines from two old Tucker Sno-Cats.

The next noise was the roar of the mountainside breaking away ten feet deep, and immediately competing with that was what sounded like a drag race as the snowcat drivers saw the avalanche coming at them and floored their machines trying to outrun it. As the slide picked up the snow machines, swept them into the trees, and turned them upside down, the straining whir of the engines was abruptly cut off, enveloping the mountain in an eerie silence.

At that very instant, Bernie Kingery was in the lift operator's shack on the top of Roundhouse, accusing Casey Jones of smelling like marijuana. Casey had been up on the mountain early, enjoying what he referred to as a morning bowlful as he watched the bombs thrown by other teams explode. The news of the avalanche diverted Bernie from his investigation, and Casey never had to find out how that moment would have gone for him. He and Bernie skied down and helped dig the snowcat drivers out.

One of the drivers was imprisoned, but safe, inside his snowcat. Inside the cab of the other machine, all the patrolmen could see was a mass of snow and an arm hanging out of the broken window. They followed the arm, dug back, and cleared the snow from the driver's face. He was already blue from suffocation, but he started breathing spontaneously.

The resort had never had a call that close before. The following winter there was another incident, when a lift at Scott Chute was opened before the patrol had had a chance to check for hangfires (the snow left hanging above the fracture after a slope avalanches). The first skier to lay powder tracks across the slope that morning set off a slide. The skier actually escaped unharmed, but in the confusion to account for everyone, the patrol set up a full probe line to be sure no one was buried. The press went wild with the story.

In March 1976, Alpine Meadows had an avalanche scare for the third season in a row, this time with deadly consequences. It had been a drought year, meaning not much snow, a weak snowpack, and a limited season for skiers. When a big storm finally hit the area in March, management wanted all of the runs open and pressured the patrol to get the slopes ready quickly. From high on the mountain the patrolmen could see cars pouring into the parking lot as tourists flocked to the resort for the fresh powder.

While deep powder is easily the best snow to ski on, in that it allows skiers to plane on it with the sensation of floating, it can also be the most dangerous. In addition, powder snow has a short shelf-life—it either settles or it avalanches. Early that morning three men traversed through Wolverine Bowl, cutting low, and triggered an enormous avalanche when they entered Beaver Bowl. All three of them were killed.

Jim Plehn had spent that season, '75–'76, working as a snow surveyor for the hydrologic sciences department at the University of Nevada, Reno, traveling along 200 miles of the Sierra Crest, charting the depth of the snowpack and collecting snow samples for analysis. He dug snow pits and trained himself to recognize what the different types of snow in the various layers looked like, tying them to the dates of particular weather sequences. In the course of that winter doing snow science, Jim learned more about snow metamorphism than he ever had as a patrolman.

When Alpine Meadows opened the following winter, it was with a full-time avalanche hazard forecaster. Jim was the obvious choice to fill the position.

Early in his childhood, Jim developed what would become a lifelong connection to the Lake Tahoe area. Raised in the affluent Bay Area suburbs of Los Altos, Palo Alto, and Saratoga, Jim spent his summers in an unwinterized fishing camp on the Truckee River that his grandfather, the head of the economics department at UC Berkeley, had built in 1911. Lake Tahoe was sleepy and relatively undeveloped in the 1950s, and when Jim was a boy, the whole area was a wide-open wilderness playground for him to explore. His bond with the place only deepened when, as an 11-year-old boy, he experienced firsthand the spectacle of the Winter Olympics in Squaw Valley in 1960.

Jim's father not only taught Jim to ski, but also infused him with a sense of adventure and an appreciation of the outdoors. Jim joined the National Ski Patrol as a teenager, coming up from the Bay Area as frequently as he could. While Jim's dad, an award-winning civil engineer, was gregarious and a legendary storyteller, Jim was the antithesis—patently shy, deeply private. Despite three generations of Cal Bears in his family, rather than attend college Jim opted for a life in the mountains. When he graduated from high school in 1967, he headed up to the place he felt most at home.

Even at Alpine Meadows Jim was known as a bit of a hermit, quite an accomplishment in a community of people who tended to keep to themselves. A gifted backcountry skier, he seemed uncomfortable in certain social situations, and at least superficially, he had difficulty communicating with people. Werner Schuster, director of public relations for the resort, said good morning to Jim every day for years without a response, until eventually he acknowledged the greeting.

Jim was also, quite likely, a genius. His dad, initially disappointed in his son's decision not to attend college, once told him that if he was not going to pursue education, he should pursue wisdom instead. Jim lived by the advice, and in doing so, over time did earn the respect of his father. Despite his lack of formal education, Jim was a curious, intellectual scientist fascinated by the analysis of snow and all its intricacies. Wiry, with long hair and scraggly pieces of beard, he even looked the part of a backwoods professor.

His nickname on the patrol was Plain Jim because it was an inversion of his first and last names, not because he was ordinary in any respect. His very nature was contradictory—he was a free spirit, but so intense. He was abrupt, stubborn, extremely opinionated, and a bit of a contrarian. He was hard to approach unless it was by someone who knew him well, and yet he was extremely difficult to get to know. It wasn't that he wasn't fun to sit around and drink beer with, he just hadn't joined the patrol to socialize. Still, he did have an extremely tight relationship with Bob Blair, who made efforts to include him in the fold.

Jim's colleagues used to joke that the aspect of patrolling he liked least was rescuing injured people—not because of the risk or the gore, but because he had to interact with them. In that respect forecasting—so individual, somewhat isolating—was perfect for him. Never a light person, Jim took on his new responsibilities with the utmost seriousness. He was wholly dedicated to the world of avalanches, to the point that it almost defined him.

A combination of science and art, avalanche forecasting involves the analysis of terrain, snowpack, and weather—and the interaction among them—to calculate avalanche hazards. A forecaster's job is essentially to predict what type and size avalanches will occur on each of many radically different slopes with diverse exposures and elevations under ever-changing conditions. Familiarity with the specific slopes is obviously critical to forecasting potential avalanche activity on them, but just as crucial is a sort of sixth sense, an instinct for a particular mountain. The seeming contradiction of evaluating the strength of a weak layer, for example, often involves more than physics. In certain conditions, Jim and other experienced patrolmen used their skis almost like antennae to tune into the tension they sensed and felt in the snow.

Having experience with the slopes in question also requires a knowledge of the past avalanche activity on them, and in this department Alpine Meadows was at quite a disadvantage. When Jim became the forecaster, the resort had only been open for fifteen years, which in terms of nature's time scale was hardly an adequate period in which to assess historic avalanche conditions. In addition, courses on avalanche prediction and safety were not readily available in the late '70s, and in a pre-Internet era, there was no easy way to exchange information. At the time, most ski resorts, except for a couple in Utah, did not have full-time avalanche forecasters.

Nonetheless, Jim set about establishing a state-of-the-art forecasting program. He attended advanced seminars designed for snow scientists and engineers. He dug snow pits in a study plot and analyzed the weather data. He delineated and evaluated contributory avalanche factors and kept painfully detailed weather records and forecasting worksheets, measuring the snow temperature both at the surface and 20 centimeters down. Twice a day he recorded and measured the minimum and maximum temperature in the valley as well as the minimum and maximum temperature on the summit. On a chart entitled "Snow-Weather-Avalanche Studies at Alpine Meadows," he entered the snowfall, if any, each day at 8 a.m. and at 4 p.m. Chillingly, there would be no entry on that chart for four o'clock on March 31, 1982.

In the days before computers, a shelf in the ski patrol office was taken up by a row of chart recorders, machines that kept track of weather conditions on the top of the mountain: wind speed and direction (from a fixed spinning-cup anemometer up there), temperature, barometric pressure, and precipitation (in this case, the rate of snowfall). Particularly visual instruments, the recorders allowed Jim to easily identify weather trends and tell at a glance which slopes were loading and how the snow was being deposited.

To keep accurate records regarding the water content of new snowfall, relevant to determining the density of the various layers, Jim would take a core sample, melt it, and measure it with a ruler. Over time, however, he could simply pick up a handful of snow and have a pretty good feel for whether it contained 10 percent water or only 6 percent. He was constantly up in the middle of the night taking measurements and making notes, and he frequently skied with both a handheld anemometer, to measure wind speed and direction, and a hand lens, to look at snow crystals up close.

Jim also modified the control routes on the mountain, adding new ones and reconfiguring the existing ones to make them more efficient. He then prioritized them by breaking them up into primary and secondary routes. With the help of an avalanche textbook put out by the Forest Service, he created an avalanche atlas, a reference guide with the principal hazard zones described and illustrated with photos so every patroller would literally be seeing the same thing. To compile the photos, he took hundreds of black-and-white shots of the various slopes, drawing potential slide paths on them in red ink.

Prior to '76, the avalanche control plan had been contained on one page. Jim established a written set of control plans that delineated, depending on the hazard and the weather conditions, what type of control measures the patrollers would do and which ski lifts and trails would be open. Plan A was implemented on days with mild storm conditions, and the plans then went up, based on the severity of the storm, to Plan D. Plan D was for intense storm problems and a high avalanche hazard to the base area, road, and parking lot. In place on March 31, 1982, Plan D entailed closing the ski resort and allowing only avalanche control crews and essential employees on-site. After March 31, the resort developed a Plan E.

Alpine Meadows was open to the public from 9 a.m. until 4 p.m. On non–avalanche control days, the ski patrolmen worked from eight o'clock in the morning until whenever they got off the mountain at the end of the day, usually around five or a little later. On control days they started, meaning booted up and ready to go out the door, at 6:30. It was unusual to get the day off on an "AC day."

Larry and Jim and the other patrollers often knew in advance when to expect an avalanche control day, but if it wasn't clear the day before whether there was going to be enough snowfall to warrant control in the morning, they referred to it as a "call day." If there was at least three inches of new snow, one of the night groomers called Jim at 4 a.m. and he in turn called the rest of the patrolmen. Since an unexpected storm could occur at any time and the patrol had to be called in to control it, as a practical matter, every day was a call day.

Prior to setting out every day, Larry and the rest of the patrolmen gathered for a morning meeting in the patrol room. Jim determined which control plan they would do that day, reviewed the hazard forecast, and detailed any special instructions. Bob Blair made the assignments for the 15 control routes (9 primary and 6 secondary). The patrollers usually finished avalanche control by nine, when the resort opened, although if need be, some of the secondary routes—in protected areas that could be kept closed and opened later—could be completed afterward.

While the most common type of avalanche control was for the patrolmen to access the tops of the slopes via the chairlifts and throw hand charges from above, that process wasn't always an option. In fierce storms when certain lifts were swinging violently in the wind and too dangerous to ride, patrolmen would sometimes trek up the slopes to place the charges. On a particularly stubborn slope, patrollers occasionally strung a row of charges together with det (short for detonation) cord and set them off all at once. To place those shots, one of the patrolmen roped himself up and drilled holes in the cornice as his partner belayed him along the mountaintop.

When the weather restricted, or prevented, Larry and Jim and the team from going up on the ridges to throw bombs, they used Alpine Meadows' artillery—a recoilless rifle and a howitzer—to control avalanches from the base of the mountain. Depending on the season, they used the rifle about a third to a half of the time they did avalanche control, sometimes as many as 20 times a winter. While the hand charges, which caused a concussion that shocked the snow near the surface, were a more reliable way to test snow stability and release avalanches, using military weapons to blast holes in the slopes generally seemed to work as well.

Alpine Meadows was responsible for the avalanche control work at the resort, but the U.S. Forest Service got involved when the gun or cannon was fired. To lease the national forest land, John Riley, one of the original founders of the resort, had secured a special-use permit from the U.S. Forest Service. (After his involvement with Alpine Meadows, over the next two decades Riley moved on to other real estate development deals, most of which fell through. By March 1982 he ended up literally back where he started, living in the parking lot of the ski area in his motor home, drinking on the deck of the lodge in the afternoons.) Under the terms of the use permit, Forest Service snow rangers were required to oversee the use of artillery (which belonged to the federal government), which meant sending an on-call snow ranger over to actually pull the trigger. In 1982, that was usually Don Huber, the head snow ranger.

The epitome of a gentle giant, Don had an intermittent stutter that only made him more endearing and accessible. He had graduated from UC Berkeley with a degree in architecture before deciding to become a ski bum. Born in 1928, he was on the volunteer patrol since 1950, then worked pro patrol for the Olympics in Squaw Valley. He was one of the first ski patrolmen hired at Alpine Meadows when the resort opened. When he arrived, he was handed nails and plywood and asked to build a six-by-six-foot wooden operators' shack to get the place ready to open.

Don became a full-time snow ranger around 1965, essentially taking over the position held by Monty Atwater, who had come to work for the Forest Service in California after his avalanche control innovations in Alta, Utah. The territory Don covered included several ski resorts besides Alpine Meadows, and his job responsibilities were diverse: making sure the resorts were skiable, inspecting chairlifts, marking timber to cut for trails, assisting in various inspections. Helping with avalanche control took up most of his time, however, and somehow that duty never seemed like work to him. Along with his wife, Roberta, who he met in the Sierra Club, he volunteered much of his free time to help train search-and-rescue dogs.

Don and senior ski patrolmen on the "gun crew" fired the 75 mm recoilless rifle (elephant guns are about .50 caliber) from a fixed, raised platform on Gunner's Knob, the knoll just above the ski area's base that Monty Atwater had originally identified as an ideal shooting location. The rifle was primarily used to control several slopes, including Beaver Bowl and Poma Rocks, to protect the base area and the facilities.

Developed during the closing stages of the Korean War, the rifle was a relic on loan (for free) from the U.S. Army to the Forest Service. It was designed without a cumbersome recoil system, but instead, it had a 100-foot "kill zone" behind it when it was fired. It was basically a 120-pound steel tube, open at both ends. Each bullet-shaped, impact-detonating missile that was loaded into the rifle weighed about ten pounds. There were two pieces to the ammunition, the propellant charge shell left behind in the rifle and the explosive warhead charge that fired. When it was shot, a blast of flame exited to the rear, propelling the warhead to arc forward and puncture an orange hole in the gloom. It was accurate, powerful, and simple.

The drawback to the rifle was that it was also dangerous as hell, with risks to the patrolmen that included fragmentation showers and shattering backdrafts. The patrol treated the situation with the level of respect they reserved for especially vital safety issues, posting signs such as "Don't fuck around with the gun or heads will roll." (The recoilless rifle was briefly banned, and ultimately retired, at Alpine Meadows after a defective round of ammunition malfunctioned and exploded in the barrel in the mid-'90s, killing a Forest Service ranger.)

Another, less life-threatening negative was that time was running out on available ammunition for the rifle. From a military standpoint, the weapon was long obsolete, and spare parts and surplus ammo were no longer being manufactured.

Since the patrolmen fired the recoilless rifle only when there was a monster storm in progress, the shooting conditions were always outrageously unsafe. Accessed by a built-in ladder, the firing platform was high in the air and completely exposed to the elements. The bulky yellow slickers the shooters wore in an attempt to protect themselves were all but worthless. The visibility was often so incredibly limited that the rangers and the patrolmen might not have been able to hit the side of the mountain, much less aim at specific shot placements on that mountain. Fortunately, Jim solved that problem by presetting the shot coordinates in good weather at the very beginning of the ski season.

The men shooting the rifle had to wear earmuffs to dampen the violence of the concussion. A handle with a push button triggered the firing pin, and if Larry or Jim or any of the rest of them gripped the handle too hard, the explosive shock could seriously injure their hand. They obviously had to stand to the side of the weapon while it shot a bright blaze of fire backward, and they would sometimes go down on their knees on the small gun mount, holding on to the supports and each other so they wouldn't get blown off by the wind and the snow.

For all that, the actual explosive in the ammunition was only about two pounds, the same as the amount of dynamite in each of the hand charges the patrolmen threw.

In 1982, the other piece of artillery used at Alpine Meadows was a 75 mm pack howitzer, vintage 1948. Also borrowed from the army, the wheeled, short-barreled cannon was originally designed to disassemble and pack on mules. (Some two decades later the government would demand that the resort return that howitzer's successor so it could be used on the battlefields of Iraq.)

The snow rangers and the patrolmen fired the howitzer less frequently than the recoilless rifle, usually only a handful of times a season. They used it to control the slide paths above the parking lot and the access road, including the Buttress and Pond Slope, wheeling it out of its storage spot in the maintenance building to fire it from specific locations in the lot and the road. It had a wooden handle and an old-fashioned nylon pull cord, and the ammunition, containing almost two pounds of TNT, was shaped like a four-foot bullet. The howitzer stirred up a lot of black smoke when it was fired, and the concussive reverberation was strong enough to shatter windshields.

The cannon could shoot miles away, but at close range it could be aimed right on target, blackening the slopes where it landed. In the early days there were a few misfires, including one time the rangers overshot the slopes of KT-22 in Squaw Valley from Alpine Meadows Road and sent a round all the way into Squaw (where it detonated without injury). Another time the forestry guys and some members of the patrol crew took the howitzer down to Highway 89 in an attempt to control the slide paths above the River Ranch restaurant. They were aiming for a cornice, but they shot a little too high and the round went over the ridge. Checking the trajectory, they determined that it likely went right into Lake Tahoe, a story that has been confirmed over the years by a string of alleged eyewitnesses.

Unlike the rifle, the firing coordinates on the howitzer could not be preset. The only way to shoot it was by manually adjusting the line of sight through the barrel, and in bad storms it was obviously a huge problem for the rangers and patrolmen to try to visually sight with little or no visibility. Another issue was the howitzer's general unwieldiness, especially in the snow. Every time one of the rangers fired it, it went rolling off all over the parking lot, sliding on ice and snow and usually lodging in a snowbank. Several patrolmen would then have to retrieve it and drag it back to fire the next round.

The kind of conditions Larry and Jim and the entire Alpine Meadows patrol worked under were unlike that of most ski resorts in the country. In general, heavy snowfall in mountain areas occurs when a mass of warm air is forced to a higher elevation as it moves over a mountain range and then cools, a process called orographic lifting. The especially immense snowfall in the Sierra Nevada range is related to its proximity to the ocean, only about 160 miles away. As tropical storms off the Pacific laden with warm, moist air move east, they rise over the mountains and mix with the cold arctic air. This atmospheric phenomenon, known as the pineapple connection, creates snowstorms of almost incomparable size.

In addition, the wind patterns in the Sierra are especially brutal, both in velocity and duration, with the canyons on the backside of the mountains essentially acting as a funnel for the cyclonic winds coming from over the ocean. The wind can cross-load slopes with snow ten times faster than snow can fall out of the sky. As a consequence of these climatic conditions tangling together, the Sierra emerges as the ultimate snow machine.

In late March 1982, the weather pattern in the Lake Tahoe region took a new twist. For reasons not well understood by meteorologists, an unusually erratic jet stream blowing east off the Pacific split in two just northwest of Hawaii, reconverging a few hundred miles off the California coast. In the past, such wayward splits were known to stabilize the path of the stream, but this time it simply aimed the jet stream and its accompanying blizzards like a fire hose at the Sierra Nevada. The northern stream brought the snowstorms and cold temperatures, and the southern one anchored it firmly in place.

In terms of snowfall accumulation, there had been a few worse storms in Alpine Meadows' history, although not many, but measured by avalanche hazard, the particularly lethal mix of snowfall, wind, and vacillating temperatures in the March 1982 storm made it the worst the area had ever seen. Earlier that season, in January, there had been a huge blizzard with lots of snowfall. February was bitter cold and rainy, with a rainstorm over the Presidents' Day weekend and only seven inches of new snow all month, and then March brought sunny T-shirt weather. The early spring thaw created melt-freeze snow, meaning the snow on the surface melted during the day and the melted water permeated the lower layers of snow where it froze at night. The end result, prior to the late March storm, was a weak snowpack draped with a shimmering layer of ice crust. And by dawn on Wednesday, March 31, that ice was coated with 87 inches of new-fallen snow.

ELEVEN

The snow was charged, electric. It was fuckin' alive.

—

Jim Plehn, avalanche hazard forecaster at Alpine Meadows in 1982

On the morning of March 31, 1982, the storm, going into its fifth day, had not only refused to let up but had actually increased in intensity. The snow had virtually not stopped falling since it began the previous Saturday evening, and Ward Peak and the steep ridges above Alpine Meadows continued to be pummeled by a seemingly endless snowstorm. That Wednesday morning the snow was coming down sideways, accumulating at a rate of more than two inches an hour at the resort and likely twice that much at the ridgetop.

Although it was a snow day for all the local children and, as a practical matter, most of the adults as well, Bernie Kingery awoke at his office (he actually slept in the first-aid room, on one of the cots). With his wife and daughter safe at home, Bernie stayed on-site, as he frequently did during big storms, to direct the avalanche control efforts.

Had it not been for the blizzard, Bernie would surely have been home having a predawn breakfast with his family. He loved spending early mornings with Julie and Kris, especially if he could be outdoors. On family camping trips he and Julie always shared a cup of coffee at sunrise and talked between themselves before breaking camp. At home all three of them often sat out on the front porch for breakfast, listening to the birds sing and watching the day wake up before Bernie headed off to work.

The decision to close the resort was made at 7:20 a.m. by Bernie and Howard Carnell, the general manager. Howard had initially wanted to open that morning, and he came to the ski area to have a look at the situation himself. It was obvious that almost no one, employees or the skiing public, could reach the resort, and that even if they could, it was far too windy to run any of the lifts. In addition, there was simply too much snow in too short a time for the patrol to effectively do avalanche control work. In the end, Howard agreed with Bernie's decision not to open.

The various supervisors then made efforts to call their employees to tell them not to come in. The phone tree at the resort was fairly primitive in those days—there were obviously no cell phones yet, and several of the workers didn't even have phones in their places. In addition, many of the employees had crashed with friends during the storm and weren't even home to receive a call. The policy at the time was storm or not, if an employee was not contacted he was expected to get to work, so some people who didn't receive notification that the resort was closed showed up there anyway. Also, the patrolmen as well as quite a few other employees—some of the groomers, maintenance workers, and trail crew—were still asked to report to work. Consequently, even though the resort was not opening that day, several dozen of the over 400 employees were present at the ski area that morning.

The daily ski report went out on radio stations in the region, advising skiers that Alpine Meadows, and also Squaw Valley, were closed. In an office in Alpine Meadows' lodge, Karen Strohmaier was available to field calls from people who hadn't heard the ski report on the radio, but under the circumstances, there were no skiers interested enough to even check.

Karen, age 27, had come to Alpine Meadows five years earlier on an internship for her major in recreation leisure studies at San Fran-cisco State University. As the ski area's communications supervisor, she ran the switchboard and the mountain radio. She was Base 1, the resort's hub—if anyone called Alpine Meadows, they talked to her first and she then forwarded the call to the information desk or a particular department. Howard called her Ace, as in his ace player.

Karen usually had Wednesdays off, but another employee was moving out of her place that day, the last day of the month, and Karen had offered to switch schedules with her. Before she left for work that morning, Karen realized she probably wasn't going to be able to get back home in the storm, so she brought a day pack with a change of clothes in it. Patrolman Tom Kimbrough also had the idea that he wouldn't make it home that night. Before heading to Alpine Meadows, he had turned off the water in his place, drained the pipes, and put antifreeze in his toilet.

The snow was falling so thickly—and so relentlessly—that neither the snowplow drivers nor the patrol could keep up with it. Another 17 inches had fallen overnight, and that morning the winds had ratcheted up, now pounding in with a hurricane force of 120 mph. The patrolmen were tempted to hammer plywood against the windows to prevent them from shattering in the storm. Jim needed snowshoes just to make it outside to the weather station at the base area. In the six years that the revamped forecasting system had been in place, it was only the second time he had rated an avalanche haz-ard as "extreme" (the first time was two months prior during the January blizzard).

The temperature fluctuations in the blizzard were following no predictable pattern, and the entire snowstorm had melded into one complicated, ceaseless, five-day event that kept changing and build-ing. It seemed like the more the patrolmen shot back at the storm, the more snow it dumped. They often likened avalanche control to com-bat, and certainly this tempest, this storm of a lifetime, was analogous to the classic siege pattern of a continuous assault. None of them could remember it ever snowing this hard for this long. The crew was exhausted and stressed beyond reason, and worse, there seemed to be no end in sight.

Out in the storm, with the sustained winds lashing a cloudburst of snow all around them, it seemed to Larry that there was almost no air left to breathe. The pressure of the wind all but prevented him from exhaling, and he had to consciously push out hard, powerful breaths. With every gulp of air he took, he forced himself to stifle the feeling that he was smothering.

Larry was battered so hard by the wind that he could barely keep his balance, and he was especially concerned about being blown over with live ammunition in his hands. He and the other patrollers groped about in the whiteout, trying not to let the blizzard play tricks on their eyes. There were no shadows, since the light was so diffuse, and all any of them could see in any direction was white on unrelieved white. The situation had moved beyond disorienting and was veering sharply toward utterly unnerving. The patrolmen's depth perception was so distorted that it made their sense of reality a little shaky—at times they couldn't even tell if they were moving or standing still, and they began to hear the murmur of their doubts over the shriek of the storm. If control work was in fact like fighting a war, they were starting to question whether this was a battle they could win.

It became clear very early that the patrol was not going to be able to access the high exposed slopes to throw hand charges. When Casey's assignment to do avalanche control on High Yellow was canceled, he and Dennis Smith, Jake's brother, went up in a snow machine to clear out some lifts. As they were plowing the bottom of the Weasel lift, Casey noticed a large amount of avalanche debris. It was obviously a natural runout, unusual without avalanche control going on, and it had also flowed farther than normal. At that point, even Casey was spooked enough to stay indoors for awhile.

Perhaps the only person at the resort unwilling to let the magnitude of the storm dampen his spirits was Jake. He was elated by the weather and fired up to be outdoors in it. Yet as much as he was joking around and acting like his typical court jester self that day, he did seem to be channeling a darker side of his humor. Early that morning he had come into the patrol room doing an imitation of a goofy skier, dressed in crooked goggles and a vest the National Ski

Patrollers wore when they were taking patrol tests. On his head he wore a gag ski pole that had been cut in half with each half attached to a headband, so that it looked like he was skewered through the head with the pole. Then he grabbed his head and groaned as if he was in pain, grinned fiendishly, and said, *"This* is a test," meaning the storm they were all facing.

Don Huber and one of the other snow rangers were at the ski area to help with the artillery, and Bob Blair went out with them into the storm to fire the recoilless rifle. Dennis Smith ferried ammunition from the armory up to Gunner's Knob for them in a snow machine. They shot Beaver Bowl, always considered an especially dangerous area, and also Poma Rocks, a seldom-skied slope with an east-southeast aspect just above the base of the resort. Poma Rocks, like all the avalanche paths at the resort, required frequent control work to remain safely diffused, but it had never caused any problems for the patrol in the past. At 700 feet high, it was considered only a medium-sized slope. The vicious winds at the top of the ridges had been scattering the snow downward, however, overloading the lower slopes, so the patrol shot Poma Rocks hard, firing repeatedly—and blindly—into the snow-drenched mountain.

Given the conditions, the rangers and the patrol couldn't see far enough to judge the results, and with the risk of being swallowed by the storm and getting lost, it wasn't a realistic option for them to venture closer to check. After they finished firing, they disassembled the rifle, laboriously cleaned all the parts, and stored it away safely. Then they headed in to try to get warm and dry before heading out into the storm again.

After the shortest of breaks, the forestry guys went back outside to start firing the howitzer. Randy Buck, a 23-year-old maintenance worker at the resort, towed the cannon down to the parking lot for them and then stayed around to man-haul it into position. When the wind gusted just the right way, Randy's bright red pants cut through the blizzard like neon. Jim headed out to help sight the targets, and another patrolman, Igor Goulaevsky, came out to assist as well.

Since he was a teenager Igor had joked that his very Russian last name was pronounced O'Toole, a quirk that went practically unnoticed among the personalities on the ski patrol. Born in Russia, as a young child Igor moved with his parents to Shanghai, China, for seven years, a plight typical of Russian émigrés at that time. The family then moved to São Paulo, Brazil, and afterward to California, where Igor's dad, an electrical engineer, got a job as a draftsman with the state. Igor was 12 when he came to America, by which point he spoke his native tongue of Russian, fluent Portuguese, and rudimentary street Chinese. He was immediately enthralled with San Francisco and adopted it as his home base for all future travels.

Igor saw Sierra snow for the first time at age 16 when the San Francisco Boys Club Band traveled to Lake Tahoe. He went back on his own several times after that, eventually joining the National Ski Patrol at Alpine Meadows in his early twenties. After graduating from college with an engineering degree, Igor went to work for Otis Elevator. Ten years later, he arranged with the company to take a year off, May to May. He traveled for the first six months and then came to Alpine Meadows, intending to pro patrol for one season. At the end of that winter, he told Otis that he wasn't returning from his sabbatical. From then on he spent his winters patrolling at Alpine Meadows and his summers in San Francisco, driving big rigs and tour buses and getting his fix of opera, jazz, and the symphony.

The other patrollers loved him, and not just because he frequently cooked for them, making soups and other Russian delicacies and lifting vodka in a toast "to those present." At Alpine Meadows he continued his habit of keeping meticulous, nearly contemporaneous journals throughout the day. In tiny but very legible handwriting he noted the mundanities of his day—what he ate, who he talked to—as well as the wild adventures of his new career.

Igor helped Jim and the rangers fire the howitzer on two slopes called Pond Slope and the Buttress that rose up above the resort's parking lot, as well as on other routes farther down the road. In the world of avalanches, Pond Slope and the Buttress were also viewed as medium-sized slopes, with vertical drops of 500 feet and 900 feet, respectively. Pond Slope had an incline angle of 40 degrees, and the Buttress, a concave slope, varied from 35 to 45 degrees. Each of them had an eastern aspect and was cross-swept by strong, southwest, down-canyon winds. Both slopes were relatively open-faced, without, for example, the cornices and couloirs of an area like Beaver Bowl. In those days they were seldom skied—there was no chairlift running to them, and they were full of bushes and small trees. The trees and underbrush acted as anchors, requiring the slopes to load with a tremendous amount of snow before they were primed to slide.

The patrol had used presettings to fire the recoilless rifle, but with the howitzer they had to manually adjust the firing coordinates by looking down the barrel. Given the visibility at this point, it was like trying to sight through gauze, but occasionally the wind would shift in a way that let them catch glimpses of the terrain, enough to make out certain trees and rock outcroppings as dark shapes. Igor went back to the patrol room to retrieve a book of aerial photos of the slopes. Jim then faced the mountain and held the photographs up in front of him, comparing them to what he was seeing through the swirling storm in order to recognize which rocks were which and determine where to aim.

As opposed to the "extreme" hazard designated to the high ridges at the upper area of the resort, the hazard on the Buttress and Pond Slope was deemed only "high" that day. In considering the potential risk from so many avalanche paths, in the patrols' experience several other areas posed a greater danger than those slopes. Still, in those merciless conditions, standard procedure did not seem sufficient to address the hazard. After firing six shots into the normal placements on the mountain, Jim and the rangers blasted an additional half dozen rounds lower across the face.

After every shot, including several that they fired from the intersection of Ginzton Road and Alpine Meadows Road, the howitzer rolled away in the murk and got stuck in the snow. The patrolmen chased it down, lugged it back, and started the process all over again. It was nearly impossible for them to tell if the cannon fire had set off any releases, although they did think they saw some snow rubble in a few places.

After putting the howitzer away, a process that entailed partially disassembling it and carefully cleaning the breech assembly and the bore, the patrolmen—cold, wet, and miserable—headed into the Summit Terminal Building. Over lunch, where he gave his pickle to Beth Morrow in exchange for her salami, Igor wrote in capital letters in his journal, "TOO MUCH SNOW." He had brought a little camera with him to work that day, an underwater Minolta that he had just discovered in his dresser under a pile of long johns. He couldn't even remember what was on the partially used film in the camera, so he just snapped some shots to use up the roll.

Larry called home at lunchtime to let Kathy know he wasn't going to make it home that night. With more avalanche control to do that afternoon and early the next morning, he told her that he was just going to crash overnight in the patrol office.

By the time the patrolmen finished eating, the wind threw yet another curve, this time easing up considerably. Despite the lull in the wind, the snowfall remained steady. At that time another weather anomaly occurred as well—in the midst of the blizzard, the temperature ticked up several degrees. That morning the temperature had been 23 degrees, but by mid-afternoon it was hovering in the high 20s. The inverted nature of the storm, turning a normal weather pattern on its head by beginning cold and ending warmer, whispered a warning of impending tragedy. A rising temperature can cause the snow on the surface to become denser, making that layer top-heavy and therefore unstable.

Unable to be out on his skis on the mountain, Jim felt a little out of touch with the conditions on the slopes. He headed out to the study plot and noticed that the composition of the snow had become a little drier. Another 13 inches of snow had fallen during the day since the morning measurement was taken, bringing the total snowfall at that point in the storm to exactly 100 inches. He took down the information in a little notebook in his pocket, but he would never have the chance to record it on the master chart. It did not matter to the snow that he was an expert.

Jim met with Bernie in the patrol office of the doomed Summit Building to decide what control measure the patrol should take next. They decided they needed to focus on protecting Alpine Meadows Road, to keep that three-mile stretch safe and clear not only so the remaining employees would have a way out, but also to provide access into the resort the next morning. Under the circumstances, the most effective way to do it would be to take a team to Squaw Valley to drop bombs over the backside of KT-22. The process, which had been done frequently in the past, meant driving some patrolmen over to Squaw, a seven-mile trip, where they would ride up the KT-22 chairlift to reach the ridge that separated the two ski resorts. Once they skied into position, the patrolmen could throw explosives down onto the slide paths of avalanches that had the potential of running onto Alpine Meadows Road.

Bernie had sent a bunch of employees home around noon, and in the afternoon he got on the radio with the following announcement: "Attention all radios, Alpine One, all employees not notified to stay are ordered to leave by three o'clock." Still, in addition to the patrolmen, there were a couple dozen other employees who had been deemed essential milling around the resort after three, mostly in the lodge and the vehicle maintenance shed—groomers, vehicle mechanics, maintenance workers, even food service workers. There were also several employees hand-picked by Bernie to stay and do road guard, a duty that involved keeping people—hikers, cross-country skiers—and cars away from the road when the patrol was setting off explosives on the mountain above.

Bob Blair, who had been at the resort all day, left right around three o'clock. He lived less than two miles down Alpine Meadows Road, so rather than try to dig out his car, he got a ride home in one of the vehicles caravanning out of the parking lot at that time.

As Bernie began to assemble the control crew to go to Squaw and the guards to stay at the resort, the last-minute shuffling of personnel was more significant than anyone could have known. One of these assignments involved Thom Orsi, the guy on trail crew who had ridden to work with Larry that morning. Bernie asked Thom to drive the team to Squaw and drop them off there—the patrol would get back to Alpine Meadows themselves by shooting and skiing their way down the backside of KT-22. The driver's job included returning to Alpine Meadows to oversee the road guards. Thom was recovering from a cold and had been in Base 4 all day helping with radio dispatch. He asked Bernie if he could remain on radio duty and stay inside where it was warm. Bernie initially agreed to have Marty Marchese, the parking lot supervisor, go in Thom's place, then changed his mind, deciding that Marty wasn't familiar enough with how to set up the road guards. "You go," Bernie said to Thom. Thom got up from his seat, the one next to Bernie, and prepared to leave the ski area.

Earlier in the day Jake had volunteered to do road guard, and Bernie asked Thom if he knew where Jake was. Rather than reveal the location of his fellow trail crew member to Bernie, Thom simply replied that he would find him. At the time, Jake was raiding the first-aid room for mattresses and blankets that he was planning to haul up to the trail crew room so he and Thom would be comfortable if they ended up having to spend the night at the resort. Jake and Thom weren't concerned about having enough food to last them through the night, since Bernie always made sure that they had plenty of emergency supplies. Every Christmas, Bernie presented each member of trail crew with a paper shopping bag full of canned fruit, vegetables, and Swiss Miss hot chocolate, telling them to keep the food in their lockers in case they ever needed it. The previous Christmas, he had put a pair of rag wool mittens in each of the bags as well.

Thom called Jake in the first-aid room and passed along Bernie's message that Jake should round up a snowmobile and get ready to do road guard. Jake abandoned the mattress project and headed back to the Summit Terminal Building to change into a dry parka and make some phone calls before heading out.

On his way into the building, Jake turned down a chance to leave. His brother, Dennis, was taking off just then with a couple of other employees in a pickup and they asked him if he wanted to ride in the back. Dennis tried to talk him into it, reminding him that almost nobody had an operable vehicle at the resort and it might be his last chance to get out. Jake told them that he was working and he was going to stay. Dennis wasn't surprised by his younger brother's response—he knew Jake wasn't about to pass up the chance to be right in the core of the excitement. "Suit yourself," Dennis said. "See you later."

Bernie also asked Beth Morrow to be a road guard. As Beth had suspected, even though she wasn't needed as a lift operator, Bernie was glad to have her there to scribe for him all day. The plan was for her to stay in the patrol office scribing for Bernie until the crew was in place at the top of Squaw. Bernie arranged with Karen to close down the switchboard in the lodge for the day and head over to the Summit Terminal Building to relieve Beth.

Bernie also tagged Tad DeFelice, 25, one of the guys who had given Beth a ride to work that morning, for road guard duty. A conscientious and enthusiastic lift operator, Tad didn't hide the fact that at that point in his life, his ambition was simply to ski.

Before he left for Squaw, Jim checked on Mariah, his German shepherd rescue dog in-training. At just over a year old, Mariah still seemed like a big puppy. She was Jim's personal dog, but he was preparing her for avalanche search-and-rescue work. He had brought her to the resort that morning and stowed her safely in the room in the Summit Terminal Building that was used as a kennel. The room was a ten-by-ten-foot space raised more than halfway up off the first floor. It had just a four-foot ceiling and was accessible only by going partially up the stairway between the first and second floors. The dog room usually also held some or all of Don and Roberta Huber's four rescue dogs, but Mariah was the only one in there that day.

After being told about the mission to Squaw, Tom Kimbrough went to get a bunch of extra hand charges for the crew from the magazine by the Kangaroo lift, passing directly under the Poma Rocks slide path in the process.

Bernie originally assigned just Larry and three other patrolmen to go to Squaw. With Thom driving the crew and unavailable to do dispatch, Bernie asked Igor to take the seat next to him in the patrol office and work the radio. At the last moment, Igor turned to Larry and asked if he could come along to do avalanche control. It was a question that would ultimately seal Igor's fate and forever tie his destiny to Larry.

"Sure," Larry said. "We need all the people we can get."

In the end, Thom drove five ski patrolmen away from the ski

resort that day: Larry, Jim, Casey, Tom, and Igor. They left just after three o'clock.

The patrolmen headed to Squaw in an Alpine Meadows vehicle, a blue Ford pickup truck with chains on all four tires. Larry and Jim piled into the cab with Thom, and the other three rode in the open back. Just a short way up on Alpine Meadows Road, the crew drove past Anna and Frank cross-country skiing toward the resort. Jim rolled down the window and asked them, in a tone that indicated he didn't care what the answer was, where the hell they thought they were going. Anna treated the remark as a legitimate question, replying that they were just going up to pick up some snow pants from the employee locker room in the Summit Terminal Building.

The groomers had cleared Alpine Meadows Road twice before noon with the blower and the grader, but they hadn't been back out to plow since then. As the truck bumped along over the new snow in the road, the patrolmen were spectators to the most astonishing sight—every road cut and gully they passed was avalanching. They could actually see the snow settling before their eyes, with mini-slides and sloughs of ripe, touchy snow releasing all around them. As surface slabs cascaded like sparkling sand down all the little knolls and depressions alongside the road, the snow looked almost fake. Even on slopes with only a slight incline, the snow was just oozing downhill. And even more surreal, as the falling flakes melded to each other and landed on the snowdrifts, they made a crackling, tinkling sound. This snow was making noise.

At that point the wind had almost completely died out. It was not uncommon to have a ebb like that in the midst of such a ruthlessly pulsing storm, and the patrolmen knew that it didn't necessarily mean that the blizzard was letting up, but still, they were buoyed by it. The wind was down, the temperature was up, and they were seemingly driving away from all the danger and drudgery of the past several days. To make the prior brutality of the storm seem especially unreal, just then beautiful, fluffy, pure stellar crystals started to fall from the sky.

As the patrolmen drove on, there was a sense of anticipation—the new snow was clearly not stable, and all they could think about was how fun it was going to be to bring down a slide big enough to bury the road. They were exhilarated again, gearing up for a fresh round of attack, ready to defy the elements after all. In their minds, despite the challenge of this one freakish, epic storm, avalanches were still theirs to create and control. They had no conception, yet, of the destruction and loss of life that would occur in a few minutes at the resort they had just left behind.

A ski patrol bomb pack—
with hand charge, evacuation
rope, and rescue shovel—
on Peril Ridge, with Beaver
Bowl in the background.
Courtesy of Jim Plehn

Larry Heywood and Jim Plehn in the Keyhole assessing the fracture line of an
avalanche set off by explosives. *Courtesy of Lanny Johnson*

A powder ava-
lanche in Wolverine
Bowl set off by a
ski patrol bomb.
Courtesy of Jim Plehn

An avalanche control slide in Beaver Bowl triggered by explosives.
Courtesy of Jim Plehn

Larry Heywood. *Courtesy of Igor O'Toole*

Jim Plehn.
Courtesy of Igor O'Toole

Bernie Kingery in his office on March 31, 1982.
Courtesy of Bob Moore

Laura, Bud, and Eric
Nelson in front of
their house in Eureka.
Courtesy of Katy Nelson

Laura Nelson as principal for a day,
fifth grade. *Courtesy of the Nelson family*

Bud Nelson.
Courtesy of Sharon Walters

David and Jeanne Hahn on vacation in the late '70s. *Courtesy of the Hahn family*

Jeff Skover's employee pass, '81–'82 season. *Courtesy of Jeff Skover*

Anna Conrad and Frank Yeatman on vacation in the summer of 1981. *Courtesy of Anna (Conrad) Allen*

Jake Smith next to a hydro at Alpine Meadows in 1981.
Courtesy of Billy Patterson

Beth Morrow with her dad, John, in the summer of 1981.
Courtesy of Janet Morrow

Mike Alves. *Courtesy of of Sandy (Harris) Horn*

Bob Blair. *Courtesy of Jim Plehn*

Casey Jones. *Courtesy of Igor O'Toole*

Katy, Laura, and Bud Nelson in their condo at Alpine Meadows in March 1982.
Eric Nelson is at the table in the background.

Courtesy of Barbara (Guinney) Schlumberger

Don Huber, Jim Plehn, and Bob Moore firing the howitzer on March 31, 1982.
Jim has photos of the slopes in his hand. *Courtesy of Igor O'Toole*

The view looking out from the doomed Summit Terminal Building at 10 a.m. on March 31, 1982. *Courtesy of Bob Moore*

Beth Morrow in the ski patrol room on March 31, 1982. *Courtesy of Igor O'Toole*

Jake Smith in the ski patrol room on March 31, 1982. *Courtesy of Igor O'Toole*

The avalanche aftermath at the Summit Terminal Building on the night of March 31, 1982. *Courtesy of Larry Heywood*

A map of Alpine Meadows ski resort. The shaded area represents the area covered by the avalanche.

The ski resort on April 1, 1982. *Courtesy of Don Huber*

The destroyed Sumit Terminal Building. The first floor and a half is completely buried beneath the snow. *Courtesy of Bob Moore*

Patrolmen inside the remains of the Summit Terminal Building.

Courtesy of Mary ellen Benier

Avalanche probes protruding from the snow in the parking lot. The areas where the tops of the cars show marks the edge of the avalanche.

Courtesy of Larry Heywood

A snowcat mangled by the avalanche with Thom Orsi in front.
Courtesy of Igor O'Toole

A front-end loader cleaning up the avalanche debris in the parking lot.
Courtesy of Vance Fox, VanceFox.com

The avalanche hazard forecasting worksheet for March 31, 1982. The bottom right corner was torn when it was pulled from the wreckage post-avalanche. *Courtesy of Jim Plehn*

AVALANCHE HAZARD FORECASTING WORKSHEET

Date: 3/31/82   Time: 0700   Observer: PLEHN

PRECIP	begin	end	form	
time	0600			
date	3/26/82			
SNOW	1600	0600	24 hr	storm
depth	8	17	22	86
water	.67	.80	2.47	
%	9	10%		
set			3	
TEMP	1600	max	min	cur
base	24	28	16 – 3/29	28
ridge	19	23	14 – 3/30	23
WIND	1600	max	avg	cur
speed	20-40	120	50	40-60
dir	220			

NEW SNOW STRATIGRAPHY   OLD SNOW STRATIGRAPHY

——— 23
10%
——— 8
9%
——— 3
0

WEATHER FORECAST INTENSE SNOW   RF

HAZARD FORECAST   H
upper – EXTREME
lower – HIGH
Scott – HIGH
road – HIGH

Rescuers digging at the site of the Summit Terminal Building. *Courtesy of Larry Heywood*

Bernard Coudurier reaching into the hole and holding Anna Conrad's hand on April 5, 1982. *Courtesy of Bob Moore*

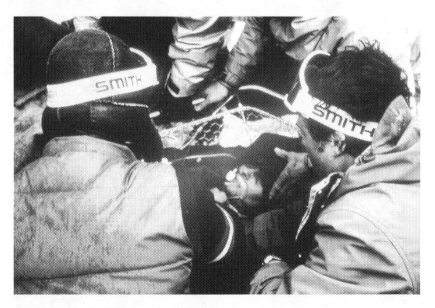

Anna just after being rescued on April 5, 1982. *Courtesy of Larry Heywood*

Roberta Huber with Bridget.
Courtesy of Igor O'Toole

A view looking up from the
hole where Anna was trapped.
Courtesy of Larry Heywood

Lanny Johnson cheering after loading Anna onto the rescue helicopter.
Courtesy of Igor O'Toole

TWELVE

I'll go with you, Daddy.

—

Laura Nelson, March 31, 1982

Six days into a vacation that was supposed to last five, on Wednesday, March 31, the Nelson and Guinney children were making the best of being snowed-in, building snow forts and tunnels in the parking lot between the condo buildings. All the family members had skied the previous Saturday and even Sunday during the storm, but since then the intensity of the wind and snow had kept them off the slopes. On Sunday the wind was so high near the tops of the runs that it was difficult to see each other, and the new snow was so deep that the kids kept falling and struggling to try to get up. Although both families had skied in the past, this wasn't the spring skiing they had envisioned for the trip. Even so, the kids seemed relatively unaffected by the change in plans—for them just playing outside in the snow was almost as much fun as skiing.

When they were inside the condo, Laura and Eric and the three Guinney boys had kept busy playing games, doing homework, and reading. During the trip Laura was reading a book called *Storm on Giant Mountain* by Frances Fullerton Neilson, with a cover that depicted, whether by portent or mere coincidence, seven people out in a blizzard. The chapters in the book happened to include ones entitled "World of White," "Deep Winter," and "Danger Descending!"

The condo was fairly spacious, with two stories and four bedrooms. The front door opened into a short entry, with the kitchen on the left. A breakfast bar faced the kitchen, and behind that was a dining table and then the living room area. Off the living room there were two bedrooms—Bud and Katy had one and Larry and Barbara had the other. Downstairs there were another two bedrooms, one for all four boys to share and one just for Laura.

Built in the early 1970s, the condo complex actually contained three sets of condos—the shingle-sided Alpine Place 1, Scott Peak Building, and Alpine Place 2. The Nelson and Guinney families, and also Dave and Jeanne Hahn, were staying in Alpine Place 2, a series of nine plainish brown buildings with dark brown trim containing a total of 49 units. Alpine Place 2 was also known as the Chalet condos or, to locals familiar with their history of repairs, the Bondo Condos. At different points over the years Andy Wertheim acted as an on-site manager for the condos. In '82, he and his wife rented out several of the units, including the one to Jeanne Hahn—an end unit with an upper balcony directly overlooking the wide driveway leading into the parking lot. At that point in the season only a couple dozen units were rented, with maybe 60 or 70 people staying there. In prior years the condos had frequently been rented to locals for the season, but by the late '70s, with the appreciation of Lake Tahoe real estate, they had been fixed up and primarily used as vacation rentals.

Early on in the vacation the Nelsons and Guinneys had been able to venture out from the condo complex. When they arrived the previous Friday, they went to Tahoe City for pizza and groceries, and Bud and Laura had gone to church together in town on Saturday evening. For the first couple of days the storm had seemed sort of like an adventure, with people from various condos standing around outside in an almost jovial mood, brooming snow off their cars and marveling at the amount of snowfall.

By Tuesday, however, it wasn't so much fun anymore. By then people were stranded, restricted. The mood among the adults in the Nelson and Guinney families had shifted first to annoyance at the inconvenience and then to concern. No one was starving, but there were nine of them altogether, and the storm showed no signs of stopping. If they were trapped in their condo for a few more days, at some point the situation was going to get a little worrisome.

A ski trip with no skiing was not Bud's idea of a vacation—he was never one to willingly sit still for long, and having to stay confined in the condo made the situation nearly unbearable for him. The two families were supposed to head home on Tuesday, March 30, but on Monday, Bud called his office around noon to tell his secretary he might not make it home as planned and to reschedule his appointments from Wednesday to Thursday. Not expecting to need more than a couple of days' worth of supplies, he made a food run that day for the two families. Despite Larry Guinney's skepticism, Bud initially planned to drive to the store in his Honda, reminding his old friend that he had lived in snow country in the Midwest. Larry gently suggested to Bud that he wasn't familiar with a Sierra blizzard, but Bud was determined in a way that Larry had long characterized as Bud's I've-made-a-decision-so-what-are-we-waiting-for state of mind. Bud fired up the car, skirted the edge of the parking lot, and drove about 100 yards before he came back, admitting to Larry that this was not the snow he was used to in Ohio.

Bud ended up going to the store that Monday in a four-wheel-drive Jeep with chains on the tires, driven by a young first lieutenant in the air force named Jay Seffern who was also staying in the condos. During the drive Jay tried to persuade Bud to go skiing with him the next day in the blizzard, taunting him with the old stand-by "No guts, no glory." Bud refused to take the bait, responding that he was a married man with a family to look after, and he didn't take risks like that. "Wait till you have a family," Bud added. "It'll change your thinking."

When they got to the store, the selection of food was pretty slim. Other people in town had clearly already stocked up during the storm; there was no bread at all, and very little milk. Most of the regular meat was gone as well, so Bud bought some high-end steaks. He collected two or three bags of food, including one carton of milk, cereal, and some lettuce. To the extent possible, he also fulfilled food requests from some of the other people in the condos. When he got back, he took Laura around with him to several units distributing food and supplies.

The next day, Tuesday, March 30, the parking area in front of the condo was completely snowed-in, and the road leading to it was impassable. Since it was clear that they weren't going to be able to get home that day after all, Katy called a friend to ask her to reschedule music lessons, a doctor's appointment, and Girl Scout snack duty. The kids played outside in the drifts, making snowmen and tunneling into the enormous piles of snow while the adults took turns freezing on a folding chair, watching to make sure the snowbanks didn't cave in on any of them.

Between one and two o'clock a snowplow cleared Ginzton Road up to the condo area, and a little later Wendell Ulberg, the handyman for the condos, plowed out the parking lot. Wendell and his wife, Kate, lived in one of the condos and he helped out at the complex, including doing some maintenance work, snow plowing, and shoveling the roofs. With only a small plow to work with and such an enormous amount of accumulation, Wendell not only couldn't stay on top of the snow removal, he had run out of places to put the snow when he plowed it. As the storm continued day after day, he also dealt with some progressively disgruntled customers frantic to get out of the condos. Four women from Atherton, an especially wealthy suburb of San Francisco, who were staying there at the time offered Wendell $2,000 to get them out by any means possible, even if that meant chartering a helicopter. He told them that he would be happy to get them out for free if he could. By Tuesday the women were becoming almost hysterical, and much to Kate's exasperation, Wendell tried to cheer them up by taking them out for rides in his snowplow.

Kate had moved up to Tahoe in '72 at age 19 from Menlo Park, a town, as it happened, right next to Atherton in the Bay Area.

A cross-country skiing instructor at Big Chief Lodge, she was an extremely capable, resourceful mountain woman. In connection with her job, she had just taken a weeklong course at Mammoth on avalanche awareness. On her porch she had a couple of avalanche probes that she had brought back from that seminar.

The combination of Wendell's plowing in the parking area and the larger plow on the road had provided a path, so on Tuesday, Bud and Katy walked up to the ski resort with Eric to ask about the storm forecast and see if they could buy food. There were two ways to walk from the condos to the Alpine Meadows resort. The first was to go down Ginzton Road and then turn left on an access road through the Subway parking lot (so named because it ended near the Subway chairlift) straight up to the lodge. The other, longer way was to go farther down Ginzton Road until it intersected with Alpine Meadows Road, then turn left on Alpine Meadows Road and walk through the main parking lot, at the base of the mountains that rose up on the right. The longer route from the condos to the lodge was just over a half mile; the Subway shortcut knocked less than two tenths of a mile off the trip.

Bud, Katy, and Eric headed out around three o'clock on Tuesday, trudging through very heavy snowfall and high winds. They walked through a channel about the width of a car and a half, with eight-foot-high embankments on either side. The road was mostly cleared, but there were still several inches of new snowfall on top of some icy compacted snow. The three of them initially turned left into the access road to the Subway parking lot, intending to take the shortcut to the lodge. It was plowed somewhat, but due to the heavy blowing snow they couldn't tell if it was cleared all the way to the lodge or even if the cut-through road went completely up to the resort. They didn't want to walk all the way to the far end only to find that they couldn't get through that way, so after walking in about 100 feet or so, they turned around and decided to take the route they knew for sure, through the main parking lot. The Nelsons went back to Ginzton Road, turning left on Alpine Meadows Road and walking through the main lot toward the lodge.

An occasional car drove past them, and as they walked through the parking lot they gradually saw more cars and people. Up in the lodge, the cafeteria was open, but not active. Katy and Bud bought all the little milk containers they could, as well as some Twinkies and several individual cereal boxes. They talked to a food service worker there who said that they didn't keep large amounts of food on hand as they received regular deliveries and didn't have much storage space, but that the kitchen usually had some extra potatoes, bacon, and eggs.

There were several people in the bar talking and drinking, and Eric was drawn to the big red popcorn machine by the windows in the bar. Bud had a beer while Eric drank hot chocolate and ate popcorn. The three of them hiked back to the condo before dark, where the two families made dinner and then all watched a beauty pageant on TV together before bed.

Jeanne and Dave Hahn had also walked up to the resort that day, but they didn't go inside the lodge. They had food in their condo and had spent most of their time curled up by the fire, but whether at home or on vacation, they loved to walk together almost every day. Their daughter Linda was supposed to meet them at Alpine Meadows the following day, but Dave called her at work to warn her about the storm and tell her not to come. Dave almost never phoned Linda at work, and at the time she thought it was odd that her dad rather than her mom had called her. She figured her dad knew that if the warning had come from her mom she might have come up anyway, but that if he was the one to call, he must be serious about the message. She stayed safely at home.

By the next morning, Wednesday, March 31, the snow was piled up to the second stories of the condos. In the Nelson/Guinney unit, there was so much snow pushing against the sliding glass door in the boys' bedroom downstairs that the adults feared it might crack or cave in. They cleared the boys out of that bedroom and made it off-limits to the kids. In an effort to conserve the food supply, everyone had a somewhat restricted breakfast. The kids hung around inside together in the morning, playing games and drawing pictures. It had been snowing every minute of the vacation, and Bud in particular, who was supposed to be performing surgery that day, was tired of feeling so cooped-up. He called in to his office to ask his secretary to just clear out the entire week and reschedule his appointments into the following week's calendar.

After a lunch of rationed food, the kids headed outside to play in the snow in the parking lot and Bud and Larry went outside to watch them. Bud was wearing a yellow Purdue sweatshirt under his jacket, and Laura was bundled up in the green ski jacket and snow pants her mom had made for her and a red-and-yellow tasseled ski cap with her name knitted in the yellow part. She didn't have any snow boots to wear, but she was trying her best to climb around on the snowbanks in sneakers.

It seemed clear to Jeanne Hahn that with the storm increasing in severity that Wednesday, it was a day to stay inside. At about three o'clock that afternoon, however, out of the sliding glass door on the second-floor balcony she and Dave happened to see a lone man walking down the hill into the condo complex on the narrowest of paths bordered by increasingly steep snowdrifts. Dave, who was wearing khakis, quickly got himself dressed to run down and talk to him, slipping on a beloved pair of brown leather Jean-Claude Killy après-ski boots. They looked like cowboy boots, and Dave had taken a fair amount of ribbing in the past from his family for wearing them. He and Jeanne hadn't seen very many people in the previous few days, and Dave thought the guy walking toward the condos might have come from the lodge and heard something about the weather situation.

The guy's name was Tim Fitzpatrick, and he was up at Alpine Meadows on his honeymoon. A 30-year-old attorney from Healdsburg, California, Tim had come to Tahoe that weekend to get married, looking in the yellow pages to find someone who was authorized to perform the ceremony. He and Dana, his new wife, were supposed to leave their condo two days earlier, but they had been held captive there for the duration of the storm just like everybody else.

Earlier in the week Tim had been having a glorious time in the storm. Growing up in Illinois as one of four boys, he had waited for blizzards just so he could go out playing and hiking in them. He even used to track pheasants in the snow, trekking out alone in big empty fields and identifying the males by the way their tail feathers brushed the snow. At Alpine Meadows he had set out in the daylight once or twice a day, ambling in the beauty of the blizzard with no one around, the only sound the crunch of his boots on the fresh snow. His new bride was having none of it, so he tramped around by himself. As accustomed as he was to snowstorms, that Wednesday he admitted that he wasn't necessarily prepared for the depth and extent of a mountain blizzard.

When Tim started out on his walk earlier that day, the snow—fine, icy particles that stung when they landed on him—was wet and falling nearly horizontally. There was no longer any visible path, and he had been forced to forge a trail through snow that was at least waist-deep. Once in the deep drifts he got scared when the wind whipped up and blocked his visibility entirely, but he was ambitious enough to want to make it to the lodge, and in his mind—incorrectly, he acknowledged in retrospect—he exempted himself from the category of people who shouldn't be out in such a ferocious storm.

As Tim trudged into the ski resort parking lot, the going got easier. The area was somewhat protected from the snow and wind, and there was less snow accumulation on the ground. Once he was more sheltered from the elements and could see the lodge up ahead of him, Tim experienced a feeling of exhilaration that he had made it. Aside from the fact that the area was flat, there was no way to tell that it was a parking lot—it could have been a field in the middle of the mountains. At the end of the lot he checked out the vehicles in the service yard, noticing a mechanic moving around up there.

When Tim reached the lodge, more than half an hour after he had started out, he was surprised to find the doors unlocked. To him, the emptiness of the huge place, especially in daylight, had the same sort of menacing, deserted-hotel-in-the-winter feeling as the Overlook Hotel in Stephen King's *The Shining*. The last time he had seen the lodge, it was filled with wall-to-wall tourists, and that afternoon, even though it wasn't dark out, the place was completely drained of skiers and staff.

Tim made himself at home in the lodge, looking for something to do while he was there. He went back into the kitchen with the idea that he would bring food to the Nelson family. He didn't know whether they needed anything to eat or not, but since they had kids and they were the only people he had met at the condos, it seemed to give purpose to his trip. He swiped some hot dogs and four 12-packs of buns. The proportions were off, since there were way more buns than dogs available, but he took whatever he could find.

The walk back was easier, almost dreamy, as Tim dragged the bags through the snow and reminisced about pheasant tracking. The wind had died down considerably, and the snow was now wafting straight down in exquisite, oversize flakes, almost like gentle hail. He stopped and just stood for a few minutes in the stillness of the parking lot, looking around at the snow-covered pine trees, awestruck by the natural beauty of a winter scene that had abruptly turned idyllic. He had brought a little radio with him to check the weather, and he put his headphones on just as the song "Leather and Lace" by Stevie Nicks and Don Henley, with its lyrics about "lovers forever," came on. He bent his head against the remaining wind and listened deeply, exulting in the feeling of being inside a giant snowglobe that had just been softly shaken.

When Tim returned to the condo area, both Dave, who had come down specifically to talk to him, and Bud, who was outside watching the kids play, wanted to hear the details of his trip. The conversation, just one of many links in a chain that afternoon, ultimately unleashed the sequence of events that would irreparably change all of their lives.

Tim gave the hot dogs and buns to Bud, who, while graciously accepting them, seemed to Tim to mentally push them aside. Admitting to Tim that he was bored stiff and going stir-crazy, Bud was much more focused on the fact that Tim had walked up to, and into, the lodge. "You can get there?" Bud asked. "You made it?"

Tim saw that his information set off instant momentum on Bud's part to go to the ski area himself. Tim told the group not to attempt it, that it was strenuous and difficult and dangerous, that it was not for kids. When that didn't seem to be having any effect, he added that they were out of their minds to think about going.

Bud didn't seem deterred, and Larry Guinney wasn't surprised by Bud's response. He knew that his friend was ultra-high-energy, always moving. Bud didn't seek out danger by any means, but nor was he overly cautious. He was the kind of man who didn't just talk about doing things, he did them. Based on what he knew of Bud's nature, Larry was convinced that he intended to hike over to the resort. From Larry's perspective, Bud was headstrong and almost cocky, although not necessarily in a negative way—more in the respect that once he had an idea in his mind, he simply wasn't going to be talked out of it. He was going to see it through.

As Larry expected, Bud announced that he was going to head up to the resort to look around for himself, and he asked who wanted to go with him. Initially there weren't any takers, and Bud seemed to register disappointment. Just then Laura spoke up, offering to go with her dad.

Laura hadn't gotten the chance to go with her mom and dad the previous day when they walked up to the lodge with Eric, and although she was having fun playing with the other kids, she was the only girl in the group and may have welcomed the chance for a break from four wild boys. She also likely wanted both to please her dad and to spend time with him. But perhaps most of all, she had a trace of her father's adventurous streak, and she might have simply wanted to experience the thrill of the quest for herself.

Eric wasn't interested in being pulled away from his snow play with the other boys, but both Dave and Larry ended up declaring that they were up for the challenge.

While Dave went up to his condo to put on some additional gear, Bud and Laura went upstairs to drop off the food Tim had given them and see if Katy wanted to come along. With Katy on board, the outing took on the trappings of a family hike, a way to partially salvage the day, if not the vacation. Laura's sneakers obviously weren't going to work well in the snowdrifts, so she asked Barbara Guinney if she could borrow her boots.

The blizzard wasn't ruining the vacation for Barbara, who had considered it a great excuse to curl up with a book and watch the snow fall outside the window. She saw Bud as their fun friend, the one who got her and Larry out on new adventures, and she viewed herself as the fear-oriented one among the two couples, always playing the role of spoilsport. In Guam, for example, she was the person asking if everyone was sure they should scuba-dive in a certain area because there were sharks, while Bud would dive right in.

Barbara was terrified of the idea of going out in the storm that day. To her it seemed obvious not to be outdoors in it, but she felt like she was the only one concerned. The way she saw it, when Bud came up to invite Katy on the walk to the resort, he didn't contemplate any potential risk purely because it didn't occur to him to think that way. In Barbara's mind, Bud wasn't looking beyond the positive aspect of taking action, the rousing stimulation that the prospect of an exploit offered.

When Laura told Barbara she was hiking to the ski area with her parents, Barbara was initially thrown. "Do you think Laura should go with you?" Barbara asked Katy. With three boys but no daughter of her own, Barbara was openly and good-naturedly jealous of Katy's intimate relationship with Laura. From Barbara's perspective, Laura seemed like the ideal child—responsible, respectful, mature— and Katy the epitome of the concerned mom, always making sure Laura had her schoolwork done and wore the right, round-collared clothes.

Katy didn't hear Barbara or just didn't answer her, and Barbara, not wanting to push the issue, offered up her tricolor brown, tan, and beige Moon Boots to Laura. Barbara had small feet, and after Laura put an extra pair of light blue socks on top of the tan socks she was already wearing, the boots came close to fitting her.

Katy didn't have any snow boots either, so she decided to simply wear the boots she had skied in. As Katy finished dressing in warm clothes, Bud and Laura went back down to the parking lot.

The light was just starting to wane as dusk slowly approached. Tim had hung around in the condo parking lot, stewing on the idea that these people were heading out into the storm based on what he now perceived to be a foolish act on his part. His father, a

John Wayne type, was Tim's role model for how to talk seriously to people. Tim was respectful to Bud, not heated, but he wanted to make his point again. He talked about the potential hazards of the storm, not in terms of avalanches, but the general risk of getting disoriented and losing bearings, of the inability of the snow to support someone if they fell into a drift.

"Look," Tim said, "this is not smart. Just because I did something stupid doesn't mean you should."

Tim didn't sense any disingenuousness in the doctor's exuberance—it seemed to him that Bud simply didn't accept that there was any danger in taking his daughter for a walk in the blizzard. Tim viewed Bud as a little smug, but very polite. He didn't argue with Tim, he merely—as Tim would later describe it—confidently shined him on.

To Tim, Bud's attitude seemed to be that since Tim had done it, they could do it too. Tim had certainly seen himself as separate from the type of person who could run into trouble or get lost in a snowstorm, and if Bud—and Larry and Dave—felt that way as well, it was easily understandable. For one thing, he had taken the walk alone, and it certainly seemed safer for several of them to go together. In addition, at that point the wind had died down somewhat, and they didn't even have to break a trail through the snow, as Tim had already done that. These were fit, athletic men who had not only been in blizzards in the past, but Bud and Dave had each taken this very walk in the storm just the previous day. One day before, the journey hadn't seemed all that treacherous to either of them. And finally, this wasn't like being advised against trekking in the backcountry or scaling Everest, this was just a little half-mile jaunt to a ski lodge through a parking lot.

When Katy came down to the parking area, Tim was incredulous at seeing the clip-in ski boots she intended to wear, and he made a derisive comment to her about the wisdom of hiking in them. Undaunted, the group set off, but before they were even out of the condo's parking area, Larry Guinney changed his mind about going. Just from trudging through the deep snow in the lot, it seemed to Larry that this was not going to be a fun walk, and on top of that, he had a niggling fear about leaving the kids unsupervised in the snow tunnels. He told Bud and Katy that he was going to stay behind to watch the boys and make sure the snow didn't collapse on them.

By this point, Dave had come down from his condo and joined up with the Nelsons. When Dave ran up to put on some additional ski clothes, he had been excited and in a hurry. He told Jeanne that the man they had seen walking had in fact just come from the lodge and that he was going to head up there with Bud and Laura. He said that Bud wanted to see about getting some food. Dave was in such a flurry getting ready and acting like the plan was all decided that he left the condo before Jeanne had a chance to realize that she wanted to come along too.

Out of the glass door of the second-floor condo Jeanne could see the group walking single-file down below her. She was dressed only in white cotton pants and a white cotton shirt, so she thought she would call down to them to wait for her to change her clothes. She had gone out on the patio just that morning to get wood, but this time the sliding door jammed and she couldn't get it open. She yanked on it several times, but it was frozen completely shut. As the line of people was moving extremely slowly, she had time to try to yell to them from inside the condo, but they didn't hear her. She watched them until they looked like little teeny people, and then she saw Katy turn around. Jeanne called a friend at home and told her Dave had just gone for a walk.

Even sticking to Tim's trail, the snow was still more than hip-deep on the men, and obviously higher than that for Katy and Laura. Katy had been clomping awkwardly in her ski boots, slipping on the ice and snow and unable to keep her balance. Feeling like she was holding them up, she decided to turn back. Laura wanted to stay with her dad. Katy handed Bud the fanny pack filled with candy, matches, money, and extra gloves that she had brought, then kissed them both good-bye. Not wanting to be last in line, Laura said, "Let me in front of you, Daddy," and Bud switched places with his daughter.

When they got near Tim's condo, at just after 3:15, he peeled off and then stopped for several minutes and watched as the little group that had committed to the walk, down to only three, disappeared into the darkening hush of the snowstorm. The lull in the wind began to seem somehow ominous, looming over the scene and infusing it with an intrinsic calm-before-the-storm feeling. Dave was leading the way. Even though they were all walking in a line, the doctor and his daughter seemed to move together as a unit.

After hiking more than halfway to the ski area, the group ran into Kate Ulberg on her way back from the lodge. With Wendell at the condos handling all manner of complaints from hungry and stranded vacationers, Kate had cross-country skied over to the resort just a little while before on a mission to see if someone there would either sell her food or bring some supplies over to the complex. She had lived in the area almost ten years by then and knew the surroundings extremely well, but that afternoon she felt like she was skiing through a completely unfamiliar, fairyland kind of place. The fresh snow had piled up as high as the old snowbanks in places, and there was no visible road. With everything covered over, she could barely tell where she was. She usually made the trip to the lodge in under ten minutes, but that time, even taking the back way through the Subway parking lot, it had taken her over half an hour.

The lights were on in the lodge when Kate arrived, and she called out a greeting, but she didn't see any people around. Just when she was starting to wonder if anyone was even there, Bernie Kingery came out to confront her, an experience she later deemed a turning point in her life. He had his Alpine Meadows jacket on, and Kate immediately assumed by his expression that he had seen her approaching the resort and had come over to have it out with her. She knew Bernie in passing, and he recognized her as a local ski instructor. He did not say hello, but proceeded to call her out on what in the world she thought she was doing there. Eyes blazing, he hollered at her for at least five minutes, mixing in obscenities, telling her that she should have had more sense. He didn't specifically reference the avalanche hazard, but he talked about safety in general, contending that she had been around long enough to know better.

When she asked him about getting some food, Bernie told her that if she needed provisions, she should call the sheriff. He made the valid point that it was not the ski area's responsibility to feed the people in the condos, then raised his voice again, yelling at her to keep "your condo people" over there. Kate tried to hit him up for information, but the most she could get from him was that the patrol crew would try to do avalanche control later, he had no idea when the resort would open, and he thought that Lowell Northrop, a local plow operator, was coming soon to plow. He was very angry and made it quite clear that she needed to go. She could tell that he was stressed and sincerely concerned, that he truly felt she had made a stupid judgment. As she started to go, he gave her a smile and a wave and told her to be careful out there. The last thing he said to her was, "Have a good ski."

Kate skied much faster on her way back. Her tracks were still there, but barely. She couldn't believe how hard it was snowing, slanting down right at her face. She lifted one ski in the air and sank up to her hips in a drift. Kate was a strong, skilled skier with years of experience and all the right gear, and yet even for her there was a moment when she feared that she might get turned around in the snowstorm. She felt she understood for the first time how people got lost in blizzards, and she contemplated how thoroughly embarrassing it would be if it happened to her.

Just then she heard what was, to her ears, the magical, wonderful sound of a plow coming down the road. Between Bernie's outburst, her brief confusion in the storm, and her excitement over the snowplow, Kate's adrenaline was coursing when a moment later she ran into Bud, Dave, and Laura. She told them that they really needed to turn around and go back, that the conditions were horrible up ahead, and that in any event, the resort was closed and the head of the ski area had just yelled at her to stay out.

Bud, holding hands with Laura, told her that they just needed to get out of their condo for awhile. "We have cabin fever," he said.

Except for the shouting part, Kate passed along the speech Bernie had just given her about the hazards of being out in the storm, not mentioning avalanches in particular but adding that she had a decade of experience with Sierra storms and still had almost gotten lost herself. In response, Bud made a comment about having survived a typhoon. She saw him as arrogant, yet she didn't even consider the possibility that he and Dave wouldn't follow her advice.

"Can't you hear the plow coming?" Kate asked.

"What are you talking to me for?" Bud replied. "If you're in a hurry, go."

Like a horse straining to get back to the barn, Kate was intently focused on going home to share the good news about the plow with Wendell. She told the group to follow her ski tracks back to the condos, and she thought that they had listened to her. She assumed they were trailing behind her as she skied away.

Bud, Dave, and Laura did not follow Kate. At that point on the walk they may well have been experiencing not just cabin fever but a bit of summit fever as well—an overwhelming desire to reach their goal since they were so close. In addition, the two men might have inadvertently provided an impetus to each other—each of them may have perceived a willingness on the part of the other one to move forward, a dynamic that ended up motivating both of them to keep going.

They might also have wanted to exert just a little bit of control over a situation in which they felt powerless, rather than to be told what to do by other people who were out doing the same thing. No one in a position of authority had informed them to stay away, and clearly a message to avoid the resort hadn't reached the condos, since Kate had not been cautioned in advance. In addition, the resort's parking lot was not closed—there were no warning signs posted or gates blocking their way.

The group did not travel the back way to the resort through the Subway cut-in that Kate had just come from. They may not have seen her ski tracks, or perhaps they took the slightly longer route through the parking lot at the base of the Buttress and Pond Slope because that was the way they knew. Possibly they stayed on Tim's trail simply because ducking into an unfamiliar shortcut in a storm seemed like a risky idea.

The last person Bud, Laura, and Dave passed on their walk

was Lowell Northrop, age 64, the owner of an independent snow removal service who was out plowing Alpine Meadows Road in a Sno-Cat loader 966c. His home was just down the road, and when he had come out earlier to get ready to start plowing, he took a look at what, at that point in the storm, was a peculiar kind of fine, light snowfall. The snow wouldn't stick to itself at all, and it seemed to be almost vibrating. Based on nearly half a century of experience in the snow business, he announced to his wife, Barbara, that he was off to get caught in an avalanche.

As Lowell plowed up Alpine Meadows Road, he saw three people walking down Ginzton Road. Laura was holding her dad's hand and reveling in the spell of the beautiful snow flurries. She waved at Lowell and he waved back. To Lowell, at that moment, they looked as if they might have been happy. He stopped to let them by, but instead they paused for a few seconds to watch him plow, waiting as the final tumbler in the lock of their fate clicked smoothly into place. Then they turned to start walking through the parking lot toward the ski area, and that was the last Lowell saw of them.

THIRTEEN

What flies without wings, strikes without hand, and
sees without eyes? The avalanche-beast!

—

Old German folk riddle, reflecting the belief
that avalanches were a product of witchcraft

Around the time the vacationing families had reshuffled the list of
people hiking up to the resort that afternoon, Jake had called Pam
from the Summit Terminal Building to tell her he wasn't going to
make it home for awhile. Afterward he hung out in the patrol room
for a few minutes talking to Billy Patterson, the groomer who ran
the graveyard shift and Jake's devoted fishing buddy. Late March
to early April was spawning season for the rainbow trout in Lake
Tahoe, and it was a tradition for Jake and Billy to go fishing together
off a pier in Tahoe Pines, pumping up night crawlers with syringes
full of air to make them float a foot or two off the bottom. The
two of them had been out fishing in blizzards at this time of year
before—they simply tipped their aluminum boat over some pilings
and cast out from beneath it. Storm of the century or not, Jake and
Billy made plans to go fishing the following morning. Just before

3:30 they walked out of the Summit Terminal Building together, Billy heading over to the grooming office in the lodge and Jake to the vehicle maintenance shed to fill a snowmobile up with gas.

While awaiting word that the control team was in place at Squaw, Jake brought the snowmobile out to the parking lot, passing Anna and Frank on his way. He and Anna made eye contact, acknowledging each other with a brief nod, and then Jake rode off.

Anna could usually walk from her house up to the resort in about 20 minutes, but in the storm it had taken her and Frank almost an hour to make it on skis. The route was basically all an uphill slant, and they pushed themselves to ski the whole time. They were both runners, often taking five-mile runs together, used to that level of exertion. Along the way, Anna had worked up such a sweat that she shed both her hat and her mittens, giving them to Frank to store in his backpack. By the time they reached the parking lot, they were messing around, being dopey with each other, feeling good about having made it.

Tom Mosher, the head of lodge maintenance, was also in the parking lot at that time, over at the west edge, trying to attach a chain to his snowbound car so he could tow it to a plowed section of the lot. Meanwhile, Marty Marchese, the parking lot supervisor who Bernie had considered sending to Squaw in Thom Orsi's place, was out trolling for coworkers to take a coffee break with him. He persuaded Tom to stop trying to extricate his car and they both went into the lodge. Once inside, Marty spied David Scott, another maintenance worker, removing snow from the upper sundeck of the lodge with a small Bobcat front-end loader. He went out and asked David to join them, but David told him that he didn't have time to stop plowing just then. After a bit of arguing, Marty convinced him to come inside for a few minutes.

Karen Strohmaier was in the lodge as well, although she was getting ready to head over to the Summit Terminal Building to scribe for Bernie while Beth went outside to do road guard duty. Karen had turned the copier and the word processor off and was just starting to shut the switchboard down when a call came in. It was a woman phoning from Marin County to complain that she was supposed to be coming up to Tahoe but the roads were closed and she didn't want to be charged for the trip. Her vacation package included lift tickets to Alpine Meadows, and since she couldn't reach anyone at the hotel or visitors' bureau, she wanted to know what Karen, the only person who had answered a phone, was going to do about the situation. Karen figured that she was the kind of woman who would write a letter to Howard if she cut her off, so she tried her best to calm her down. The caller was furious and rude, and she kept Karen on the phone for over ten minutes, almost certainly saving her life.

With Thom and Igor both gone, Bernie was running the radio in the ski patrol office by himself. The office was in the northeast, downhill corner of the Summit Terminal Building off the large patrol room. A room about 12 by 14 feet, its exterior walls were a foot thick and supported by steel I-beams. There were two gray, metal desks facing each other in the room, one for Bob Blair and one for Don Huber, although when Don wasn't there, his desk ended up being used by whoever needed it at the time. Bernie's desk was over in his own office in the lodge, but during avalanche control, Base 4 was the nerve center of resort, and he worked from there.

Beth was alternately sitting in a chair at Don's desk and leaning back against the wall with a clipboard, scribing for Bernie while she waited for Karen to come take over. In preparation for going outside to be a road guard, she had put on white bib ski pants, rubberized yellow overalls, and her Skadi avalanche beacon. Bernie, pacing around the office, didn't have his beacon on him at the moment, but he had it out on the desk.

Around 3:30 the patrol crew called in on the radio from Squaw to report that they had reached the bottom of the KT-22 chairlift and would be starting up soon. The next transmission was from Howard, who had left the resort not more than 15 minutes before, calling from Alpine Meadows Road to report that some snowbanks had sloughed onto the road and needed to be plowed out. When Howard drove away that afternoon, Bernie had not, as he had in the past, given him a hand charge to throw up on the mountain on his way down the road. It was clear that this situation was going to require a more comprehensive strategy than that.

Normally Bernie was invigorated by storms—each one came in differently and he loved to watch them, sit up with them as they unfurled. Avalanche control was something like a chess match for him, keeping track of everyone's location on the mountain, checking how deep the snow was getting, asking the patrollers if there was electricity coming off their skis. He was constantly challenging himself to see if he could outsmart the avalanche, plotting his next move while striding around the patrol office, pounding one fist into the palm of his other hand. He was clearly stimulated by this storm as well, but that afternoon his energy was mixed with a bit of fatigue and a slight sense of worry.

Around the time Bernie was fielding radio transmissions, Jeff Skover and Randy Buck drifted into the patrol room to see what they could do to help out. Jeff, age 23, had grown up in San Francisco. He was extremely attractive in a slacker sort of way, with expressive bright blue puppy-dog eyes, a beard, and wavy dark hair. A junior at UC Berkeley, for the second winter in a row Jeff took the semester off from his zoology classes to come up to Alpine Meadows to ski and work. He started the season in night maintenance, but then moved to a position as a night security guard. His shift, which ran from late the previous evening until that morning, was long over, but he stayed to work wherever he was needed as well as to do a bit of snow-diving (jumping off roofs into enormous piles of snow) with Randy.

Randy, the maintenance worker who had helped with the howitzer earlier that day, seemed to feel that the lodge was plenty clean, and he wondered if Bernie wanted some extra help closing the road. A former professional skateboarder and amateur mountain climber, Randy had moved to Alpine Meadows from Sunnyvale, California, three years earlier to support his skiing obsession. Red pants aside, Randy usually looked like quite the mountain man in rotating plaid shirts and a bushy dark beard.

At that point a call came in for Bernie on the land line. Patrolman Lanny Johnson had a rare day off, and that afternoon he was out in front of his home preparing to go cross-country skiing. On a whim, he went back inside his living room and called Bernie to see

what was going on at the resort, which slopes had slid and which
hadn't. As they talked, Bernie seemed especially bothered by the
overloading in Beaver Bowl. It was a valid concern—in '65, before
the Summit Terminal Building had been built, Bernie had been at
the resort when a huge avalanche flowed down from Beaver, taking out the Summit chairlift and coming up to the edge of the old
lodge. Lanny assured Bernie that Tom was quite certain Beaver
Bowl had released the day before.

"Hold on," Bernie suddenly said to Lanny.

Anna had just poked her head into the patrol office and called
out a greeting. After coming up the stairs to the second floor, Anna
and Frank had first stopped into the employee locker room, but
before she changed her clothes, Anna wanted to let Bernie know
she was there. Since it looked like she and Frank were going to have
to wait around at the ski area while the patrol did avalanche control
on the road, she thought she'd see if she could help with anything.
Frank waited in the locker room at the opposite end of the building
while Anna walked over to the patrol room.

Bernie strongly believed that people did not have enough of an
appreciation for their own safety, and to a large extent he was right.
Only 15 minutes earlier in the lodge he had given Kate Ulberg a
lecture about the hazard involved in cross-country skiing through
avalanche terrain to the resort, and now here was Anna, having
done the same thing.

Anna had just said hello to Beth and barely begun to comment
on how thrilled her friend seemed at the chance to be helping out in
command central when Bernie came out into the main patrol room
and started yelling at her. Raising his voice, he started in on a tirade
that would ultimately last several minutes, questioning whether
Anna realized the risk she had taken by crossing through avalanche
zones in the storm.

Anna's hair was dripping wet and her jeans were soaked.
Uncomfortable about being chastised in front of the other people
in the room, she didn't say much in response other than to apologize and defend herself by saying that she had called to verify that
the road was open. In this midst of his genuine concern for Anna,

Bernie made the inaccurate declaration that the road was only open to cars, not cross-country skiers, then spat out that she could have been killed. To emphasis his point, he stalked over to the map table in a corner of the patrol room and began jabbing his finger at a map of the area, saying, "You did this, you did this," as he pointed out which specific avalanche paths she had passed under on the road and in the parking lot.

Bernie's speech lasted long enough for Randy to wander out of the room and over to lift operations, where he saw Frank, his backpack shrugged slightly off his shoulder, looking out the window by Billy Davis's office as he waited for Anna.

With his anger finally expended, Bernie told Anna to stay put, expressing to her what he, and everyone else associated with the resort, believed to be true—that it was safe inside the building. He went back into the small patrol office, and Randy, Jeff, and Tad DeFelice followed him in.

Randy and Tad, who was waiting to be given his road guard position, walked to the back of the room across from Beth. Randy took a seat at Bob Blair's desk, and Tad stood next to him. The counterweight for the Summit chairlift, a ten-foot-high, six-foot-thick, 22-ton solid mass of concrete, was directly behind them. Jeff was over by the doorway to the main patrol room.

When Anna left the patrol room, she crossed through the building and went back into the locker room. Frank was patiently waiting at the far end of the hallway, facing away from her as he read the employee bulletin board. As much as she wanted out of her wet jeans, Anna's first priority was to reach Frank to tell him about the conversation she had just had with Bernie. She walked about halfway down the hallway, maybe ten yards away from Frank. She never made it to him.

After Anna left, Bernie picked up the phone to continue his conversation with Lanny. "One of the lift ops was here," Bernie told him. "I read her the riot act." They had just started to pick up their discussion about avalanche control when the radio started crackling and Bernie put the phone down a second time.

"Hold on," Bernie said again to Lanny.

It can be as simple as the weight of a skier or a snowmobiler, or the explosives used in avalanche control, but with an avalanche, there is always a trigger. In a naturally occurring avalanche, the storm itself is the trigger—that final, delicate snowflake drifting down from the sky and landing on top of the mountain.

It was 3:45.

The radio transmission was a garbled message from Jake. The content was desperate, but the tone nothing less than heroic, delivered by a man whose instinct in the throes of impending disaster was to call in a warning. Only one word of Jake's transmission was audible, and that word was "Avalanche!"

"Ten-twenty, Jake?" Bernie shouted into the mountain radio, asking Jake his location.

In response, there was a snatch of fragmented words, then static, then silence. Jake did not come back on the radio. As Bernie strained to hear a reply, he took a step into the center of the room, then one back toward the window. Jeff moved farther into the room.

The lights in the building flickered, then went out.

Beth recorded the word "Avalanche" in the logbook, five seconds before the building blew apart.

FOURTEEN

I saw a wall of white—it engulfed the running figures
and swept them away.

–

Mike Alves, mechanic at Alpine Meadows in 1982

The deceptively named maintenance shed at Alpine Meadows was
a sturdy dark brown cinder-block building across from the main
lodge. Two stories tall, it was large enough to house not only all of
the resort's various yellow snow removal and grooming vehicles,
but also the howitzer used for avalanche control. Approaching the
lodge from the main parking lot, the maintenance building was a
bit off to the right, nestled into the base of the mountains and surrounded by trees.

By Wednesday afternoon, the seven or eight vehicle maintenance guys inside the shop were exhausted and the slightest bit disgruntled. Most of them couldn't make it to and from work due to
the hazardous road conditions, so they had ended up sleeping in the
building Monday and Tuesday nights. To try to compete with the
immense amount of snowfall, they had started in the early morning hours and worked all day. They were keeping the routes in and

out, but they were getting behind—the snowbanks were starting to close in on them and they were beginning to lose the parking lot. Just before 3:45, Rich Baker was talking with the crew about having a 7:30 dinner at the River Ranch restaurant at the end of Alpine Meadows Road and wondering whether, because of the inaccessible roads, there was a chance the resort would pay for any of them to get a room for the night at the hotel attached to the restaurant.

At the same time, Mike Alves, a mechanic on the road crew, was outside in the vehicle yard, talking to Cliff Fraser about the snow removal plan and trying to get one of the Austin Western graders to start. A big power horse of a machine, the grader had four-wheel drive and four-wheel steering with a blade in the middle. It was used to move snow and peel the pack down to the asphalt while another guy drove the blower, scooping snow and sending it spraying a couple hundred feet up and out in an enormous arc. Cliff was supposed to be down in the parking lot with the grader already, but the mechanical problem was holding him up. Mike had been heading home, as he had come in at midnight and already put in more than a 15-hour shift, but he stuck around to help Cliff because with snow removal, you did it until the job was done.

Mike wasn't thrown by the repair. His family had long been in the snow removal business in Placer County, and he grew up fixing and operating Norland 966s and Caterpillars with wing blades. Tall and lean with a muscular build, Mike had light brown hair that curled onto his neck and a trim mustache that he would later grow out in a Fu Manchu style. He had strong, charming eyes and a lazy smile to match his unhurried, easygoing nature. On his days off, he spent a lot of his time tinkering with his own personal equipment, a rapidly growing collection of vehicles that at the time consisted of four cars and six motorcycles.

Meanwhile, Ray Overholt, a longtime groomer, had already left the service yard. He was in the cab of a snowblower in the parking lot below, anticipating his role in the snow removal process. He had been expected at work at noon to relieve Mike, but conditions being what they were, he hadn't arrived until three o'clock. Ray idled the Norland's two motors, one for the engine and one for the blower, and looked out at the expanse of the whiteout as he waited for Mike and Cliff to resolve the issue with the grader.

The service yard where Mike and Cliff were talking over the repair was located above parking lot level, between the maintenance shed and the main lodge. Mike, over near the service entrance, noted two people trudging in his direction from the parking lot, one a little distance behind the other, sort of dark shadowy figures in the wind-thickened roil of the storm.

Immediately afterward, his attention was pulled by the sound of a small cracking noise in the midst of the howling wind. From Mike's location, the avalanche's more dramatic announcement, a sharp blast or boom, was likely lost to the ratcheting storm. The sound Mike heard wasn't a rumble or a roar. It was a noise like twigs or wooden matchsticks breaking, but it was not actually twigs at all, but hundred-year-old trees with trunks a yard thick being snapped by a massive curtain of snow surging down the mountain.

The mountain had unzipped itself all the way around, the boundary sharply defined by a thin crack that arced across the slope. The tear, more than a half a mile wide, yawned wider as a plate of snow fifteen feet thick lost its grip on the mountainside. For just the briefest of freeze-framed moments, the snow on the mountain paused and held, and then it fell as one complete windowpane.

Mike, looking up to the face of the Buttress and Pond Slope to identify the source of the sound, saw a sight that few people have lived to describe. In a motion too fast for his eyes to track, the snow was turning loose all at once, melding the mountain and the sky into an undifferentiated smear. The slope shattered into a buckling snarl of smaller shards until the entire sky was obliterated by a wall of white, a churning, boiling swell that grew larger and larger until it became the only view.

The avalanche pounced on the mountain like it was crushing a can, not just knocking trees down but shredding them. Part frigid river of lava, part icy bubbling cauldron, the avalanche slid down the mountain in a mad whirl, destroying or entombing everything in its way. In front was a spectacular 40-foot-high powder cloud with its billowing leading edge blasting against displaced air and suspended snow particles. Within the seemingly cottony cloud, boulders of snow spun and collided and disintegrated. As the avalanche raced down the slope, it vacuumed up immense quantities of new, loose snow in its path, growing more massive and powerful as it went and moving with shocking, unprecedented velocity.

The source of the speed, and the distance, and all the death to follow, was—if judged solely on destructive capability—the flawless design of the avalanche. Once the slab ruptured off the mountain, like a chunk of plaster cleanly popping out of a wall, it leapt over the downslope staunchwall fracture and roared down the rest of the mountain. Usually, at that point an avalanche is slowed up somewhat by confrontation with the surface it is running on—rocks, vegetation, the remaining layers of snow.

That slab, however, was riding on top of an overinflated cushion of air in the form of several inches of puffy, light stellar snowflakes. As it plunged downhill, the avalanche built momentum on the new layer of fluff, actually lifting right up off the slope. And once it jumped its track into the air, the avalanche was soaring resistance-free. There was no friction to arrest its descent, no friction at all.

As a result, the slide was capable of traveling not only faster but also farther—astonishing, unimaginable speed combined with the potential for unparalleled distance in the runout zone. The phenomenon gave Mike Alves a front-row seat to one of the most awe-inspiring sights in nature—an airborne avalanche literally flying down a mountain.

In what seemed to him like some kind of horror-show slow motion, Mike forced his focus back to the figures in the parking lot, who by this point had progressed to within 40 feet or so of the lodge. Relatively sheltered by the wind in that area of the parking lot, and with the lodge right up ahead and only a foot or so of snow on the ground to wade through, they had picked up their pace somewhat. They were close, just so close—maybe thirty seconds, maybe fifteen—to the edge of safety.

Involuntarily, Mike took time to process the thought that these people were not familiar with the mountains, that they hadn't heard the approach, they weren't looking the right way, they weren't aware of, weren't reacting to, the monster bearing down on them. And then, in just the briefest of moments before his own delayed survival instincts kicked in, he saw the two figures run.

There were, of course, actually three people in the parking lot—Laura, her dad, and Dave Hahn. Two of the figures were likely so tight together that they seemed to be only one, with Laura just ahead of or behind her father.

From his perspective in the snowblower at the edge of the parking lot, despite the intensity of the blizzard, Ray Overholt was near enough to be able to make out all three figures. As he watched through the swirl, he saw Laura, in her oversize boots, slip and tumble onto the ice. And in that moment Ray was privileged to witness a display of paternal instincts so powerful that they overrode all concern for personal safety. Bud's identity as a father was so inextricably tangled with his beliefs, his faith so intertwined with his love for his daughter, that hesitation was never an option. Bud did the only thing he could do to save her. He stopped in his tracks, turned back, and raced to Laura's side to help her up.

Just then a tantrum of snow from the avalanche periphery slapped onto Ray's windshield, obscuring his vision. Mike, with a bird's-eye view, saw the rest unfold.

Just a few dozen feet to the edge of the parking lot and only slightly ahead, almost certainly having paused to confirm that Bud had Laura, Dave sprinted for safety. Bud and Laura were close behind him, perhaps holding hands as they ran, maybe Bud screaming at his daughter to go faster, possibly even sweeping her little body up in his arms as he ran, quite literally, what was to be the race of his life.

It was all over, start to finish, in under ten seconds.

Millions of tons of roiling, swelling snow hit the parking lot like a tidal wave crashing into shore, but this snow wave did not recede. Shoving a hurricane-force wind in front of itself and traveling at almost 200 mph, the torrent flowed mercilessly forward.

Helpless in a way no one ever fully recovers from, Mike watched the men and the little girl try to outrun the avalanche. An instant later, he witnessed it overtake them and bury them alive under twenty feet of snow.

FIFTEEN

The noise an avalanche makes is often described as a growl or a roar, but to the survivors in the ski lodge at Alpine Meadows, when the avalanche destroyed the Summit Terminal Building it was more like the sound of 10,000 kids with roller boards all racing across a gymnasium and slamming into the wall at the same time.

As the air blast hit the building, the whole structure began shaking violently, the massive steel beams bending a foot and quivering as if they were made of rubber. Then, like water gushing through a hose, the snow flooded into the building and exploded out of the walls and windows that were trying to contain it. Every part of the 100-foot building was blown out, stripped away, leaving only a skeleton—some beams and a few sections of wall flapping precariously in the wind.

In a classic and heartbreaking example of what wildly capricious killers avalanches can be, when the snow stopped moving, two of the seven people in the building ended up on the surface. A few feet either way literally meant life or death for the employees in the patrol room. Randy and Tad survived by the sheer freak luck of their position in that room. They were essentially leaning against the downhill side of a 22-ton rock when the avalanche hit, and the ocean of snow simply flowed around them.

As the building began to vibrate, Bernie scooped his avalanche beacon off the desk. Jeff, instinctively relying on his San Francisco earthquake training, grabbed a wooden countertop and dove beneath it. Randy stood up from his seat just in time to witness a scene out of some kind of lurid nightmare. As time became distorted and chillingly hyper-focused, he watched as first Beth, then Bernie, were launched out the window, almost sucked out as if through a shattered window on a suddenly depressurized airplane. Almost instantly, they were swallowed up by the white abyss. Shell-shocked, Randy dropped to the floor and curled into a ball behind the desk, covering his face with his hands.

The air blast detonated inside the building, picking up whole walls and carrying them away, filling the air with flying debris. Immediately afterward, a barrage of snow surged into the building, tearing holes in some walls and flattening others. The torrent engulfed the area near Randy, pushing him around and buffeting him like he was caught in surf, but it did not pick him up and carry him off. He felt a current in the snow, like fast running water. As the movement slowed down, the avalanche started to crush him.

As Randy felt his life being squeezed out of him, he instinctively kicked out with his feet. He felt something solid beneath him— part of the floor, as it turned out—and with that leverage, he broke the surface and was able to heave himself out of the snow. At that moment, his sensation was more a feeling of accomplishment than elation at being alive—everything was happening too quickly for him to think about death. He saw Tad right next to him, buried up to his waist in the snow, half hanging out of the building. Everything else, and everybody else, that had been in that room was gone.

Tad's leg was pinned under the snow by some skis, and despite being jacked up on adrenaline, Randy wasn't able to get him out.

Randy essentially triaged the situation, determined that Tad's injuries weren't life-threatening, and with Tad's blessing, left him there while he looked for the others. He saw building debris spread out over hundreds of feet, but no sign of any of the people he had been talking to in the patrol office moments before.

Despite injuries later diagnosed at the hospital as a broken rib and a compression fracture in his lower back, Randy continued searching and digging as the rescue efforts unfolded around him. Within about three minutes of the avalanche, he was joined by several employees who streamed down into the area from the lodge, struggling over the debris and stepping up to the search-and-rescue role they suddenly found themselves thrust into.

Although time has usually run out for an avalanche victim while search teams are formed, in this situation it was even more extreme—the people who would normally take charge of a rescue were not immediately available. Bernie was missing, Bob was at home, and the remaining members of the ski patrol crew had been sent to Squaw.

Billy Patterson, Jake's fishing buddy, was one of the employees who had come on the run from the grooming office in the lodge. In the fading light and the blur of the continuing storm, he scanned the area, weighing speed against thoroughness and trying to be both quick and complete at the same time. In the midst of the wreckage, over 100 feet away from where the Summit Terminal Building had been, he saw a bare hand sticking up from under the snow. Randy heard the shout when Billy found Jeff.

Jeff Skover was on his back under about a foot and a half of snow covered over by plywood. Billy and Scoop Skalinder, the grooming supervisor, dug feverishly to free him. Jeff was unconscious, but he came to and started talking almost as soon as they lifted him out of the snow. The events unwound in slow motion in Jeff's mind—after ducking beneath the counter, he had clung to it as the wall behind him disintegrated. Then the force of the pressure charge ripped his grip away and whipped his body back and forth, blasting him across the room and hurling him through whatever was left of the building. The last thing he remembered was a vortex of wind and white. He landed out in the direction of the Bell Tree, so named because the ski school instructors rang a bell on the tree to round up their students, where he disappeared under the snow, invisible except for a single hand.

In addition to a concussion, Jeff had a deep gash just above the hairline on his head that was bleeding profusely, cuts on his face, and bruises all over his body. His white Santa Cruz surf shop sweatshirt was doused in blood. He seemed incoherent and in fairly deep shock. While Billy and Scoop continued searching for survivors, other employees led Jeff to the lodge to get him a blanket and warm him up.

After demolishing the Summit Terminal Building, the avalanche had slammed into the lodge as well, bursting out all the windows and swarming inside, dumping several tons of snow in the lounge and cafeteria on the second floor. The avalanche submerged the sundeck, sweeping up the Bobcat loader that David Scott had been operating moments before and slamming it down a set of stairs, where it landed on its head. Much later, when Tom Mosher next saw the parking lot, the car he had been attempting to dig out was buried beneath tons of snow. In just one of the many quirks of fate associated with the tragedy, had Marty Marchese gone to Squaw in Thom Orsi's place, he wouldn't have been at the resort to tempt Tom and David away from their positions in the path of the avalanche.

The employees inside the lodge at the time of the avalanche, all of whom survived, hadn't necessarily recognized the disaster as an avalanche right away. It was so out of the bounds of their imaginations for a slide to have enough force and mass to enter the lodge that many of them initially thought they had experienced an earthquake. When the snow poured in, the lights blinked out and the fire sprinklers on the ceilings went off, drenching the employees with freezing water.

In her windowless office, soaking wet from the sprinklers, Karen had crawled along on the floor in the dark, feeling for the extra handheld radio she had in her desk. She always kept a spare radio hidden from Bernie, who never charged his and was always grabbing one from her. She first tried to reach Bernie, but obviously got no answer. Within a minute, Billy Patterson called her on the radio to tell her what had happened and calm her down. Karen knew she had to call for help, and since the base radio wasn't operable with the power out, she used her handheld radio to communicate with the patrollers in the Summit lift shack on top of the mountain. She relayed a message to them, and through the radio up there they sent word to Howard Carnell.

Within a split second of the avalanche hitting the parking lot, Mike Alves shook himself out of his shock with the realization that if the avalanche had wanted to kill him, it would have. Perhaps it was slowed up some by the trees above the maintenance building or by the structure itself, but for whatever reason, the avalanche didn't seem to want to bother much with the maintenance shed or the vehicle yard just downhill from it. It swept completely around the building on each side, streaming into the upper parking lot on one path and striking the Summit Terminal building on another path. Nearby, the slide had tossed and played with several pieces of heavy equipment, leaving them mangled in a heap, but aside from some broken windows, the maintenance building itself and the people in it were virtually untouched.

As the runout settled, Mike stared out over the expanse of parking lot. The entire lot, from the maintenance building down to Alpine Meadows Road, was enveloped by a load of snow over 600 feet wide, several hundred feet long, and ranging between six and 20 feet deep. The figures he had seen were just simply gone. They had vanished beneath the snow so completely that it was almost incomprehensible that they had ever even been there at all. Knowing that every minute was incredibly crucial in this type of rescue, Mike forced himself to suppress his hysteria and focus. He desperately scanned the surface looking for the heel of a boot, the fingers of a glove, a piece of clothing or gear that could offer a clue as to where the avalanche discarded the people after it swept them up, but the snow wasn't giving up its secret. There was literally no evidence of them whatsoever.

Mike knew he needed help, and he first ran up to the maintenance shed to get it, screaming as he went that there were people buried. Inside the solid building, the first sound of the avalanche the mechanics had heard was the splintering of a window 13 feet off the floor. As some snow spilled in that window, the crew came outside to see what had happened and found themselves confronted by a near-manic Mike yelling at them to grab whatever they could find to dig.

About half a dozen vehicle maintenance workers snatched shovels from the building and went out to the parking lot. Mike indicated the last-seen point, telling his colleagues that before they disappeared, the figures were very near the edge of the slide.

Every fragment of energy Mike had left, after the trauma of the events mingled with the stress of working 16 hours straight through since midnight, was directed toward getting employees out to the parking lot to help the people whose burial he had witnessed. Mike was frantic in his efforts to find them—seeing them alive and then seeing them covered made him think that he could do something to save them. He raced around corralling as many people as he could find, and between the garage shop, lift maintenance, and lodge maintenance, he sent several more people out to the lot to search.

Mike knew that rather than dig blindly, the searchers were going to need to probe for the victims. Avalanche probes, a crude but effective method of finding a victim under the snow, have been used to look for people in the Alps for hundreds of years. The probes are narrow, rigid, lightweight poles, typically made of aluminum. They are usually 10 or 12 feet long but fold up to much shorter lengths so they can be easily carried.

There are two general methods of probing: a fine probe, which is essentially for body recovery; and a coarse probe, used when there is hope of finding a victim alive. Probing is most effectively done in horizontal lines using a grid spacing. The searchers stand about two feet apart, elbow to elbow, and on an order spoken by a probe line leader, each searcher thrusts his pole into the snow, first at the top of his left foot, then at the top of his right. Then, with almost military precision, the line systematically advances forward a small step. The searchers repeatedly follow the command "Probes down, probes up, advance" until one of their probes hits something that gives resistance.

It takes quite a bit of muscle to penetrate the snow with an avalanche probe. The motion needs to be less spearfishing than the application of steady force. Once a searcher connects with something other than snow, he leaves his probe in place while another searcher slides his probe alongside it to see if he encounters the same sponginess. Assuming there are enough people to search, the probe line is ideally followed by a shovel crew that leaves the probes in the snow and digs all the way down.

The coarse probe basically balances the probability of finding someone against the time they have left to live beneath the snow. By any calculation, the chance of success is very low. On average, it would take twenty searchers four hours to coarse-probe an area roughly twice the size of a football field, and they would have a 70 percent chance of finding the victim on their first pass. A fine probe, with smaller spaces between the searchers and the steps, would yield a higher probability of locating the victim, but it would also take several times longer. If there are enough searchers, it is more time efficient to run multiple coarse-probe lines.

Victims are often found only after a second or third pass over the same area. For one thing, depending how the victim is positioned under the snow, it is possible for the probes to miss him entirely. In the late '60s at another resort, a ski patrolman was buried under the snow on his side, with his skis still on. The only probe to hit him was one that connected with the metallic side of his ski.

More likely, however, despite heightened senses in an emergency situation, searchers—especially inexperienced ones—don't recognize the sensation when they have struck a person. Often bushes, muddy ground, or even a layer of slush can have a similar feel.

Another downside to the probes, particularly in a huge avalanche, is that the victims are often buried deeper than the length of the poles. If a victim is ten feet down, a searcher would only find him if he pushed a probe all the way down to a handhold. If the victim is deeper than that, the pole wouldn't even reach him.

Although avalanche probes were ideal for the situation in the parking lot, in a cruel irony, the cache of hundreds of probes at the resort was unavailable. The probe poles, along with all of the other rescue equipment, had been stored in the Summit Terminal Building and were, at that point, buried under the snow themselves. Initially Mike didn't have any idea what was happening on the other side of the resort, but a vehicle mechanic named Rich Hutchins had seen enormous pieces of the Summit Terminal Building soaring through the air when he first came out of the maintenance shed.

Realizing that accessing the stash in the headquarters building wasn't going to be an option, Mike instantly determined how the crew could improvise. He handed off the key to a storage room in the maintenance garage to Rich with instructions to grab all the long rods of electrical conduit he could find. The half-inch conduits, already cut in 15- and 20-foot lengths, were used to run electricity to the ski lifts. They were the perfect items to utilize for avalanche probes, especially given the depth of the snow in the parking lot. The makeshift probes arrived in the lot almost instantaneously—in the urgency of the moment, the mechanic's shaking hands couldn't quite manipulate the key into the lock, but he made up valuable seconds by breaking the lock right off.

Since Mike could identify approximately where the victims were located when they were caught—a piece of information rescuers usually don't have—he knew they were buried anywhere from that point on through the end of the runout zone. He took a wide view of the scene, looking at the general flow characteristics of the avalanche itself to try to determine if the victims were likely swept left, right, or straight ahead.

On a mountainside, there are sometimes assumptions about where to search based on where someone could potentially be trapped, such as snow ridges or concave areas. In the broad, flat expanse of the parking lot, there were no such markers, except the hills of snow the groomers had been piling up in the middle of the lot. Those snow storage piles had been about 20–30 feet long and 10–12 feet tall. It was possible that the victims were caught against them, but the piles had been so covered over with fresh tons of snow from the avalanche that they were indistinguishable from the rest of the expanse of white. Mike and the rest of the searchers had to rely on their memory to determine the pre-existing location—and shape—of those various man-made mounds of snow. The first improvised probe pole stabbed the snow less than five minutes after the victims had been swept away.

Despite the employees' valiant attempts at organization, the scene at the two rescue sites—the parking lot and the Summit Terminal Building—was beyond chaotic. In addition to the 15–20 feet of snow blanketing the area and building debris scattered throughout the base of the resort, darkness was closing in, the only available light source was from a few headlamps and flashlights, and heavy snow was still falling. The storm obviously didn't stop or slow down just because the mountain had avalanched, and in fact, it was busily reloading the slopes with fresh snowfall. The disaster was not like a tornado in that once it moved through the area the danger was essentially over. In this situation, the employees had no idea what had slid or what might slide next. Not only were they unsure of the stability of the slopes, they realized that the storm and the additional snow accumulation were only making the circumstances more precarious. Rather than dealing with the aftermath of a disaster, the employees were still very much in the midst of one.

Inside the lodge, the scene was operating on a slightly lower frequency of frenzy, although there was no power, no heat, no phones, and no water, except for what was pouring down from the sprinklers. The place was covered with snow, strips of bark, pinecones, and broken glass from the windows. Some of the employees set a bunch of candles around—the intent was to provide light, but the effect was to add a creepy, cultish atmosphere to the unreality of the scene.

The guy who ran food service, usually so particular about rules that he wouldn't allow rescue dogs in the bar, did his part in the only way he knew how—he unlocked the liquor cabinets, pulled the alcohol out, and left it all on the counter.

Although the storm was blowing right through the gaping holes in the lodge where the windows had been, it was the best the employees had to work with as a temporary first-aid station. The actual first-aid room was packed with avalanche snow, so several of the employees shuttled supplies up to the restaurant in the lodge.

The mattresses and blankets Jake had been collecting to sleep on that night ended up being used to treat the survivors.

At some point David Scott ran down to check on John Riley, age 74, the original planner and promoter of the ski area who lived in his motor home in the parking lot by the lodge. The avalanche had not reached the area of the lot where he was parked, but he was passed out inside and seemed to be suffering from some sort of panic attack. After David brought him to the lodge and covered him with a blanket, his vital signs soon returned to normal.

One of the groomers was also an EMT, and he was helping Jeff Skover, who at this point was going back into shock. He looked increasingly dazed, and he was losing a lot of blood from his head wound. He also kept wanting to go to sleep. The groomer put a compression bandage on his head to stop the bleeding and kept him warm and calm while Karen Strohmaier, now sliding seamlessly into position as a nurse, made sure he stayed awake.

Despite the broken bones in his spine and his rib, Randy knew how many people were still out there under the snow, and he played the dual roles of victim and rescuer for over an hour until his pain was too much to bear. He had immediately given the searchers a head count of the people who had been in the building, as well as their locations as best he knew it. At one point Randy found a shovel and went back to help dig Tad out, and then the two of them probed the area with shovel handles.

The searchers in the area of the Summit Terminal Building didn't have any probe poles, but the vast amount of wreckage at that site rendered probing useless anyway. The groomers and other assorted employees, about seven or eight of them altogether, did organize a probe line with some shovels they found in the lodge, running outside with them right through the shattered windows in the second-floor cafeteria and on top of the mound of avalanche snow. They started at the far end of the debris field out toward the Meadow chairlift, several hundred feet away from the site of the Summit Terminal Building. They worked their way along the edge of the slide to about the Bell Tree, but after only 15 minutes or so it became obvious that the effort was pointless. As the searchers probed the snow, within two feet their shovel handles connected with parts of the building and its contents—boards, beams, furniture, and all sorts of other rubbish.

At that point they gave up the line and started to search individually, looking under boards and trying to find items that looked like they came from the patrol office, knowing that both Bernie and Beth had been in that room. That method of searching, the most effective under the circumstances, would continue into the night. Earlier, Billy Patterson had reached Bob Blair on his radio at home and, upon realizing that search-and-rescue teams couldn't access the resort, jumped into the first snowcat he could find that hadn't been crushed by the avalanche and went down to get them.

Meanwhile, after Mike made sure the poles were secured and got everyone pointed in the right direction in the parking lot, he joined the probe line himself. There were no engines, no machines, no conversation, just a riotous, encompassing silence as the probe poles methodically sliced through the snow. As twilight turned to darkness, in the face of the storm and the path of the avalanche, Mike and the other mechanics did not waver from their search for the strangers lost in the runout zone. Later that evening, Mike would leave the line to plow the road in an attempt to make it easier for more searchers to reach the scene. Over the course of his rescue efforts that night, he collapsed twice and had to be helped to his feet.

The mechanics had no way of knowing if there were more people buried beyond the two Mike had seen—other people walking in the parking lot, or shoveling out their vehicles, or even sitting in their cars. It wasn't until it all got sorted out over at the condos as to who was missing that the rescuers realized that there were really at least three victims. Two people versus three didn't matter in terms of their search efforts, though—they were looking as hard as they could as fast as they could. And, as it turns out, they were looking in almost exactly the right place. With a runout zone encompassing several acres and no surface clues, the men from the vehicle yard still found the first person in the parking lot just 40 minutes after the avalanche had descended.

SIXTEEN

Jake was out being a boy on a snowmobile.

–

Larry Heywood

The Alpine Meadows ski patrolmen had been at the base of KT-22 putting on their skis to board the chairlift that afternoon when some unusual transmissions began coming over their radios. The Squaw Valley ski area had seemed deserted when they arrived. Normally Thom would have just dropped the crew off and left, but when Jim got out of the truck that afternoon, he made a point of telling Thom to wait there until he called him to confirm that they were able to get on the lift.

When a lift operator showed up to crank up the chair for the patrolmen, he told them that an avalanche had ripped through some houses along Sandy Way in Squaw Valley, badly damaging one house while a person was inside taking a bath. Most of the Squaw Valley patrollers had abandoned the resort to respond to the scene. No one was killed in that avalanche, but the press immediately picked up the story, and the timing of that slide ended up lending a extra layer of confusion to the news that was disseminated from the Lake Tahoe area that day.

The handheld walkie-talkies of that era didn't have much range or power in the best of circumstances, and trying to hear over the clamor of the storm was an added complication, but when Jim and Larry picked up a transmission from Howard Carnell, the resort's general manager, they were both quite sure that they perceived urgency in his voice. That drew their attention immediately, because Howard was not a man who panicked. They couldn't catch the whole message, and Howard didn't use the word "avalanche," but through the static there was a moment of clarity on the channel long enough for them to make out a sentence. It was Howard's voice again, saying, "Get the dogs, get an ambulance."

The crew didn't know who Howard was directing those instructions to, but they initially assumed that he was talking to Bernie. Jim called Bernie at Base 4 and got a busy signal. He then called Base 1, the main office in the lodge, and the phone just rang through. Despite the limitations of the radio, Jim realized that he should have at least been able to raise one of the base stations. He asked the lift operator to get him an outside line, and he dialed every extension he knew at the resort—the various departments, individual offices, the first-aid room—and every one of the lines simply rang and rang with no answer.

Phone lines often go down in a storm, but the patrolmen, as a whole, instinctively sensed that there was something very wrong at the ski area beyond a mere telecommunications problem. Even Howard's request for emergency help didn't necessarily indicate anything about the scope of the tragedy, but somehow they all felt it.

On the chance that Bob Blair had taken his radio home and was monitoring it, Jim called him at his house in Alpine Meadows. When he answered the phone, without providing any details, Bob made it pointedly clear that the crew should return to the resort immediately. He had realized from the radio traffic that there had been an avalanche, but he had no sense of the magnitude of it until a few minutes later when Billy Patterson radioed him from the ski area and described the scene.

The mood among the patrolmen in the truck on the ride back was somber. They knew complete darkness was less than an hour away. Jim still couldn't raise Bernie on the radio, and Bernie loved to talk. All of them recognized that the situation at the resort was dire, but beyond that they had no idea what they were going to see when they got there, in part because none of them could imagine a disaster that complete.

Even in an era before cell phones or the Internet, news of the avalanche began spreading around Alpine Meadows and filtering throughout Lake Tahoe within minutes. All around the area, whether they had been specifically called to report back or not, patrolmen, Alpine Meadows employees, locals, and even tourists were inextricably drawn to the ski area to try to help any way they could. Road closures all over the region slowed the travel time down considerably, but people journeyed toward the resort, no matter how long it took.

Lowell Northrop spread the word virtually instantaneously. He was just across the bridge on Ginzton Road, driving away from the mountain in his snowplow, when the avalanche hit. He was within a few seconds, a few yards, from being caught up in it, and as it was, snow from the runout splattered all over the back of his loader. He immediately drove his plow to the condos and told Wendell Ulberg about the slide. Wendell contacted the sheriff, who was caretaking the nearby Stanford Alpine Chalet, then began gathering shovels and organizing a rescue group from among the people staying in the condos.

The electricity was already out by the time Kate Ulberg got back to the condo complex. When she was told that there had been an avalanche at the resort at the moment she was skiing away from it, her reaction was to grab the probe poles off her porch and head back to the scene.

After Lanny Johnson's phone went dead during his conversation with Bernie, he tried calling back to the patrol office, but the line was busy. He simply assumed the phone lines had gone down, so he took off cross-country skiing with his wife. When they reached the Lucky store in Tahoe City, Lanny ran into a firefighter outside the grocery who seemed incredulous to see him there and explained that Alpine Meadows was calling for assistance for a huge avalanche that had hit the base area of the resort. Lanny started to say that that wasn't possible, that he had just been talking to Bernie on the phone, then trailed off as he remembered how their connection had been abruptly severed. He headed straight for the ski area.

Jake's brother, Dennis, was still on the road going home when the radio cut in with a broadcast of an avalanche at the resort. Since avalanches fell harmlessly in the Sierra with some regularity, news bulletins reporting them were often viewed with nonchalance if not outright disregard. In a city, it would be analogous to hearing a report of a car accident on a busy highway—the odds were remote that there would be a fatality, much less one involving someone known to the listener. In addition, some of the news stations erroneously reported that an avalanche at Alpine Meadows had destroyed the Summit lift shack rather than the Summit Terminal Building, an event that would have been unlikely to yield tragic results. Nonetheless, whatever Dennis heard was serious enough for him and his two coworkers to turn the truck around in the blizzard and go back.

Don Huber's wife, Roberta, was listening to a recap of the avalanche in Squaw Valley on a scanner when Don came home from the Forest Service office. A few minutes later, they received word to bring their avalanche rescue dogs to Alpine Meadows. As soon as the couple grabbed their gear, Bridget and Smokey were already at the door, ready to begin the search.

Longtime patrolman Gary Murphy had just walked into his home in Truckee when his wife told him that Bob Blair had called with some news. Before she even finished conveying the message, he gave his newborn daughter a quick kiss, then contacted the patrolman he drove home with to get a ride back. The California Highway Patrol had closed the road at Squaw and the patrollers didn't have their employee passes with them, but they managed to talk their way back in.

At the time the avalanche was destroying much of Alpine Meadows, Nick Badami, the owner of the resort, was with Werner Schuster, the head of public relations, at a hotel in Reno in a meeting discussing the possible expansion of the company into a new ski resort development. Their meeting was interrupted by a bellman who handed Nick a telephone. Howard was on the line, calling to let him know that there had been a big avalanche at the ski area but that he didn't yet have many details as to the level of its seriousness. Nick told him that he and Werner would wait there to hear more. When, a short while later, the bellman handed Nick the phone a second time, he listened for a moment, then ended the meeting abruptly. He and Werner attempted to drive back to Alpine Meadows that evening in the storm, out of phone contact and unable to receive updates on the situation until they arrived home.

Larry and Jim and the other patrolmen coming back from Squaw had only driven a short way down Alpine Meadows Road before they ran into Howard's blue Blazer parked sideways in the road. He was strategizing a rescue plan with Bob Blair, who had walked there from his house. With Bernie missing, in the chain of command it fell to Howard to be the rescue leader, while Bob would go up to the resort as the on-site commander. Howard decided to set up rescue headquarters in the nearby water district building, where he could be near telephones and radios and arrange help from within as well as outside the community.

It was too dangerous for search-and-rescue teams to proceed down Alpine Meadows Road to the resort that evening for two reasons. First, it would entail crossing under several uncontrolled avalanche paths. At that point it was unclear what had slid, but there were several active avalanche paths above the road, and the crew that went to Squaw had been called back before it had finished—or even started—its mission to control those routes. Second, despite the immense peril, on his way out of the resort Billy Patterson had attempted to use the main road but quickly realized that it was impossibly treacherous, and slow, due to all the power lines snarled in the snow. The patrol was going to have to find another way up to the resort, and Bob and Billy already had a plan in motion. The patrolmen arranged for a roadblock on Alpine Meadows Road, then skied up into the bordering subdivision to rendezvous with Billy.

Bob's house was in the labyrinth of back streets in the neighborhood off the main road and Billy had lived there in the past, so between them they picked a specific location on John Scott Trail to meet. The roads were completely impenetrable for conventional vehicles, but Billy had been able to punch his way through in a snowcat. The actual snow grooming machine he chose was a Packmaster 3700, generically referred to as a snowcat but known among the grooming staff as a hydro because it was hydrostatic—it had no drive train and was fueled by hydraulic fluid. The hydro was a broad, massive piece of equipment that made monster tracks. It had a blade to plow snow in front, a one-person cab in the middle with two joysticks, a big hood, and a short flatbed. In the back was a compactor bar to smooth down the snow with arms that articulated out and looked like wings.

On his way through Bear Creek Estates, with the ten-way blade on the compactor bar fully folded back to be as wide as possible, the only way Billy could tell if he had hit a car was by the amount of snow that sloughed down. There were 20- to 25-foot high snowbanks on either side of him, and the hydro was like a pinball bouncing off them, the whole machine shifting over to one side of the road, then correcting itself back. Days later, when Howard asked Billy how many cars he had hit in his frantic effort to transport rescuers to the scene as fast as he absolutely could, Billy looked at the general manager with amazement. "I hit 'em all," he replied.

Coming down the subdivision, Billy knocked out a chain blocking access to the road without a problem, but he had a moment of concern when he came around an S-curve and reached the one-lane bridge over Bear Creek. He knew he wasn't going to fit, but there wasn't any choice. What flashed through his mind was whether the bridge could support the weight of the hydro, and then he was across it, full-speed, the safety rails on both sides of the bridge demolished and flung out of the way.

By the time Billy reached the meeting point in the subdivision, residents in the neighborhood had poured out of their houses dressed and ready to help. Most of them had shovels or ski poles or other tools they thought might be useful in the search. In a scenario not unlike running back into a burning building, these volunteers were willing to advance into a disaster scene that was still smoldering.

There were far too many people for Billy to take up the mountain in one trip. The solution was obvious to the patrolmen—they had their skis with them, and they used the evacuation ropes in their packs to fashion an ad hoc ski tow. They secured several long lengths of rope to the hydro and tied knots in the other ends as handholds. Larry grabbed one rope, and Igor and Jim grabbed another. As the hydro took off, the patrolmen were essentially water-skiing over the snow behind the snow grooming equipment. The setup was an aberration of skijoring behind cars, which Howard Carnell, as well as many of the patrollers, had delighted in during their youth.

Casey and Tom swung up onto the compactor bar. Bob crammed into the cab with Billy, five or six of the volunteer rescuers piled on top of the hood and hung on as best they could, and the machine began bulldozing its way to the ski resort.

The snowbanks on either side of the hydro were enormous, and as the edges of the compactor bar rubbed along the sides, it knocked loose snow backward over the patrolmen as they hung on to the rope tows. The second the blade touched the banks, the snow peeled off. It was wild snow, hissing and sizzling with electricity and seemingly lit from within. The banks were cascading off into the road trench in such volume that it was like a continuous avalanche flowing down around the skis of the patrolmen as they tried to stay in the tracks of the machine. The light was flat and dim and it was snowing like crazy, so the patrollers couldn't see very far ahead. As the road got narrower and the berms began to close in on them, they had the claustrophobic sensation of skiing in an increasingly constricting maze.

At one point the hydro lurched on its way up a hill and Igor, holding on to the rope in front of Jim, fell down, causing Jim to tumble as well. Just at that moment Billy, apparently stuck in a rut, began backing the hydro up to get better traction. As the machine rolled back toward them, the patrolmen—each with at least 30 pounds of dynamite on his back—were trapped behind it in the compressed path, still grasping the rope, unable to get up on their skis fast enough. Billy couldn't see them and didn't know they were down, and Jim was convinced that he was going to die the ignominious death of being backed over by a snowcat. They started screaming, which at least caught the attention of the people on top of the hydro, who then started beating on the cab to alert Billy. On a heightened level of adrenaline, all of the rescuers proceeded to the ski resort.

After winding its way through the back roads, the hydro came out on a street known as Bear Creek #3 that intersected the base of Alpine Meadows Road. The engine of the hydro suddenly started whining with a shrill *whaaa* sound as it mounted an unexpected and extraordinarily steep incline, and Larry realized they were climbing up the edge of the avalanche runout zone.

As they reached the pinnacle of the debris pile, the sensation was like stepping onto a glacier. Twenty feet up from the level of the road, the patrolmen caught their first glimpse of the consequences of the avalanche. The sheer unnatural scope of the devastation was staggering. The parking lot was gone. In its place was a seemingly infinite plane, awash in an ocean of snow. Massive ponderosa pines that had stood for a century were fractured and peeled, toppled onto the ground like a giant's game of pick-up sticks. The telephone poles that hadn't been snapped off like raw spaghetti were leaning at broken angles, with the power lines entwined in the snow and the trees. Larry, Jim, and Igor were forced to ski a high-stakes slalom course, zigging and zagging to avoid getting twisted up in the electrical wires.

The extent to which the environment had been redesigned, and the harsh solidity of that change, was incomprehensible to the patrolmen. They could barely recognize their surroundings, and they strained to get their bearings amid a miasma of shock and utter disorientation. There was no sense of finality or safety in the aftermath—it was as if a force was still crouching in the snow, biding its time before it pounced again—yet their instinct was only to push farther into it.

It was almost, but not quite, dark. When Billy turned the hydro around the corner onto Ginzton Road, the first thing the patrollers noticed was a mangled, partially buried snowmobile with the Alpine Meadows logo on it in the middle of the road. They didn't wonder which employee had been riding it; they knew instantly that it had belonged to Jake.

As the wind shifted and rolled the omnipresent snowfall over the bleak moonscape of avalanche debris, the rescuers skimmed their eyes across the road, the parking lot, the Ginzton Road bridge. Where Jake should have been had been wiped off the map. There was no tranquillity to the desolation, but rather a disturbing, hushed stillness. And there was no sign of Jake.

Bob gave Casey the terse instruction to find Jake. Both Bob and Casey dropped off at that point, as well as Igor, and the hydro continued on to the resort.

The night was just beginning for Billy Patterson. He would make several more trips with the hydro shuttling people through the subdivision up to the resort, and later he would use the machine to search through the rubble of the building. He skimmed a foot of debris at a time off the top of the pile and pushed it all the way out toward the Meadow chairlift, while people watching from the side intently scanned the mass in front of his blade. He tried to peel the layers thin, but even so, he dreaded the possibility of a head or other body part rolling up in front of him.

The fact that the avalanche had pitched the heavy snowmobile on top of the snow while burying Jake beneath it was not an unusual phenomenon. In a slide, large objects have a tendency to sift to the surface of the snow, much like the way shaking a bag of chips filters the smaller pieces to the bottom and leaves the biggest ones on top. Casey assumed, correctly, that Jake would be wearing his avalanche beacon, and he searched for him that way, pinpointing his location—about 40 feet away from the snowmobile—within a minute.

Avalanche beacons, otherwise known as avalanche rescue transceivers, were invented in 1968. They have continued to grow in popularity ever since, and have become smaller and more effective over the years. Referred to as a Skadi, the 1982 version was a yellow box about the size of a television remote, with a red panel and lanyard. It ran on rechargeable batteries and it could pick up a signal from a distance of 50 feet or so.

While beacons often provide the best chance of locating a victim, their potential downside has always been the false sense of security they create in people who believe that merely carrying a beacon is sufficient protection against dying in an avalanche. The beacon's signal enables a rescuer to identify the location of a victim only if certain factors are aligned: the victim is wearing a beacon that is switched on to transmit a signal, the rescuer himself has a beacon to receive the signal, and the rescuer knows how to use the beacon. Operating these devices is obviously second nature to ski patrolmen who routinely travel in avalanche terrain, but their knowledge comes from extensive training. An emergency in the backcountry is no time for someone to pull out the instructions on a beacon for the first time. Even if every member of a group knows how to use the beacon, a victim caught in an avalanche while wearing one could still be killed by trauma, or, more likely, run out of air before rescuers could shovel him free.

The beacon transmits an invisible electromagnetic pulse that radiates out in the shape of butterfly wings from beneath the snow. To locate the signal, the searcher on the surface flips his beacon to the receive mode and begins a grid search. Every other searcher also has to manually switch his beacon to the receive mode so that the rescuers don't pick up each other's signals. When the person conducting the search hears a beep, he turns the volume down to hone in on the sensitivity of the signal. He continues to walk around on top of the snow, and as he gets closer to the victim's location, the beeping gets louder again.

Beacons can generally tell a rescuer distance, but not necessarily depth. The signal Casey picked up was coming from the area of a creek that had been buried by the avalanche, but there was nothing there—no surface clues whatsoever to give away Jake's hiding place. Skadis could theoretically locate a victim to within a few feet, but there was a zone of inaccuracy involved in a deep burial. To try to figure out whether Jake was directly below them or angled down and away in a certain direction, the patrolmen pulled probe poles out of their packs and quickly probed the area. They inserted the ten-foot poles down into the snow until they were just grasping the tips of them in their fingers, and still they did not connect with Jake. Casey, Bob, and Igor knew only that Jake was nearby, and very deep.

They started digging furiously, but the snow had set up like cement. By then other volunteers—from the condos, the nearby development, a second hydro operated by Scoop Skalinder—had arrived at the scene to help. There were about six to eight people digging, including a doctor from Sacramento who used to teach at the ski school. Some of them were shoveling from under the bridge, an area that hadn't been completely compacted with avalanche snow, attempting to get to Jake sideways, since digging to him later-ally was less likely to collapse any airspace he might have had. The various strategies and tactics of digging a hole—one big enough for the rescuers to get in and for Jake to get out—came easily to the patrolmen, but they were acutely conscious of the passage of time as valuable minutes ebbed away. As they dug, the low droning beep-beep-beep of the Skadi was like an insistent alarm clock reverberat-ing in their heads, driving them to move faster, push harder.

At one point Lowell Northrop rumbled over the road just above the rescuers with his snowplow. The motion sent snow pouring over the sides of the bridge, initially prompting the fear that the moun-tain was avalanching all over again and injecting an extra bolt of panic into the existing crisis.

The men knew they could find Jake, and they thought there was a chance they could save him. The snow, extremely hard and heavy, was not a blanket in any poetic sense. Most of the crew was digging with shovels—Casey and Igor had them in their packs, and many of the volunteers had brought them—but some people, including Bob, whose pack was at home, were clawing at the snow with their hands.

The rescuers began CPR on Jake before he was even free of the snow. He was in a standing position, leaning back slightly and look-ing north, about 15 feet deep. The patrolmen worked on his head first, scooping their fingers into his mouth to empty it of snow and clearing his airway, and then the volunteer doctor crawled into the hole to give him mouth-to-mouth resuscitation. Meanwhile, the other rescuers continued to dig him out.

Jake was broken and blue, and his body didn't look quite right. He was cyanotic, his coloring the dull, dark blue-gray of faded denim. His legs were bent a bit, as if he were in the act of jumping. In the decades to come, Jake's vertical position under the snow would only enhance his mystique, providing confirmation in the eyes of his friends that he was tough enough to stand up through an avalanche. He was intact, but he had traveled a long way, and he had some traumatic, high-velocity injuries in addition to being crushed. He had also been buried a long time—it had been almost an hour and a half since he called Bernie on the radio. Even though he was wearing a beacon and the rescuers knew almost exactly where he was, it still took over half a dozen men approximately 35 minutes to dig to him in the roadside creek bed.

When the patrolmen had Jake totally out of the snow, they moved him under the bridge and set him on a platform made out of skis, where they continued CPR. Weeks later, when she came back to visit the scene, Pam found some change, keys, and bolts under the bridge. She realized that wasn't the place where he had been found, but even before Casey told her they had moved him to that location, she knew the items belonged to Jake.

The patrolmen repeatedly checked Jake for a pulse, allowing extra time for the slowed heart rate of a very cold person, but it was too late. It was 5:15 when the doctor announced that further efforts to revive Jake would be futile.

Igor, stunned at the sight of Jake's dead body, felt like he had been hit in the stomach with a hammer. Earlier he had been elated when Casey was able to pick up Jake's Skadi signal, and he hadn't even allowed for the prospect that they wouldn't pull him out alive. Expressing the emotions every one of the rescuers felt, Igor knelt down and cried, the first time he had done so since he was a child. Knowing there was nothing more they could do for him, the patrolmen covered Jake and temporarily left him under the bridge while they went to search for more victims.

Days afterward, some of Jake's colleagues wondered why he was at that location at the moment of the avalanche, since there seemed to be no real reason for him to be there just then. He hadn't yet been posted in position as a road guard. It would have been a bit premature, but it was possible that he was doing a preliminary sweep of the area to clear out traffic and pedestrians. More likely, however, according to coworkers familiar with his patterns, Jake couldn't resist taking a quick, blissful swing around the high snow-drifts in the parking lot on the snowmobile.

Jake had a little 110 camera with a pop-up flash in his jacket pocket when he died. There had been one shot taken, and initially his family wondered if he had somehow taken a photo of the ava-lanche as it was coming at him. Later, when they developed the roll, there was no image on the film, and it seemed that the camera had merely gone off on impact. As far as taking the opportunity to photograph the avalanche before it overtook him, Jake was too busy at the time. His sacrifice was certain and unmistakable—to operate the radio hanging from his chest, he had to remove his hand from the snowmobile's handlebars to push the transmit button, precious seconds he spent warning others rather than trying to save him-self. Then, as the people who loved Jake like to believe, in his last moments he turned and gunned the snowmobile, riding away into a white and endless horizon.

SEVENTEEN

Out of the silence and the darkness,
these Nordic ski gods just appeared and
skied up full-speed like they were born on skis.
Quintessential ski patrol rescue heroes.

—

Tim Fitzpatrick, guest at the Alpine Place 2 condos, March 31, 1982

A rescue mission is always, at best, controlled chaos—a fight against time, distance, terrain, and the elements—and the ski patrolmen were well trained to handle disasters. They hadn't, however, practiced a rescue drill in the dark with no equipment, a limited crew, a missing leader, and the threat of additional avalanches.

As the hydro towed Larry and Jim closer to the resort, through the murkiness of the scene Larry noticed some people digging over on the right in the parking lot. He initially thought they were shoveling out their cars, and he was livid that in the midst of the catastrophe their priority was to find their vehicles. What he witnessed wasn't a search for cars at all but the last stages of a desperate rescue attempt by Mike Alves and the other mechanics and Alpine Meadows employees.

In the end, the depth of the snow prevented the rescue crew from reaching any of the victims quickly enough in the dwindling twilight. After locating Dave Hahn beneath the snow with a probe after only 40 minutes, it took several vehicle maintenance workers, digging furiously, another 40 minutes to shovel ten feet down to get him out.

Dave was found just on the edge of the avalanche, on the right side of the upper parking lot near the maintenance shed where the employees traditionally parked their cars. He had been pinned very tightly in the avalanche snow, with his arms extended over his head. The searchers extricated Dave at almost the exact moment that the rescuers near the Ginzton Road bridge were exhuming Jake. After almost an hour and a half under the snow, Dave was nearly frozen, his pupils fixed and dilated. The employees cleared the snow out of his airway and repeatedly performed mouth-to-mouth resuscitation and heart compressions on him, but they were not able to bring him back.

The men who found Dave carefully loaded him onto a sled and pulled him to the first-aid room in the lodge. Avalanche snow had poured into the small room like whipped cream and it was ice-cold inside, but it functioned well for its temporary purpose. They laid Dave down on a bench and covered him up. The first-aid room operated as a makeshift morgue that evening, ultimately holding three bodies when the search was suspended later that night. Never again would Larry be able to enter that space without being brought back to that moment, the night when the little room designed to dispense bandages and treat broken legs was instead blanketed in the distinctive smell of death.

From their vantage point as they approached the ski lodge, Larry and Jim had not yet been able to see the remains of the Summit Terminal Building. When they reached the breezeway in the lodge, the overturned Bobcat taunted them with an inkling of the destruction beyond. Massive piles of snow in the tunnel blocked their way, so with their dread intensifying, they skied back around the lodge and through the vehicle maintenance yard. Larry and Jim came up on the pinnacle of the site in unison, silhouetted together in the moment, shoulder to shoulder against the frozen sky.

The millions of tons of snow that had fallen on the resort

muffled almost all sound, and despite several dozen people spread around the area searching for victims, the landscape was deathly silent. The storm blocked any view of the moon. The remnants of the Summit Terminal Building were illuminated only by the headlights and rotating beacons from a couple of snowcats, and the diffuse light cast an eerie pall over the entire proceedings.

Jim's first view of the obliterated building made him physically sick to his stomach. The first floor and much of the second floor were completely buried under the snow, with just a shell of the partial second story and the top story reaching up to the sky. His initial, visceral reaction was followed by the thought—not knowing that three people from the building had already made it out alive—that there was no way anybody could have survived.

As they surveyed the ruins, Larry and Jim were overwhelmed by the unqualified power of the avalanche—stripped trees and building debris encased in snow were spread out farther than the length of a football field. Several large snowcats had been carried for hundreds of feet and then dropped, twisted and crushed, back onto the ground. The avalanche had completely transformed the topography of the area—the surface of the runout zone was not level, but waved out over several acres in various hills and valleys.

By that point there were several people on a probe line in the vicinity of the building. Despite the seeming futility of probing amid the wreckage in that area, once additional searchers arrived, the employees had again organized a line. The groomers and other staff members had been joined by Kate and Wendell Ulberg and a group of people staying at the condos, including Tim Fitzpatrick, the honeymooner who had brought hot dogs from the lodge to the Nelson family. There weren't enough avalanche probes to go around, so many of the volunteers prodded the area with ski poles from the rental shop. They were cold and scared and probing in near darkness. They didn't know if one slide meant that more were likely, but they were all unnerved by the possibility.

Tim had returned to the ski resort that evening in response to a request for volunteers to search for victims of the avalanche. As he headed back out into the blizzard, following the same path he had taken an hour or so earlier, he saw rescuers lifting Jake out of the creek, a vision that lent razor-sharp focus to the gravity of the situation. Several other men responded to the call for help as well, including a black man from Oakland on vacation with his family. The only footwear he had with him was a pair of sneakers, but he asked Wendell to lend him some boots (which he mailed back weeks later) so he could join the search.

With the building itself and all its contents scrambled up and scattered throughout the base area of the resort, the rescue effort was nearly destined to fail. In trying to pierce the surface of the snow, the searchers—told to feel for something with the consistency of a pillow—hit pine branches, doors, boots, ski parkas, papers. Kate Ulberg's thoughts drifted between calculating the odds of another avalanche coming down to wondering where the hell Bernie was.

As hard as all the searchers were trying, from Tim's perspective he felt there wasn't the slightest chance he could distinguish a pair of balled-up powder pants under the snow from a body. Plus, it didn't seem at all clear how they were supposed to extricate someone if they did find a victim. In some ways the exercise seemed perfunctory, purely a formality, but within the unreality of the situation, all the volunteers were doing the best they possibly could to assist. There was an oddness to their perception—they were concentrating on their task but also attempting to absorb and assess the events, and in the process, the passage of time seemed somehow suspended.

The atmosphere was steeped in gloom and despair, with none of the volunteers on the lines talking. The employees showing them where and how to probe never used the word "bodies," saying only that there were people buried somewhere under the snow and they should hurry. There was a definite sense of urgency on the probe lines, a mission to find victims who might be dying, but deep down the searchers all knew that the people were gone. They weren't pretending that they were going to help anyone. Everyone probing, even the most inexperienced volunteers, shared an unspoken belief that no one was alive beneath that snow—it was just too deep.

Among all the horrors of that day, the arrival of the ski patrol is the single strongest image Tim Fitzpatrick carries with him a quarter of a century later. As he probed, out of the darkness ski patrolmen suddenly appeared without a sound and skied right up to the wreckage. They looked like hippies from central casting, but they were focused and purposeful, and they flashed an immediate air of authority and experience. Until then, nobody had really been in charge, and the searchers could sense the need for it. If inside Larry and Jim felt like they were scrambling, they certainly did not let on. To Tim it didn't seem as if they showed up and then figured out what to do, but that they already had a plan for this particular set of circumstances.

There were, in fact, no clear backup procedures in place to handle a situation in which the headquarters building was demolished, the rescue equipment was buried, and the mountain manager was presumed dead. Another component to the scenario was that the main access road was so unsafe that emergency equipment and machinery could not be brought in from outside the area. For all their experience, an avalanche of this magnitude was wholly beyond the scope of the patrolmen's knowledge or understanding. Years of training had been under the assumption that the rescue headquarters and equipment would be intact and available, but that is not the way the tragedy unfolded. The patrolmen worked with what they had, and in large part what they had was the gear they were carrying on their backs and a poised and well-developed leadership instinct.

When Larry and Jim and the rest of the patrol came on the scene—no-nonsense and organized—Kate Ulberg felt like the troops had arrived. Larry told her they needed a head count of anyone missing from the condos, and asked her if she would go back and help with that. As he watched the patrolmen take control, Tim had no doubt that if he was lying helpless under the snow, he would have wished for these brave, impressive men to be searching for him.

In addition to being sleep-deprived and physically exhausted, the rescuers were emotionally ravaged as well, but they remained calm and reasoned throughout the night. Bob Blair set up an incident command center in the lodge, which by then resembled a Buddhist temple, with candles burning all around. He tried to sort out the scene, deciding who was going to do what, where, and with what equipment.

The situation was theoretically in Bob's job description, but actually doing it, juggling the logistics of putting it all in place and protecting the search teams, was another matter entirely. He needed to determine what resources the rescuers needed going forward, but they were isolated at the resort, marooned at the end of three miles of dangerous road. In addition, even if the patrolmen were able to control the access road the next day, the surrounding roads, including Highway 80, the main highway to north Lake Tahoe, were still expected to be closed due to the storm. Leigh Rovzar, chief of the Alpine Springs Fire Department, Sergeant Kent Hawthorne of the Placer County Sheriff's Department, and Placer County Supervisor Larry Sevison were instrumental in coordinating the resource requirements.

Bob realized that nobody at the scene felt safe. In no way did the rescuers believe that the disaster was over—the sensation among them was more akin to fighting a forest fire that was still raging out of control. Yet in addition to the hopelessly deep snowpack, the scene also involved a building, and the idea that there could be airspaces gave them a little hope. There were a few people staggering around inside the lodge, still in shock. Bob gathered witnesses and directed people to conduct another so-called hasty search of the area around the building, looking, as was the literal case with Jeff Skover, for that proverbial hand poking out of the snow.

It was obviously essential for the rescuers to determine just how many people were in the area when the avalanche hit and exactly how many were still missing, but it was a nearly impossible task. The patrolmen had no idea if there were other victims buried among the acres of avalanche debris out in the parking lot. The rescue crews learned from the survivors of the Summit Terminal Building that Bernie and Beth, as well as Anna and her boyfriend Frank, had been in the building just prior to the avalanche, but they didn't know if any other employees had been inside as well. The staff at the resort had been gradually reduced all day as people headed home at different times, a dynamic that added to the confusion of who was still on the clock at the resort at 3:45.

There was a part-time trail crewman who no one could account for—some of the employees thought that he had been at the resort, but no one could find him. As it turned out, he wasn't even at the scene, but with the area later evacuated and people scattered throughout the state, it was a week before his safety was confirmed.

Bob assigned Larry to be in charge of the search and rescue of the base area surrounding the Summit Terminal Building. Larry, who demanded high standards from everyone else, himself stepped up to the role. He made sure the shovels and collapsible probes from the patrolmen's packs, as well as a small cache of extra probe poles recovered from the first-aid room, were distributed among the workers at the two search sites—the building and the parking lot. After sending an additional team of about a dozen volunteer searchers to the parking lot to probe, he then focused on the vicinity of the building.

Larry thought (correctly, as it turned out) that Beth might be wearing her Skadi in preparation to be a road guard, and he was initially hopeful that a search team could find her that way. He directed the rescuers to conduct a beacon sweep of the area over and over, spanning hundreds of feet in every direction to account for the beacon's range, but they did not pick up a signal.

As a test, Larry had the searchers try to locate the locker of beacons that had been in the ski patrol room. Employees left their beacons in the locker to charge overnight, and while the Skadis didn't transmit while they charged if they had been turned off, inevitably at least one or two people left them in the on position. The searchers couldn't raise a signal from the Skadis in the locker either.

The rescuers hadn't used the Skadis much in searches involving debris other than snow, and they weren't necessarily aware of the beacons' signal strength or capability if they were blocked. In the end they believed that the metal of the building was somehow interfering with the signal or, more likely, that the signal couldn't penetrate all the wood and other wreckage.

Throughout that night Jim was extremely quiet and deliberate, trying to determine what slope or slopes had slid and protect the rescuers from harm by evaluating the future hazard. He was obviously concerned for Mariah, his puppy lost in the rubble of the

Summit Terminal Building, but given the situation, he was forced to suppress those emotions. Later that night he spent a few hope-less moments calling for her, looking and poking around, but he couldn't find any sign of her.

Once Lanny arrived, Jim grilled him as to the details of his con-trol work with Tom Kimbrough on Beaver Bowl the previous day. Jim and Lanny went out to look at the direction of the debris path as best as they could with headlamps. It didn't seem like the slide had come from the direction of Beaver, but they couldn't tell for sure. Jim knew that if the avalanche hadn't fallen from Beaver Bowl, the hazard to the search-and-rescue teams at that point was expo-nentially higher. With all the new snowfall it was possible for that slope to slide imminently, and if it fell in any kind of similar propor-tions to what they were dealing with, the runout zone could wipe out the entire rescue operation. The patrolmen had no illusions—it was insanely dangerous for them to be there.

Contributing to their unease was news of yet another avalanche that had occurred at about 4:30 that day at the junction of Highway 89 and Alpine Meadows Road. Although no one was killed, the slide was powerful enough to trap a California Highway Patrol (CHP) officer in his vehicle and stuff the two women he had been talking to underneath it.

As the backup generator had failed to get the phone lines working, the only means of communication outside the resort that night was the radio. Radio transmissions were sporadic at best, with patchy reception due to the storm. Despite the communication restrictions and the lim-ited access to the site, by 6:30 there were at least 60 rescue workers on the scene, including members of the Tahoe Nordic Search and Rescue Team and various snow rangers, CHP officers, Placer County sheriff's deputies, and firefighters from all of the North Shore stations.

Don and Roberta Huber had arrived with their German shep-herds just after five o'clock on one of the first hydro trips, Roberta and her dog Bridget sharing the cramped one-person cab with the driver. Bridget and Smokey, both familiar with rescue missions, were comfortable riding on the snowcat—in prior searches, they had rap-pelled out of helicopters strapped to their handlers.

The dogs searched the parking lot first, then headed up to the area of the ruined Summit Terminal Building. In the parking lot, the snow was likely too deep and too dense for them to pick up much of a scent beneath it. Around the vicinity of the building, all the human smells inside the hundreds of lockers mixed in with the debris confused the dogs somewhat, and they alerted falsely a few times on sweaty clothes and old lunches.

As more rescuers came on the scene, there was again a shortage of avalanche probes, but one of the patrolmen remembered that there was a stash of 20–30 poles in the back of the attic in the maintenance shed. Dennis Smith had just arrived back at the resort, and he scrambled up to get them. They were mostly flattened, but they still worked. Filthy from crawling around in the attic, Dennis passed them out and then joined a probe line in the parking lot. When he first showed up Dennis had asked a few employees where his brother was, but people seemed to avoid the question and he just assumed that they didn't know. It fell to Casey, who had led that rescue, to tell his good friend that Jake was gone.

Sometime after Casey had pulled Dennis aside, patrolman Gary Murphy arrived at the ski area to find Dennis wandering around between the main building and the lodge, annihilated by shock, saying, "You know that was my brother." Gary then proceeded to the lodge, where he was greeted with the chilling report that nobody could find Bernie. Bob appointed Gary to be the parking lot site commander, and Gary headed down to supervise the search there and yell out cadences for the probe lines.

By that point the searchers in the parking lot were working in the pitch-darkness without enough flashlights and headlamps to spread among them. They were so focused on probing that for the first hour or two after the slide, many of them hadn't even realized that the Summit Terminal Building had been destroyed right behind them.

At Gary's request ten more volunteers were sent down to the parking lot. He set up two probe lines, each with about 10–15 people. One probe line worked from the maintenance shed into the parking lot, and the other line was farther down in the parking lot, moving its way up toward the building. Even the extra-long electrical conduit was often not long enough to probe all the way through the snowpack. In most spots, the regular 12-foot probes were barely able to hit the tops of cars. There were at least a couple dozen cars in the parking lot, and whenever the rescuers connected with one, they dug down to make sure no one was in it.

Kate Ulberg returned to the resort shaken, having gathered a report from the condo complex confirming that the two dads and the little girl she had passed on Ginzton Road were indeed missing.

"There's nothing for me to do here, right?" she asked a group of rescuers at large. "Everybody's dead, right?"

Someone muttered a response to her: "Yes, everybody's dead."

Larry walked over to Kate and told her firmly that if she was going to talk and not work, she had to go home. Her grim mission complete, Kate headed back to the condos for the final time that night.

The whole time Tim Fitzgerald had been probing by the building for victims, he hadn't given a thought to the doctor and his daughter, simply assuming that they had returned to their condo long ago. Even when word began to spread that at least two people were buried in the parking lot, Tim still didn't put it together. Then, in the course of accounting for missing people, information filtered back to him that Bud, Laura, and Dave hadn't returned to their condos yet. He was dazed by the news, and overcome with sadness. It had been too long. If the doctor was safe, he knew that someone would have seen him by that time.

Several rescue workers searching on a silent probe line dug Bud Nelson's body out from almost 20 feet of snow at seven o'clock that evening. Two men gave him CPR, but they could not find a pulse. Like Dave, Bud had his hands raised above his head, and he was ice-cold. The searchers transported him to the first-aid room in the still-swirling storm, then came back to continue probing.

The massive amounts of snow padded the scene against noise, cushioning it in a protective cocoon of near stillness. While certain sounds—the soft whoomp of a slope giving way beneath them—could signal death for the rescuers, it was also a tool they used to manage the snow. Once the snowcats began searching through the wreckage, the shriek of their engines was deafeningly, piercingly loud against the silent fear of a snowbound community.

Over the next few hours it continued to snow heavily, with several inches of new snow coating the scene and wiping out any point of reference. In a fresh sea of white, the rescuers could barely make out where the avalanche debris ended. The search-and-rescue teams were wet and cold and both physically and emotionally spent. They didn't know what was above them, and the cross-loading on the slopes overhead was escalating the threat by the minute. In the inky blackness, the scene seemed to have turned into a suicide zone.

Bob and Jim knew that the first rule of rescue was not to make a bad situation worse by killing more people, and just before eleven o'clock they made the decision to abandon the search for the night. There were no signs of life among the debris. By then they didn't have much hope that they could save the victims, but they did believe in their ability to keep the rescuers alive.

The patrol then began the slow and complicated process of pulling out, ensuring that everyone was transported back to safety over dark and unfamiliar terrain. Jim and Bob transferred the three victims (Jake had been moved up from under the bridge earlier in the night) from the first-aid room onto a Thiokol snow tractor with a pickup bed. Their bodies had been sculpted by the avalanche into poses, frozen in whatever position they had landed under the snow. A few limbs extended out in awkward angles, making them difficult to maneuver. The patrolmen took their time, using the last of the bedding Jake had been gathering earlier that afternoon to wrap him and the other victims up as best they could. There was some snow remaining on their faces, and Jim reached over and gently brushed a little of it away.

As the last of the rescuers left the scene, five more people lay buried beneath the merciless snow, dying or already dead.

EIGHTEEN

No, no, not my Bud and Laura.
We're here on a family vacation.

—

Katy Nelson, March 31, 1982

When the lights went off in the condo complex at 3:45 p.m., the people staying there had no idea that the power outage had been caused by an avalanche. They couldn't see or hear the disaster from half a mile away, and initially all they knew was that it was getting dark and they had no light or heat. Katy and Barbara went outside to tell Larry Guinney to bring the kids inside so they wouldn't get too cold or wet.

When Larry came in, he turned on a little portable radio and heard a report about an avalanche at Alpine Meadows. It was a preliminary broadcast with only sketchy details as to the scope of the catastrophe, but even so, an immediate sensation of doom washed down over him. He shared the report with Katy and Barbara, but kept his feelings to himself.

For some reason the phone in the nearby condo of Jay Seffern, the air force first lieutenant who had befriended the Nelson family a few days earlier, was briefly operable that evening. While Jay went to the resort to see if he could help with the aftermath of the avalanche, Katy used his phone to call her parents and tell them they were all okay.

As the minutes and hours went by and Bud and Laura didn't show up, Katy and the Guinneys sat around trying to come up with rational versions of what could have happened and why they weren't back yet. And there were, of course, so many plausible reasons to explain their delay.

At first Katy was not overly worried, thinking that they might have stopped in at Dave's condo on the way back to chat and have a beer. Even if they were at the resort at the time of the avalanche, it didn't make sense to her that Bud, who was eager to get outside and do something, would have turned back just as an event occurred to break up the monotony of the storm. He would have at least wanted to stick around and watch the proceedings, and if at all possible get involved in helping with whatever needed to be done. If there was anyone injured at the scene, Katy assumed that Bud, with his medical training, would be at the site treating people, perhaps even resuscitating victims. She figured that Laura was warm and safe in the lodge, drinking hot chocolate and waiting for her daddy to tell her what to do.

As it got darker and colder, the Guinneys were increasingly concerned about Bud and Laura's safety, believing that if Bud was okay he would have returned to the condo, or at least sent word back. To Katy, however, Bud was all but invincible, and her mind refused to bend around worst-case scenarios.

One credible argument was that the group had been told to remain at the resort rather than return to the condos over dangerous terrain. As the evening stretched on, Katy thought that maybe it was too cold and snowy for them to make it back and they decided to stay at the lodge overnight.

But perhaps the most compelling reason for Katy to believe her husband and daughter were alive was that people did not get killed by avalanches in the parking lots of ski resorts. People who died in avalanches were caught high on mountainsides in the backcountry or pushing the limits on steep, out-of-bounds slopes. Victims swept up in avalanches were extreme skiers and snowmobilers, not tourists taking a walk.

And in any event, the odds were so astronomically against this group of three being buried at the base of the ski resort—if they had been in a slightly different spot *in either direction,* they surely would have survived. It was so much more likely that they had walked a tiny bit faster or a little bit slower and had been anywhere but that exact location at that specific moment.

As Bud, Laura, and Dave had hiked to the resort, along the way people with the best of intentions unknowingly worked almost in concert to delay them just long enough to ensure that they were in that place at that time. If people had not tried to help them, they might have inadvertently saved them by allowing them to make it to the resort more quickly. It was ultimately the things designed to keep Laura safe—the warnings and the boots—that ended up killing her. And then again, the half minute they paused to watch Lowell plow the road essentially cost them all their lives.

The first few hours after the avalanche were a fuzzy time, with people coming and going from the various condos. At some point Kate, Wendell, a sheriff, and Andy Wertheim, the Realtor who had handled Jeanne Hahn's condo rental, came to the door, flashlights pointing harshly upward to illuminate their faces, to ask if anyone was missing. When the Guinneys told them that Bud and Laura were not back yet, right at that instant the scenario clicked together for Kate and she understood that the two men and the little girl she had run into on Ginzton Road were the people the rescuers were digging for in the parking lot.

"Did they take a walk?" she asked. "Was one of the men wearing cowboy boots?" Kate knew the answers before the questions were even out of her mouth. Without definitive information to give, one of the people in Kate's group simply mumbled that there had been a big avalanche and maybe some people had been caught in it.

By the time Kate and the others left, it was freezing and pitch-black inside the condo. Larry made a fire while Barb and Katy tried to play a game with the boys. Around that time Jeanne arrived at Katy's door with the news that Dave had not returned yet either.

After the power went out, Jeanne had sat alone in her condo for a long time. As darkness descended and Dave still hadn't come back, she went over to the unit next door. There were some women and children inside, and one of the kids had just fallen and cut his lip. Over the boy's bellowing, a woman told Jeanne that their husbands were over at the resort helping with the avalanche. Unclear what they were talking about, Jeanne found a working pay phone in the hallway of the condo complex and dialed the sheriff's office. She had just begun to explain that Dave was missing when she heard the operator, talking to someone else in the background, say, "Oh, my God, this woman thinks her husband was up there."

The sheriff's department either didn't have much information to give or wasn't willing to share it with Jeanne, so she stumbled across the parking lot in the dark to Katy's condo. At some point she ran into Andy Wertheim, who lived in a house near the complex, and he came with her.

Barbara knew that Bud and Laura were gone the moment the people had come to ask if anyone was missing, but Katy still would not accept it. The options had hardly been exhausted, and she and Jeanne spent the rest of the evening agonizing over various scenarios in detail. There were obviously other men from the condos volunteering at the ski area. No one had gone to look for Laura and their husbands at the resort and returned to report that they were *not* assisting there. In a dark, chaotic rescue scene, Bud and Dave might have blended into a search team. They could have been working on a probe line or treating a injured victim anywhere throughout the area.

And if they had covered the last dozen or so yards of their walk a few seconds faster they *would* have been over at the site helping— Bud treating Jeff Skover's head wound and Dave looking in the rubble of the Summit Terminal Building for victims. Laura likely wouldn't have been drinking hot chocolate as Katy had first suspected, but she might well have been in the lodge gathering blankets and first-aid supplies. These were two generous men of integrity, and based on their natures, if they had been propelled into a position of trying to save lives, they almost certainly would have joined in the rescue without taking time to send word back about their own personal safety.

Despite all the logical reasons to believe they were safe, as the hours dragged by, the anticipation and hope of earlier in the evening had mostly been replaced by the intensity of a somber dread. When Tim Fitzpatrick stopped in at Katy's condo at the end of the night, he walked into an anguished, funereal atmosphere. Although there had not been any official notification, by that point it seemed as if they already knew what had happened and were just waiting for someone to tell them it wasn't true. The kids were playing games and everybody was doing regular stuff, except it was very clear that they were merely going through the motions of normalcy.

Tim tried to talk to Katy privately in the kitchen, but she turned her head away, almost refusing to listen to him. He felt he needed to convey what he could about the situation, and he told her as carefully as possible that he didn't believe her husband and daughter were aboveground, that someone had seen them in the parking lot just before the avalanche. Although Katy did not respond to his information verbally, to Tim it almost seemed as if the fact that he didn't have proof of their deaths in some way provided encouragement that they might still be alive. Even at that late hour, without understanding the force and magnitude of the avalanche, there seemed to be possibilities for their survival. Perhaps they were hiding under a vehicle in the parking lot or had lunged inside a car just as the avalanche began to flow down the mountain. There was a certain raw comfort in not knowing, in waiting and speculating, that Katy was in no way ready to let go of yet.

Around 10:35 there was another knock on the condo door. The instant Katy saw the sheriff, she completely unraveled.

Wendell had driven Jay Seffern and a Placer County sheriff from the resort to the condos in a snowcat. Jay had been on a probe line in the parking lot all night, and he had identified Bud's body in the first-aid room. The men had come to the condos to notify two women on vacation that they were widows.

The deputy set Bud's fanny pack, his ring, and his Seiko watch—still ticking—on the table and gently asked Katy if she could identify them.

Through her initial waves of hysteria, Katy managed to get one question out. "My daughter too?" she asked.

The men met her eyes, but no one answered her. Barbara had always seen Katy as a private woman who kept her emotions restrained and under control, but the night she found out that she had lost her husband and daughter, Katy became utterly unglued, wailing, pounding the table, refusing to believe.

"I love him," she said to Barbara. "I love him so much."

The deputy gave Katy a form indicating receipt of Bud's personal effects, an act that set off fresh gales of sobs. She initially refused to sign the document, feeling that doing so was an admission that he was dead.

Jeanne, who already knew how this story would end for her, quietly spoke up and said that her husband had been with Bud. The deputy asked her what he had been wearing, and she described it—a dark blue ski sweater with light blue stripes down the shoulders and arms, and a dark blue down vest. In response, the deputy merely told her how sorry he was.

In contrast to Katy, Jeanne's reaction to the shock was to just shut down. The color went out of her face and the emotion left her voice. She kept her feelings to herself for the most part, outwardly appearing almost jarringly calm. Both women seemed to have a general sense not of denial exactly, but of disbelief at the news—that it couldn't be real, that it couldn't be happening there.

Adding to the horror of the circumstances—if that was even possible—the storm was still raging furiously. The roads were impassable. All the phones in the condo development had stopped working hours before, and it was impossible for Katy or Jeanne to communicate with the outside world. There was no heat and no light. They were completely trapped in the cold, dark condo with no way out. Their night went on forever.

At some point earlier in the evening, the boys had gone to bed. Eric was tucked into Katy and Bud's bed on the main level rather than in the downstairs bedroom where the sliders were piled up with snow, and with all the commotion right outside the bedroom door, it had been impossible for him to sleep. In the late hours of that endless night, Katy crawled into bed with her six-year-old son and told him that his daddy and sister were not coming back. In a small voice, he simply responded that he had heard.

Jeanne seemed almost sedated—her husband was gone and she was unable to reach her daughters to tell them what had happened to their dad. In a room full of virtual strangers—including a woman who had also lost her husband and was out of her mind awaiting official confirmation on the fate of her daughter—the options for seeking warmth and comfort were limited. So it was that Jeanne spent that night on the floor, holding on to the guy who had rented her a condo.

Back in Los Altos Hills, Linda Hahn, having not traveled to Alpine Meadows that day on the stern warning of her dad, was unaware of the avalanche. As her mom couldn't call her, the news of her father's death came instead from a particularly insensitive member of the press. At around two o'clock in the morning Linda was awakened at her parents' house by a call from a reporter who she thought identified himself as working for *The Sacramento Bee*.

"Are you the family of the Dave Hahn killed in the avalanche at Alpine Meadows?" he asked.

As she tried to process the enormity of that question, Linda could only reply that she didn't think so. She didn't know what was true at that point—she couldn't get through to her parents and she couldn't seem to find any answers elsewhere. Her thoughts circled around the idea that if her dad was gone, her mom could be dead too. It wasn't until the next day, after her sister, Stephanie, had boarded a flight home from college in San Diego, that their dad's death was confirmed and they learned their mom was safe.

In the hours after the avalanche, Sandy Harris was left to wonder what had happened to the three people who had left her little cabin in Alpine Meadows earlier that day and never came back. More familiar than most people with the tragic turns that fate could take—a few years prior, her 19-year-old brother was killed when his motorcycle collided with a horse one dark night—she nevertheless discounted the first avalanche report she heard. At 3:45 p.m. the power went out, but her phone was still working. When a friend called to gush about how glad she was Sandy had answered the phone because she heard a massive avalanche had hit the ski resort, Sandy told her to stop being so dramatic. She assumed that the press had blown a minor incident way out of proportion.

As darkness fell, however, and Anna, Frank, and Beth hadn't returned, Sandy began to get uneasy. The local radio stations had scanners, and they picked up and broadcast the content of some of the radio traffic about the disaster, but not much news was getting out. It was a different era as far as receiving and relaying information. Without the benefit of answering machines or call-waiting, much less the Internet, as the information trickled in, Sandy ended up acting as a one-person message center that night.

At some point Sandy spoke to Casey Jones, who described the scene to her. He told her that all three of the people who had woken up in her house that morning had been in the Summit Terminal Building at the time of the avalanche, and the building was gone. "You've got to prepare yourself," he said. "Nobody is walking away from this."

One of the calls Sandy answered that evening was from Frank's mom. Marie Yeatman had just finished preparing dinner at home when she heard a story about the avalanche on the news. She remembered that Frank had hoped to go skiing with Anna sometime that week. She wasn't sure where he would have been skiing or even if he had gone at all, but she did feel with absolute certainty that her son had been caught in the avalanche. As she got up to dial Anna's number, her husband told her she was being foolish. Marie called anyway, and Sandy confirmed that Frank and Anna had skied to the resort earlier that day. Sandy did her best to sound calm, and offered hope that perhaps they had stopped somewhere along the way, but Frank's mom already knew the truth.

Beth Morrow's dad, John, stayed awake all Wednesday night trying to think of reasons why Beth, normally an extremely conscientious person, hadn't called to let them know she was all right. Driving home from work at the public defender's office that day, he had heard the news about an avalanche at Squaw Valley. Later that evening he and Del caught another report of a severe avalanche at Alpine Meadows. They called Beth's number all night with no answer, then tried unsuccessfully to get information from the sheriff's department and the hospitals. Finally someone picked up the phone at Beth's house. Initially John's heart jolted when he thought it was his daughter, but then he realized the voice wasn't right. It was Beth's neighbor who had answered the phone, and all she could tell the Morrows was that Beth had been up at the resort and that all the roads in the area were closed.

As scared as they were that night, Beth's parents tried to convince each other that Beth couldn't call them from wherever she was because the phone lines were down. John stayed home from work the next day. There was a leaky outdoor faucet that had frozen at the house and he let the plumber in to fix it.

Beth's sister Carol lived in the area, and early that morning John telephoned her to tell her that Beth was missing and she needed to get home. When she got to the house, her dad was out driving aimlessly. Carol had recently bought a Charlie Chaplin doll with a porcelain face for her sister as a surprise, and she thought that if Beth was hurt, she would bring it to her in the hospital to cheer her up.

Late that afternoon John's supervisor called to say he was so sorry about what had happened. John didn't immediately grasp the significance of the comment, and he didn't ask for clarification. A little while later he and Del were sitting on the couch, their hands folded in their laps, watching a news report about the avalanche on television. Carol walked into the room just as a shot of a covered body on a stretcher appeared on the TV. Simultaneously with that image flashing on the screen, the Morrows' doorbell rang. As Beth's parents spoke to the Sparks police officer, her brother ran back to Beth's bedroom and put on a John Denver album. After that, from Carol's perspective things got kind of swirly.

At home in Lafayette on the day of the avalanche, Jake's mom heard about the slide on the evening news and immediately panicked. She lit a prayer candle that she always kept in the kitchen window, then called Pam and Dennis's wife. It was clear early on that Dennis was safe, but there was no news of Jake. While no one seemed to know where he was, everyone assured Bettigene that he was probably on his way home when the avalanche happened. When Jake's sister, Kathe, stopped by that evening with baby Jeff, she tried to console her mom by telling her that Jake was likely right in the hub of all the action. Still, Bettigene paced in the kitchen listening to the news until late that night when Dennis's wife finally called to tell her that her youngest child was dead.

At the scene, the rescuers battled exhaustion to work deep into the night, with no way to get word out to their families that they had not been buried in the avalanche themselves. There were no cell phones in 1982, communications had been knocked out at the resort, and emergency radios were bad to begin with and made worse by the storm.

Larry's wife, Kathy, and his son Shawn, age 12, were home at 3:45 that Wednesday afternoon. Larry had left the house at 4:30 that morning and Kathy hadn't woken up with him. The last she heard from Larry was at lunchtime, when he called to say that he was going to do avalanche control that afternoon and then spend the night in the Summit Terminal Building.

Kathy spent part of the day trying to keep on top of shoveling the fresh snowfall, but there was so much of it that whenever she opened the door to get wood for the fire, more snow just poured inside the house. She was folding laundry with the radio on in the background when the newscaster interrupted the broadcast to announce a major avalanche at Alpine Meadows in the employee building. Kathy called all the numbers she could think of at the resort, but the phone just rang with no answer. Shawn stayed by his mom's side, telling her not to worry, assuring her that Dad was going to be okay.

Kathy then called Kris Marvin, Bob Blair's girlfriend, to ask if she had heard any news about Larry. Kris said that she didn't have any information but that she would call her back if she did. Kathy also called Jim's wife, Ellen, who was snowed in at their cabin on the Truckee River. It was the first Ellen had heard of the tragedy, and she tried to get whatever updates she could from the radio until the search was suspended for the night and Jim finally got a chance to call her.

As the hours went by in the Heywood house, Kathy alternated between feelings of panic and helplessness. She wanted to go look for Larry herself, but with all the new snow accumulation, she knew she would never even make it down the road. While she imagined that Larry might be dead, she also knew him well enough to know that if he wasn't, he would be in the midst of the rescue and so busy that he wouldn't stop to call her. Bob's girlfriend, Kris, called her back long after dark, and Kathy realized that she hadn't lost her husband when Kris told her that that she had just heard Larry's voice over the radio.

Larry eventually called home close to midnight, from the safety of Bob Blair's house, and Kathy heard his voice for herself. Once they left the scene, the rescuers' grief for those that were lost and the dread of what was to follow overcame them. The relentless endurance the patrolmen had exhibited that evening, combined with little sleep and the pressure of making a constant succession of rapid-fire decisions over the previous five days, all took their toll. Kris made some food for Bob and Larry, but they both passed out long before they could eat it.

NINETEEN

There was a flat snow field,
it used to be a place
people came to have fun
on what is now a shattered mountain.

There are cars mixed up in every direction
with anxious men with long sticks and shovels
probing the snow
hoping not to find
anyone they know.

—

Shawn Heywood (son of Larry Heywood) at age 12

April 1, 1982, began with a bluebird morning. The storm had finally broken, albeit temporarily, and the weather was sunny and clear. The skies were so bright blue, in fact, that the deaths the day before and the prospect of recovering more bodies seemed like one huge, bitter April Fools' joke.

Billy Patterson had parked a hydro in the Bear Creek subdivision the night before, and early that morning, while Bob and Jim were in a meeting to coordinate next steps, Billy drove Larry up to the scene. For both men it was an exceptionally creepy sensation to be standing at the ski area in daylight with no people around and no sound or movement of any kind. There weren't even any ski tracks on the mountains—just clean, fresh snow.

With the sun out and no snowfall, Larry and Billy were able to see the devastation much more clearly than they had the evening before. The crown of the avalanche was 15 feet tall and spanned the width of ten football fields. The snow up on the mountain had been cleanly sliced through, like a spatula cutting Jell-O. That morning a vast, sharp edge remained on the slopes, clearly displaying where the slab had broken free and fallen. Later in the day the sunshine crumbled the fracture line a bit, and while it remained evident, it no longer stood out in such vivid relief as it had at that moment.

The avalanche had not released from Beaver Bowl after all, but from Poma Rocks, the Buttress, and Pond Slope—three massive avalanches moving sympathetically, and simultaneously, together. It was a once-in-a-century catastrophe, an event of geologic time—the confluence of that particular snow and those specific winds and that precise temperature interlinking with the exact angles of those slopes.

Days later, the patrolmen excavated the snowed-over fracture and determined that in a phenomenon known as a step fracture, the avalanche had gone to the ground, breaking deep below the melt-freeze crust into old snow layers and taking almost a season's worth of snowpack with it down the mountain. The result was a stifling amount of snow plunging into the ski area—100 inches of new snowfall plus a couple more feet of snow beneath the sun crust.

In a conventional storm, Poma Rocks, the Buttress, and Pond Slope, all with separate avalanche paths, would have behaved individually. In this epic storm, however, they essentially became one, with a single continuous fracture line. They were some of the lower slopes at the resort, ranging from 500 to 900 feet high, the ones wind-loaded with snow from higher up on the mountain. Relatively shorter avalanche paths like those could not normally have built up enough speed to travel out into the parking lot and the base area of the resort. The combined mass of the sympathetic avalanches certainly increased the distance of the slide, but more significantly, the staggering length of the runout zone was created by those light, beautiful, deadly, pure stellar crystals. They tempted and lured innocent people out into the storm like a tantalizing winter Siren, only to offer up a feathery layer of snow for the avalanche to fly faster and farther on, airborne and friction-free.

The avalanche actually caused damage well past the point where the sliding mass stopped. A Volkswagen and a Ford van had been pancaked and thrown forward substantially beyond the runout zone into the lower parking lot. Looking up at the mountain, Larry and Billy realized that the avalanche had flattened not just huge stands of mature timber but had also demolished both the Summit and the Kangaroo chairlifts. The slide had taken out over two dozen utility poles in the parking lot and the road. It had descended with enough force to pick up a snowcat, carry it over the vehicle maintenance building, and drop it on the other side. As the two men walked through the area, they noticed a few other anomalies caused by the avalanche: A door at the lodge prominently marked Keep Closed at All Times had been blown wide-open, and an aluminum thermometer from the ski patrol room was embedded high in a tree, its glass tube and ball intact.

The rescue operation that day and in the days to follow turned into a massive cooperative effort among several different agencies. Working from the headquarters at the water district, Howard Carnell and Nick Badami opened various lines of support and received the total backing of everyone they contacted. The fire and sheriff's departments assisted in lining up rescue equipment, lights, and portable generators. The CHP provided traffic screening and roadblocks in the area, and the power company installed extra phone lines at the water district. Although the furor of the ongoing storm prevented the patrol from safely controlling Alpine Meadows Road on the day after the avalanche—complicating the deliveries of rescue equipment, including explosives—the California Department of Transportation and the Placer County Road Department assisted with road maintenance in the surrounding area and helped clear the access road the following day. Once the search crews were allowed back into the resort, the Red Cross set up an aid station inside the lodge to dispense sandwiches and coffee to the rescue workers.

In addition, neighboring ski resorts sent over patrolmen to help on the search-and-rescue teams. As much as the Squaw Valley and Alpine Meadows crews had been rivals in the past, in times of emergency the two patrols backed each other up totally. In addition to personnel, in the days following the avalanche Squaw Valley provided a great deal of dynamite to the Alpine Meadows patrol. Other firepower was brought in from Reno and from Alpine Meadows' sister resort in Park City, Utah. Explosives were also trucked in from Sacramento, which entailed transporting them over Donner Pass, closed to traffic at the time, with the aid of a police escort. Heavenly Valley ski resort offered the use of its helicopter so the patrol crew could throw bombs onto the slopes from above.

Attempting to control the avalanche paths leading to and overhanging the disaster scene was an incredible challenge for the ski patrol. They were unable to reach the howitzer ammunition, stored in a magazine over by Scott Meadow, so using the cannon wasn't an option. In addition, the breech for the recoilless rifle had been stored in a safe in the patrol room and had been lost among the avalanche debris. Since every recoilless rifle had a custom-fitted breech, a whole new rifle and breech had to be somehow transported to the scene.

Heli-bombing was the most effective method of control under the circumstances. Helicopters had never been used for control work in the past at Alpine Meadows, due to the expense as well as the extreme danger of flying in storms. On the morning after the avalanche, Jim and Lanny Johnson waited at the corner of Highway 89 and Squaw Valley Road for Heavenly Valley's helicopter to arrive. When they saw a helicopter in the sky, as they had prearranged with Heavenly, the patrolmen popped smoke signals so the pilot would know where to find them. As it turned out, the helicopter that landed next to them was a news copter from Channel 3. Out of smoke to wave down the correct helicopter and losing the window of clear weather to shoot from the air, Lanny and Jim simply commandeered the news helicopter.

After the patrolmen tersely explained to the pilot that he had obstructed the search and was delaying rescuers from getting to the scene, he agreed to take them up. Lanny instructed him to take the door off and to dump everything out of the helicopter, including the cameraman and his cameras. Jim and Lanny then piled in hundreds of pounds of bombs packed in cardboard boxes. When the pilot asked what was in the boxes, in unison Jim and Lanny replied, "Explosives." To his credit, the pilot stated that he didn't need to know any more.

Lanny was in front acting as the spotter, directing the pilot where to fly, while Jim sat seat-belted in the back, cases of bombs at his feet, lobbing dynamite out of the open space where the door had been. They peppered the road route going into the resort with charges, hoping to regain some level of control over the road so that emergency vehicles could access the site safely. The results were spotty and inconclusive, with the patrolmen expecting avalanches that they didn't get.

By then the storm began to move in again full-force—the skies darkened to gray, the wind picked up, and once again the snow began to fall heavily. There would not be another break in the blizzard for four more days.

As the weather prevented the patrolmen from doing much control work on the slopes above the rescue site, they were on edge, knowing that the search efforts that day would be conducted under the still-heightened—and increasing—risk of another avalanche. Bill Williamson and the other two patrollers who had spent the night in the Summit lift shack did throw hand charges that morning from their position at the top of the mountain, primarily in Wolverine Bowl, but the slopes did not release. Despite the hazard, once the patrolmen stopped their control work, a couple hundred people flooded into the area around noon to help with the search.

The volunteers were split among the two search areas, but even so, there were so many people helping that at some points they were almost stepping on each other as they worked. The search crews gave up on traditional probing in the area of the Summit Terminal Building and resorted to trenching with shovels and snowplows instead. They used wrenches and cables to access the remains of the building itself. The search-and-rescue teams were spread out over acres of debris, alternately using shovels and over-snow vehicles to carefully move tons of hard-packed snow and structural material from the area.

Early on, one of the rescuers contacted the Forest Service for chain saws to cut away the debris but was told that they were all broken. Rusty Witwer, a Forest Service snow ranger on the scene at the time, looked the other searcher right in the eye and said, "Well, I can make chain saws." As a firefighter for the Forest Service in the summers, Rusty and his colleagues were constantly in need of operable chain saws, and by necessity he had become an expert at cobbling them together. At Rusty's request, the Forest Service sent over every broken chain saw they had to the scene. Rusty went to work cannibalizing parts from them and from other equipment, promptly producing several working chain saws for the crew.

The rescuers first used the chain saws to cut away heavy, barely attached remnants of walls protruding up into the air to prevent them from falling down and crushing the workers crawling around the site. As the rescuers sifted through the tons of debris, periodically yelling down into the wreckage as they worked, they found a bizarre assortment of random junk hard-packed into the snow. In addition to an immense amount of winter clothes and shattered skis, the items they found that day included a dartboard and three darts, a skillet, a flowered purse, a bottle of window spray, parts of TVs and telephones, and a poster of a cat peeking into a mouse hole.

The various papers the crews found were frozen rather than soaked through. Early that day Larry had set out a few industrial-sized garbage cans and told the teams to use them to save any paperwork they found. Some of the documents came out of the snow wrinkled or shredded, and the searchers didn't find them all, but most of the weather records from the patrol office were eventually recovered.

The teams found evidence of Bernie everywhere, including some of his notes and a yellow time sheet with his initials on it, but they could not find the mountain manager himself. The first few times a rescuer found a man's boot, they thought that Bernie might be nearby, but it turned out that there were dozens of pairs of ski and hiking boots underneath the snow. All of the footwear that was found, along with ski gear, street clothes, and a few wallets, was brought into the lodge and spread out on the floor for employees to claim.

When the volunteers first began searching that day, they were all instructed that they could not smoke, eat, or urinate near the search areas so as not to distract the rescue dogs. As it was, the dogs had plenty of scents to divert their attention. Don and Roberta Huber were back searching with Smokey and Bridget, and several other dog teams had reported to the scene as well.

The Hubers were members of a California search-and-rescue dog organization called Wilderness Finders, known as WOOF. There were no words for the O's in the acronym—the O's just stood for two dog eyes. There was no other word like it on the radio, and the group knew that it was a name that law enforcement agencies wouldn't forget.

Founded in 1975, WOOF was a private nonprofit association formed with the intention of using the dogs for area and disaster searches as well as avalanche work. The dogs searched by air scenting, which was particularly valuable in avalanche rescues where there was generally no trail to follow.

The organization started out with seven dog teams, and had about 20 by 1982. At the time of the Alpine Meadows disaster, the practice of using dogs to search for victims lost in avalanches was in its infancy in the country. No dog had ever located a live avalanche victim in North America. The reason for this was simply one of time—even if a rescue dog group was called immediately, by the time a dog and its handler were transported to the scene, it was too late to save a victim buried under the snow. Instead, the dogs functioned as a valuable resource to recover hidden bodies.

In the early '80s, WOOF received an average of two search requests a week, the vast majority of which involved people lost in the wilderness. When the group started there were no other dog rescue groups in the southwest United States, so over the years calls came in from 36 California counties as well as Arizona, Colorado, Oregon, Nevada, Idaho, Wyoming, Wisconsin, and Alaska. In most instances the teams were transported to the rescue sites by military or CHP helicopters.

The group involved a volunteer commitment of about 20 hours a week. A small amount of funding came from California ski resorts, including Alpine Meadows, and the local sheriffs at a search scene would usually feed the handlers and occasionally fill up their gas tanks, but much of the cost of training and radios was supplied by the handlers themselves.

There were other husband-and-wife teams in addition to Roberta and Don, and about half the WOOF handlers were women. Several of the female handlers, including Roberta, were members of the National Ski Patrol. The handlers had to be in excellent physical shape and also free to leave home on emergency notice, as many of the searches involved sleeping on the ground and cross-country skiing for days in rough terrain.

WOOF looked for dogs with a strong working background and preferred to use dogs with double coats of fur so they didn't become hypothermic during lengthy searches in the snow. Shepherds generally seemed to be the best candidates, although WOOF also used Labrador and golden retrievers (which Roberta derisively referred to as "goofy goldens"), bloodhounds, and mixed breeds. They tried to train various sled-dog breeds, but they tended to alert at squirrels and then take off chasing them.

Roberta's first rescue dog was a nearly all black German shepherd named Windjammer Annie. For Annie's second pregnancy, the Hubers mated her with a purebred shepherd named Baldur. That litter was almost born on their bed—when a very pregnant Annie crawled up on it, which she almost never did, Roberta knew she was ready to give birth. She quickly moved Annie to a box she had set up with an infrared light and stayed awake all night with her. Annie had nine puppies in that litter, but four of them died shortly after birth.

Roberta's young son and daughter helped their mom pick names for the surviving puppies from a baby name book. The runt of the litter was black and tan, with coloring a little lighter than that of her siblings. The family named her Bridget as a bit of a nod to Roberta's French heritage. When she was only a day old, Bridget stopped breathing. A registered nurse, Roberta immediately gave the tiny puppy mouth-to-mouth resuscitation and was able to revive her within a minute or two.

Even when she was a puppy, it was clear that Bridget had the ideal temperament for a rescue dog. She was very obedient and responsive, but beyond that she was highly curious and intelligent. She wasn't passive or overly aggressive. Assessing her nose and her attitude during puppy games, Roberta was thrilled with the way Bridget acted and reacted.

Early on, Roberta concealed items around the house for Bridget to find, always using positive reinforcement. Sometimes she hid and had Bridget find her, and other times she asked Bridget to locate the children. Bridget could essentially find everybody by herself, so Roberta simply reinforced her dog's natural skills. Like all WOOF dogs, Bridget also frequently practiced agility work: balancing, jumping, climbing. The point of the training process was to constantly encourage the dogs and praise them with a favorite game or treat. When Bridget made a find, Roberta rewarded her with a game of fetch the stick.

The next phase of WOOF instruction was to set up mock searches for Bridget with volunteers unknown to her. In avalanche training sessions, people posing as victims were buried under the snow for her to find. As much as possible, WOOF dogs were trained in reality circumstances, with a vast array of situations and terrains. Sometimes the handlers asked their dogs to locate just a single bone they had hidden in snow or debris. The dogs were precise, and given enough time, they could seek out anything.

It took about a year to train a WOOF dog to perfect its search skills, and often longer than that for a handler to learn how to read the dog's signals. There was a talent to observing the nuances of a dog's behavior and interpreting its body language. The organization stressed the importance of the handlers believing their dog, which wasn't always easy to do.

Once Bridget was fully trained, she participated in about 70 WOOF searches a year. She loved the attention and she thrived on the work. Whenever Roberta picked up her rescue pack, Bridget beat her to the door. She also developed an adorable personality apart from her rescue skills. She frequently snuck up on the couch after the family went to bed, then pouted when Roberta scolded her. Bridget was very conscious of when a camera was aimed at her, and she made a point of posing and showing off.

When Bridget found a live victim in a training session, she tended to double back to prod her nose deeper into the snow, scratch at the snow surface with her front paws, bark, and wave her tail like a flag. In a real search when she located a dead body, her reaction was more subdued, but Roberta tried to make that event somewhat of a game as well. It was important for the dogs to find dead bodies, too, and essential for the dogs not to become depressed by the work.

Many of Bridget's searches involved looking for lost or injured hikers in the wilderness. Once she found a hunter who had suffered a fatal heart attack, and on another occasion—despite the presence of a large cinnamon bear on the scene—she located a plane-crash victim. One time she sought out an elderly victim of dementia who had wandered away from her house in a rainstorm and died of hypothermia. A particularly sad search involved a young ski instructor at Mammoth who had been caught in an avalanche when a cornice broke off a slope. Once Bridget arrived at the scene she found him immediately, but he had died in the time it took Roberta and Bridget to fly in from Truckee.

As Roberta and Don's children became teenagers, they began to train their own search dogs. In 1982, between Bridget, Don's dog Smokey, and the children's two dogs, there were four rescue dogs in the Huber household. At age nine Bridget was still actively searching, but she was beginning to wind down her career.

The conditions of the two search areas at Alpine Meadows were particularly frustrating for the rescue dogs. While the WOOF dogs were trained to ignore the commotion of a search and concentrate on scents wafting up from below the snow, the debris of the

Summit Terminal Building included locker rooms with clothing and gear from more than 200 employees. In addition, the wind was circulating the diesel fumes from the machinery used in the search, and the exhaust temporarily burned the dogs' noses and deadened their sense of smell.

The parking lot, where Bridget was primarily searching on the day after the avalanche, had fewer competing odors, but the depth of the snow in that area presented its own challenge. Dogs have over 200 million scent receptors in their noses, compared to 5 million in humans. Under the right circumstances Bridget could pick up the scent of a victim as far away as a quarter of a mile, but dense snow provided exceptional insulation. While in general it takes about ten minutes for a human scent to permeate several feet up to the surface of the snow, when a victim is buried deeper than that, he gives off very little scent. At an avalanche rescue site in the past, Bridget's half-brother Smokey alerted all the way down a mountain—the dog could tell where the victim had been, but the final resting place was too deep for him to pinpoint.

Despite how dedicated the dogs were to the search, rescuers found the bodies of Beth Morrow and Frank Yeatman without their aid. They located them within a few minutes of each other—Beth about 150 feet away from the Summit Terminal Building, and Frank inside the wreckage of the building.

Searchers trenching in the area of the Bell Tree had first discovered a desk and some office equipment. Around three o'clock, after clearing away a thick load of mangled plywood, they picked up a signal from an avalanche beacon. Apparently the heavy debris had prevented Beth's Skadi from transmitting a signal the previous evening. Once the rescuers followed the beeping, they located Beth's body about fifteen feet beneath the snow, up against a partial wall from the building. Her left leg was broken.

Lanny and several other rescuers found Frank's backpack just before they spotted his body. They were working on the side of the building that the avalanche had first entered, using cables to pull back a wall at the far end. Frank's body was wedged into a corner, pinned under a wall and crushed against some lockers and a wall heater. His official cause of death was suffocation, but based on his injuries it was unlikely that he would have survived even if he had been found within minutes.

Over at the other search area in the parking lot, patrolman Gary Murphy organized approximately 90 searchers into probe lines, focusing on the end of the parking lot where Dave and Bud had been found. Every so often the teams would hear the muffled boom of explosives from the Squaw Valley side of the ridge, causing them to glance up at the mountain apprehensively. Whenever a searcher hit a vehicle, they marked it with an orange flag and a shovel crew came along to dig it out. Although there had been no additional reports of missing people, the potential still existed for someone to have been trapped inside their car or truck. There was an anxious moment each time a rescuer cleared off a windshield and peered in, but ultimately they found neither survivors nor bodies in any of the vehicles.

Just a few minutes shy of 24 hours after the avalanche had descended, a searcher on one of the probe lines signaled a possible find. He had inserted a long piece of conduit into the snow until it almost disappeared, and it connected with something that felt different from the surrounding snow. With a sick, sinking feeling, the rescuer asked several other members of his probe line to come over and feel the pole. At a spot about twenty feet away from where the employees' vehicles were parked, the shovel crew dug 12 feet down. As the rescuers tenderly removed the body of a small, freckle-faced girl in a homemade green snowsuit, Laura's death was official.

Laura's body, located very close to where her dad had been recovered, was found on April 1. April Fools' Day, normally a spirited holiday around the Nelson household marked by lots of practical jokes, would never again be celebrated by the surviving members of the family.

Out on Alpine Meadows Road, Anna's roommate Sandy came out of her cabin with a blanket wrapped around her body and her head in her hands. Casey Jones, in the area to coordinate access into the site from the staging area, noticed Sandy sitting on the edge of the road and went over to talk to her. When he received a radio call, he briefly turned away from her to take it.

"Some of the answers are coming down the road now," Casey said. "They found a girl, we don't know who." He convinced Sandy to go back inside so she wouldn't have to see the coroner's wagon drive past.

Sandy had received a call from Anna's parents early that morning. At home in Glendora, California, Anna's mom, Joan, had heard a news report the previous evening about an avalanche in Squaw Valley, and she commented at the time that she hoped Anna was where she was supposed to be. She and Gene considered calling Anna then, but they knew she tended to go to bed early and they didn't want to bother her. By that morning, Joan had heard the news that three people were confirmed dead at an avalanche at Alpine Meadows, and she called Anna and Sandy's house at six o'clock in the morning.

When Sandy answered the phone, Joan calmly asked to speak to her daughter.

"She's not here," Sandy said cautiously.

"What about Frank?" Joan asked next.

"He's not here either," Sandy replied.

Joan next asked where they were, and when Sandy finally broke down and admitted that she hadn't seen them since they had gone up to the resort the afternoon before, Joan dropped the phone and screamed for Anna's dad.

While awaiting word, Anna's parents decided to go to their respective jobs that day. Joan, a substitute teacher, spent much of the day crying, and the children in her class responded to her trauma with their best behavior. Gene, a researcher for the Forest Service, drove 45 miles to his office in Riverside, walked in, and was immediately approached by two coworkers who asked him if he had heard about the avalanche at Alpine Meadows.

"My daughter's buried in it," he said, and headed back home. Later, flying into the area, just the sight of snow from the air made Anna's mom cry.

On the day after the avalanche, the only sign of life beneath the snow came from Mariah, Jim's German shepherd puppy. Late in the afternoon, an Alpine Meadows ski instructor was cutting away a piece of the building with a chain saw when he thought he heard whimpering and muted yips from under the snow.

Tunneling down into the building as far as he could, the ski instructor recognized the unmistakable sound of a dog whining. He radioed Jim with the news, and Jim and some of the other searchers cut away a section of the floor. Once they had access to the lower level of the building, they began picking their way through a jumble of snow and boards. Except for the snow coating all of the debris, the procedure was very much like searching through ruins caused by an earthquake or a bomb.

Finally a shovel broke through a tiny air pocket and Jim took off his glove and extended his arm down into the hole. He felt a cold, wet nose. The nose briefly retreated, then came back again, first sniffing Jim's hand, then licking it. Seemingly convinced that the hand belonged to her owner, Mariah bit down hard on it and would not let go.

After yelling at his dog to release him, Jim and a few other rescuers carefully excavated her. It was nearly dark when they lifted her out. Jim carried his dog into the lodge, where a volunteer ski patrol nurse took care of her, bundling her in blankets and giving her warm water and milk to drink. Mariah was hypothermic, dehydrated, exhausted, and clearly suffering from shock. She fluctuated between panting with a glazed look in her eyes to sitting up agitatedly. Despite being buried up to her neck for more than a full day, she ultimately survived.

Although Mariah's rescue proved that there were spaces below the wreckage and gave the searchers some hope that Anna and Bernie could have survived the avalanche, the official word, picked up by newspapers around the country, was that the two of them were "presumed perished." When the search was suspended on Thursday evening, Werner Schuster, in charge of public relations for the resort, was asked by a reporter to access the likelihood of the teams finding any survivors at that point. Werner, who possessed an intimate familiarity with avalanches by virtue of having grown up in Immenstadt, Germany, near the Swiss and Austrian border, gave this response: "It's very, very remote. I'm sorry."

On the following day, Friday, April 2, another 18 inches of snow fell. The sheriff evacuated several homes in the area, and Anna's roommate Sandy was forced to leave their cabin. She got a ride out of town, and at a roadblock at the end of the road a sheriff's deputy keeping track of the residents stopped them and asked Sandy to sign out.

"Is there anyone else at home?" the deputy asked.

Completely worn down at that point, her eyes brimming with tears, Sandy fought to control her voice as she answered the deputy's question.

"No," Sandy said. "Just me."

Several dog teams went into the scene early on Friday morning, two days after the avalanche, in an attempt to pick up the scents of the remaining victims before the heavy equipment and masses of searchers arrived. Bridget was assigned the area of the Summit Terminal Building.

Almost as soon as she got to the site, Bridget scrambled through the debris and took off toward the ski lift bull wheel. She appeared to pick up an air scent, and sniffing as she went, she followed the smell around the building, ultimately squeezing herself into a tiny opening in the wreckage. The gap Bridget slid into was between the floor of the locker room and several collapsed walls covered over with at least eight feet of compacted snow.

Bridget disappeared for a very tense minute and a half, long enough for Roberta to wonder if she would ever see her dog again. Then she surfaced out of the hole face-first, meaning that she had had enough room to turn around in the space.

She bounded over to Roberta, giving unmistakable signals that she had found someone. The dog was ecstatic, frolicking back and forth, leaping up and down, licking Roberta. Bridget communicated with her handler in every way she possibly could, wagging her tail, pricking up her ears. In a final attempt to emphasize her point, she acted out the stick game that Roberta always played with her as a reward. She ran to the wreckage, grabbed a wood scrap, and threw it joyfully at Roberta.

In the past when Bridget found a dead body, she would move

into a point. Her behavior in this situation was so palpably different that despite the odds against it, Roberta was convinced that her dog had found someone alive under the snow. Just as the rescue teams moved in to dig, word came over the radio that all the searchers had to evacuate the area and wait in the basement of the lodge while patrolmen and snow rangers blasted the slopes above the base area.

Jim and Lanny were back up in a helicopter, this time a big black commercial one from a company in Reno. The somewhat impetuous pilot, known only as Cowboy, seemed to swoop around a great deal more than he had to, including a signature landing move that involved flying straight up in the air before coming down. Despite the rockiness of the ride, the patrolmen were satisfied enough with the results of the control work to briefly open Alpine Meadows Road. Even Cowboy wouldn't go all the way up to the ridgetop in the storm, though, so the patrollers were unable to shoot the higher slopes above the base area, including Beaver Bowl. They did throw bombs throughout the lower slopes, but rather than releasing avalanches, they got only potholes.

In an effort to control Beaver Bowl, the patrolmen determined that they needed to shoot it with a recoilless rifle. The Forest Service office in Truckee had an extra one, so Don Huber loaded it onto a helicopter and, in an unauthorized and highly illegal maneuver, flew it into the area. The helicopter was swaying in the wind, and the pilot was insecure about the landing. He ultimately performed a one-skid landing onto the snow in the area of Gunner's Knob, but he didn't want to cut the power. The pilot held the helicopter as steady as he could in the gusting gales of wind while Don and another ranger heaved the recoilless pieces, the ammunition, and their packs out onto the snow. They had barely leapt out themselves when the pilot was airborne and away. The snow rangers shot as much of the mountain as they could reach with the rifle, but they did not trigger any slides.

As soon as the control work was finished, the rescue teams returned to the remains of the Summit Terminal Building, desperate to resume digging. A crew dug a shaft about 15 feet north of Bridget's alert point so as not to obstruct any potential airspaces.

They shoveled at least ten feet down through hard-packed snow and building wreckage, using chain saws and picks to get through the collapsed walls and lockers.

If Bridget had in fact found a victim, based on the location in the building it was almost certain to be Anna, so the rescue team kept yelling her name down into the wreckage. At one point someone thought they might have heard something—pounding, or cries for help—but the rescue machinery operating nearby was so loud that it was impossible to tell for sure. The searchers shut the equipment down almost immediately, but by that time—despite several silent, suspenseful moments in which the workers practically held their breath as they strained to pick up any kind of sound in the ruins—no one could hear a thing.

When the crew finished shoveling out the shaft, Roberta released Bridget and without hesitation she again indicated at the same spot. It was at that moment, just after noon, that the search-and-rescue teams were told that due to an off-the-scale avalanche hazard they had to suspend the search for the day.

By then the storm had worsened considerably, with several inches of fresh snow falling every hour. Already the snowfall was overloading the upper bowls to a treacherous level, and the weather report called for an intensifying blizzard with another mass of clouds brewing additional storms right behind it.

If Tom and Lanny were correct, Beaver Bowl had released, at least partially, the day before the avalanche, three days earlier. Since then, the slope might or might not have slid on the morning of the avalanche, when the gun crews fired artillery in near-zero visibility and weren't able to see the results. In any case, an avalanche had not been triggered in Beaver Bowl for at least 48 hours, and since that time several feet of new snow had quickly accumulated on the ridges, adding a nearly unbearable amount of weight and stress to the existing snowpack. The searchers digging in the ruined Summit Terminal Building were directly in the base of that slide path. Norm Wilson, the mountain manager at the resort before Bernie, was at the scene as an avalanche consultant, and he unconditionally agreed that it would be reckless to further jeopardize the lives of the rescuers.

Before the search teams left the scene, Jim met with Roberta to discuss Bridget's behavior. Roberta was convinced by Bridget's reaction, adamant that this dog, for the first time in the country's history, had found a live avalanche victim. Jim was incredibly torn, and forced to make the most excruciating decision of his life. He weighed the reality that the rescue dogs had alerted falsely in the past few days, and with hundreds of human scents floating around in the debris he couldn't be positive that Bridget wasn't alerting on an old pair of socks. In addition, the teams had been searching for days, and there had been no other evidence to indicate that there was anyone alive in the wreckage.

In the end, the decision to temporarily evacuate the site rested on the compelling fact that in the time it would take rescuers to search the area Bridget had indicated, it was not unlikely that another avalanche could descend from above and kill them all. As certain as Roberta was that Bridget had found a live victim, and as frustrated as she felt with the circumstances, Roberta concurred with the decision to pull out.

The rescue crew boarded up the shaft with plywood to protect it from the storm as much as possible. Likely no one at the scene except Roberta, who knew her dog well enough to trust her implicitly, had any real expectation that Anna could be alive, but just in case, the searchers yelled down into the rubble that they were coming back for her.

As it turned out, they were not able to return for 71 hours.

TWENTY

She just knew she'd done it.

—

Roberta Huber, Bridget's handler

Contrary to weather reports, Monday, April 5, 1982, dawned bright and clear. The past three days had dumped almost another four feet of snow on the area, and although search-and-rescue teams had made daring, nearly life-threatening attempts to get back over the weekend, the intensity of the ongoing blizzard had made a safe return to the area impossible. Over the weekend over 300 people were evacuated from their Alpine Meadows and Squaw Valley homes because of extreme avalanche danger, and the Red Cross opened a shelter in Truckee to help house the evacuees.

The previous Saturday patrolmen had again attempted to do avalanche control from the sky, but high winds grounded the helicopters altogether. Despite the still-raging storm, many of the rescue workers attended Jake's funeral in Tahoe City that day. It was blustery and miserable throughout the service. As Jake had requested, his friends and family had red roses everywhere, and they played the Kinks' "The Last Assembly," with lyrics including "As I walked to the last assembly/There were tears in the back of my eyes/And I saw all my friends all around me/They were there to wish me good-bye."

Jake was buried in one of his plaid shirts with a fly-fishing rod in the casket, and laid to rest in Trail's End Cemetery in Tahoe City. His grave is next to that of Timothy Grimes, a local 13-year-old boy who died on the night of the avalanche when he jumped from the roof of his two-story house into the snow below and was swallowed by the drifts.

If it was possible for someone to live a full life in 27 years, Jake's mom believed that her son had surely done it. He would have wanted to go out in a big way, and this ending—valiant, heroic—fit him. Any other death would have been wrong for Jake.

Shortly after Jake was killed, both Pam and his sister, Kathe, felt his presence nearby. Kathe had a powerful sense that he was in the room with her, and when she said his name aloud, she was convinced that she heard her brother call her "Cake" in response. Pam was at home when she experienced a jolt of electricity run through her, like a lightning bolt. She knew it was Jake saying good-bye.

The day after the funeral, Sunday, April 4, the patrolmen again attempted to access the rescue scene. As none of them wanted to fly with Cowboy again, the resort made arrangements with a different helicopter company, out of Carson City, Nevada. This pilot, who had flown in Vietnam, met Jim at Squaw and took him up with two cases of quad bombs at his feet. They were only halfway up the valley when a sheet of clouds and snow coming down the canyon forced them to turn back.

With the morning sun shining briefly on Monday, the patrol finally thought that they might have a chance to get back in. By this point in the storm it had snowed nearly as much since the avalanche as before it. The snow was still falling intermittently, but it was calm enough at 7 a.m. for Bob and Jim to call in two helicopters. Bob was in a helicopter with Tom Kimbrough, and Jim and Norm Wilson went up in the one flown by the Vietnam vet pilot. Each bombing team threw eight-pound charges, four times the standard size, and this time the snow responded to the explosives. They set off several unusually huge slides, including one on the Five Lakes cliffs with a 20-foot crown that buried the base of Alpine Meadows Road near the resort, carving a new swath through mature timber and taking down a fourth of a mile of electrical lines and poles. Jim's pilot had the grace to wait until they were back on the ground to tell him that it was the first time since his firing missions in Vietnam that he had experienced flashbacks—set off by the smell of the fuses—while he was flying.

The site was officially deemed secure at around noon, and the waiting search-and-rescue teams were let into the area. The storm had picked up again by then, with almost another two inches of snow falling every hour. Larry was at the scene, and Bob, and almost all the rest of the ski patrolmen. The search quickly resumed, beginning at exactly 12:22, but after being away almost three full days, the mood among the nearly 100 searchers was not one of anticipation.

While it was clear to just about everyone on day five that the rescue effort had turned into a mission to recover Anna and Bernie's bodies, there was at least one person, and one animal, treating the scene as if they were there to hunt for survivors.

Roberta had not given up hope of Anna's survival. Over the weekend she couldn't keep her mind on anything for long, her thoughts constantly drifting back to the young lift operator. She'd start a project, then have to put it down. Bridget, on the other hand, had more sense than to worry or sulk. She behaved like a regular dog over the weekend, but when she saw Roberta gather her rescue gear on Monday morning, she immediately became agitated.

As soon as Bridget returned to the scene, she broke away from Roberta at the lodge and took off, leading her handler more than 100 feet to the spot where she had indicated a find three days before. As Roberta was catching up to Bridget, the dog kept running back and forth from that place to Roberta. Apparently considering her part of the job complete, Bridget then climbed on top of a snowbank and lay down, intently watching the rescuers dig.

Most of the searchers were unaware of this dynamic playing out, or, unused to relying on canine instincts, didn't give it much thought. The atmosphere remained somber, almost grim. In the midst of it, Lanny Johnson would yell down into the debris from time to time, then listen for a response that never came. Falling back on their mountaineering training, Lanny and Tom Kimbrough both wore helmets as they scrambled around the unstable debris.

Shortly after the avalanche Lanny had been almost obsessed with the idea that Anna could be alive, but he had become less optimistic by the following day when he and some other searchers found her boyfriend crushed amid the debris. At that point his hopes for Anna, who presumably was somewhere near Frank at the time of the slide, began to fade. Soon after extricating Frank, Lanny found Anna's locker and her jacket, labeled with her name, in an area where the walls were all completely smashed down to the floor. The farther he and the other searchers trenched down that hallway on the day after the avalanche, the more they expected a grisly scene. Now, four days after Frank had been found, Anna's chances just seemed impossibly slim.

On that Monday afternoon the searchers shoveled for awhile, then brought in a small snowcat to move away the wood and debris so they could dig deeper underneath. Lanny was digging side-by-side with Bernard Coudurier, an Alpine Meadows ski patrolman originally from France. As they worked, Meredith Watson, the lone female member of Alpine Meadows' ski patrol, came around from where she had been crawling beneath the rubble to report that she hadn't found anything. Lanny and Bernard were working in unison deep in a trench, about 15 feet down, Lanny on Bernard's left. They had just finished hauling snow off a blown-in wall of the building when together they began to yank back on a huge section of white plywood in the wreckage.

Lanny had been photographing much of the rescue effort, but in an attempt to get a better grip on the piece of wood, he threw his camera up to patrolman André Benier at the top of the trench. As he did so, Bernard, who clearly wanted to see something in the rubble, started to imagine that he had. He thought, for the briefest of moments, that he might have glimpsed a hand, but then it went away. As it was snowing heavily, plus snow was getting thrown around from all the digging, visibility remained low. Bernard wondered if it really could have been something, or if it was just a trick of his imagination in the flat light. He told Lanny that he thought he had spotted a hand and that he was going to check it out. Bernard got down on his knees and extended his arm deep into the dark hole. As he moved his own hand around blindly in the chasm, he suddenly felt something squeeze it. Bernard, who quite definitively thought that he was looking for a corpse, flew backward in shock.

At that moment, a skinny little live hand came out from the hole, grasping for a thin film of snow that was floating down.

Lanny yelled down into the opening for Meredith to knock it off, stop messing around. Then he caught sight of some movement at the edge of his vision, and he slowly turned around. Meredith was crouching directly beside him.

Holy shit, he thought. It's Anna.

In as steady a voice as he could manage, Lanny shouted, "Anna, is that *you*?"

"Of course it's me," was the reply that filtered back out of the darkness.

It was 1:05 p.m., just 43 minutes after the search had resumed that day. Anna had been buried alive for the past 117 hours.

She had been knocked down headfirst by the avalanche, landing, by the rarest of chances, under a wooden bench just a split second before a bank of wooden lockers crashed on top of the bench. The lockers supported the approximately fifteen feet of snowload and debris that piled up and filled in the area above her. If any one aspect of this domino effect of intricate timing had happened even the slightest bit differently, Anna would have been mangled in the wreckage. She was locked in a V position, like a jackknife, in a very small enclosed area, approximately five feet long, a yard wide, and two feet high. The space that created Anna's air pocket was, eerily enough, about the size of a coffin.

Three days prior, searchers had been within maybe three feet of her. Due to the peculiar way sound is stifled as it travels up through snow, the search teams hadn't been able to hear her screams, hadn't known that she was beating her frozen feet against the walls of her hole.

She told the patrolmen, later, that she had heard them calling her name three days earlier. She listened as they yelled for her and then, when she couldn't make out their voices anymore, she realized that they were leaving, abandoning her in her snowy grave. She endured her lowest moment when she heard the muffled crunch of snow above her as their retreating footsteps faded away. She never once, however, wavered in her belief that they would come back and find her.

At the moment of her rescue, her voice weak and hoarse, Anna offered a few more words to the patrolmen above her: "I'm okay, I'm alive."

As choruses of "She's alive, she's alive" started to spread backward through the waves of searchers, at first there was a gaping, stunned silence, the crowd unsure for a moment if this was some sort of ski patrol black humor taken to the extreme. When it quickly became clear that the news was true, the rescuers turned simply euphoric, jumping up and down, throwing themselves onto the snow. Bridget, who would be presented with her very own steak for dinner that night, was doing her personal version of a victory dance, clearly and triumphantly communicating to everyone at the scene, "I found her, I found her, I found her."

Bob Blair, working at the other side of the building at the time, initially heard the commotion via his radio. As thrilled as he was that Anna was safe, his very first thought in response to the news was a renewed hope that they might yet find Bernie alive.

In the midst of the frenzied scene, the patrollers experienced a brief flash of fear tied up in their conviction that they couldn't let Anna die. She was still trapped amid wood and rafters, and there were jagged pieces of metal all around. In addition, at that point the patrolmen had no idea what her injuries might be. While one of the searchers radioed for the rescue helicopter, someone said they should wait for the fire department so they didn't crush her by moving the wrong thing.

"Like hell," Tom Kimbrough said. "We're getting her out."

And then all the patrolmen on the scene began digging like fiends. Larry and the team that had been searching for Bernie by the Bell Tree came over to assist with the rescue. It took some work to get the building off Anna, and involved a chain saw, but to the patrollers it seemed like they had her free within seconds.

Officially, Anna's rescuers cut her completely clear of the hole by 1:38, just over a half hour after finding her. There had been no shortage of manpower with shovels, so Bernard opted to stay close to Anna during the process, holding her hand the entire time. Severely dehydrated and closer to death than anyone, including Anna herself, realized, she drifted in and out of consciousness while the patrolmen dug her out. She talked a little, requesting a drink and asking if she could crawl out on her own, to which she received answers of no and no.

Lanny passed an oxygen mask down into the gap to Anna, which in the chaos of the moment was initially put on upside down. While digging, he kept up a constant stream of endearments to her: "We love you, we're so glad you're alive, we're coming to get you." At one point Anna responded with, "Okay, I'm hanging on."

When they pulled her from the opening, all of the tough rescue heroes had tears in their eyes. They gathered around her, affectionately hugging and kissing her. She looked beat up and worn out. Five days without food in the extreme cold had taken 20 pounds off Anna's five foot six, 135-pound frame, and she had a black eye where the avalanche had smacked her in the face. The injury was caused not by flying debris, but purely as a result of the sheer force of the wind and the snow. She had several scabs on her forehead where the pressure of the wind was so potent that it actually pulled her skin back and split it open.

When Anna had first regained consciousness after being knocked out by the air blast, she awoke to total blackness in a cocoon of snow and wood. Having less faith in her house than in the ski area, her initial thought was that there had been an explosion somewhere in her home. She heard blasting, likely what shook her out of her concussion, but she couldn't understand what the noise could be.

Despite intense head pain, Anna tried to find a way out, but the bench above her was pinned securely by the lockers. She twisted her body in the tight space, crawling as much as she could up into the wood lockers and clawing at them. There was no opening to the outside. Feeling around in the dark, in the bottom of one of the lockers Anna found a pack of matches with three matches left in it. When she lit the first one, she was able to peer through a crack and make out a lock high over her head. She couldn't make sense of that discovery at first, since she didn't have a lock at her house. Then she started to remember.

Even then, when Anna understood where she was, she still didn't know what had happened, and assumed that the bombs used for avalanche control had accidentally blown up inside the Summit Terminal Building. All the time she was under the snow, she never realized that an avalanche had caused the building to explode.

Anna was able to drag some clothes out of the lockers that had ripped open around her, and she pulled them over herself as best she could. She had no gloves or hat, since Frank had been holding them for her in his backpack. As cold as she was, Anna's feet seemed especially freezing to her, and she feared that they were severely frostbitten. The floor of her tomb was carpeted, and relatively dry. The sheer fluke of her lying on carpet under the bench, and not in a pool of icy water, likely saved her from dying of hypothermia. She couldn't sit up, but she could move her limbs slightly, and she was able to roll a bit. To try to help her circulation, she took off one cross-country ski boot at a time, massaged her numb foot as much as possible, and then put the boot back on. Even with that strategy, by the fourth day she had lost all feeling in her feet.

Anna slipped out of awareness and slept much of the time, but during tormented periods of wakefulness, she thought about her family and friends, especially Frank (who was, unknown to her, already dead). Throughout the five days she maintained a powerful tool of survival—in an incredible trick of memory suppression, she simply did not remember that Frank had been with her in the building. The moment she was rescued, the memory of their being together in the locker room flowed back in a torrent.

Despite her terror of being trapped, of dying in the cold, dark space, Anna's fierce endurance was coupled with her absolute faith that the ski patrol was coming to save her. She never gave up hope that her colleagues would rescue her, and despite the days that passed, she had no doubt that she was going to survive.

At the beginning of her confinement Anna ate as much snow as she could find, but her body temperature melted much of it. After a few days, there was nothing left. She would scratch at some snow and pretty soon she was just scraping at dust. As a result she was becoming increasingly weak and dehydrated, and she knew she couldn't hold out much longer. On the final day, she realized that she was very sick, her body shutting down, and she prayed that the patrolmen would find her soon. She remained convinced they would find her before she died, but her mind was looping on the thought that she wanted to be conscious to thank them.

In a state of near delirium, Anna didn't realize what was happening when Lanny and Bernard removed the final piece of timber above her. Lying on her back, she perceived a flash of light behind her head, but she was so far gone that she didn't process the concept that she was being rescued. She just saw snow wafting down into her hole and instinctively, she reached up to grab it.

As the patrolmen loaded Anna onto a stretcher, she asked them about Frank. They pretended they didn't know who she was talking about, and attempted to distract her by asking if she knew how long she had been missing. She was only off by a day. She had tried to keep track of time by counting when the ski patrol was bombing the mountain, and even though the avalanche control had been sporadic throughout the storm, she still calculated that she had been buried for about four days.

When the patrollers questioned Anna about her injuries, she just said that her head hurt a little and she couldn't feel her feet. They poked her left foot, clad only in a wool sock, and asked her if there was any sensation. They knew something was wrong when Anna, in confusion, suggested they take off her boot.

While Anna was being extricated, members of the grooming crew had snapped into action, flattening a makeshift helicopter pad over by the base of the tattered Kangaroo chairlift. On instructions not to land until Anna had been completely removed from the wreckage, the rescue helicopter had arrived and was hovering nearby. Bridget, who had abandoned her celebratory dance to keep a protective vigil near Anna, apparently realized that her find was about to be taken away to safety. Without warning, and before Roberta could restrain her, she leapt forward. In a moment of unadulterated possessiveness, Bridget licked Anna right across the face, oxygen mask and all, a kiss as only a German shepherd can give.

Like the Grinch gazing down over Whoville, Jim watched the scene unfold from high up above. He had earlier been dropped off by a helicopter at the top of the Buttress to analyze the fracture line of the avalanche up close. He was monitoring radio traffic while he worked, and he picked up something about rescuers having Anna. From his perspective looking down over the wreckage five days after the deadliest avalanche ever to strike a ski resort in North America, Jim was witness to the most surreal sight. He saw a Care Flight helicopter land to pick up a survivor.

While the patrolmen were loading Anna into the helicopter, all other movement on the ground came to a stop. The crowd, acting as one, remained utterly silent, intensely focusing on the act of Anna's transfer.

The Care Flight helicopter had landed at 1:50, and it left the ground at 1:53. As it lifted off, the silence was shattered.

Over the course of the previous five days, the emotions of Larry and Jim and all the rest of the ski patrolmen had transformed from joyful exuberance to cold, tired, sober fear. March 31 was a day they were prepared for, to the extent they could ever be prepared for such a loss, but the apparent futility, the thanklessness of what they had done in the days leading up to the disaster, and each day afterward as they found one dead body after another, had carved irreparable trauma into each of them.

Now here, at the end, there was gratification, wonder tangled with tragedy. In this moment, hope against reason had become faith fulfilled. The rescuers—ragged, unwavering heroes who ignored the cold and the fatigue and the danger to keep searching even when survival no longer seemed an option, to hope when there was no reason left to hope—were triumphant on this day.

As the helicopter took flight, the rescuers, drunk with relief and rapture, erupted into a collective and wholly spontaneous cheer that swept up to the top of the mountain, and the hands of every one of them reached to the sky in celebration.

TWENTY-ONE

Sometimes I have a nightmare that the snow
just keeps falling and falling and fills the
valley up to the top until everything and
everyone is buried, trapped beneath it.

—

Kate Ulberg

Yeah, I have that one too.

—

Wendell Ulberg, Kate's husband

Less than two hours after Anna was rescued, ski patrolmen found
Bernie's body, buried deep in the snow beneath the ski school Bell
Tree. The dogs had tried to search for him, but he was so frozen and
so far down that the scent was very faint. Bernie had his arms raised
above his head and one fist clenched, a sign to those who knew him
that he was fighting to the end.

He had been severely injured, with extensive head trauma, making it clear to the coroner that he had died almost instantly, either by
hitting a steel beam on his way out of the building, or by smashing

into the tree where he landed. He was about 150 feet from the Summit Terminal Building, approximately ten feet from where rescuers had located Beth. His avalanche beacon was discovered nearby.

The rest of the searchers were especially subdued while the patrolmen dug Bernie out. Once he was clear of the snow, all the patrolmen on-site circled around him to pay their respects. The reverence and compassion with which they moved him was a pure tribute to their leader. In a way it was fitting that Bernie was the last to be found, as if somehow the rescuers' time was meant to be spent looking for the others first. It almost seemed as if Bernie was watching over the people around him one final time, doing, even in death, whatever he could to try to protect and save them.

With Bernie located, the search effort was declared officially over. As soon as he was removed from the area, front-end loaders and other heavy equipment moved in to excavate and clear the scene, looking like Tonka Toys as they crawled over the massive piles of snow and debris. There were no other bodies uncovered in the parking lot, just about 30 employee vehicles, most of which had 50 or more mini-hammer dents on their roofs from the probe poles.

On the way to the hospital, above the whirring of the helicopter's rotors, Anna had been able to hear the roar of the rescuers' cheer. In response, she told the flight nurse that she wanted to go to the hospital in Truckee (Tahoe Forest Hospital), the one closest to the friends who had saved her. During the flight, the emergency personnel slit open Anna's jugular vein to get fluids into her as fast as possible. They called her "Annie" as they worked, and she was clearheaded enough to state that her name was Anna. The nurse responded that the press had been calling her Annie, the first time Anna got a sense of the enormity of the tragedy.

Anna's roommate Sandy had been in Nevada earlier that day, attending Beth's funeral. Homeless since being evacuated after the avalanche, she asked a friend to drive her to Alpine Meadows in hopes of getting back into her house or at least digging out her car. On the way she considered the dilemma of Frank's car, still blocking hers in the driveway. She wondered if Frank had left his car keys at the cabin before setting off for the resort with Anna, and if not, where they would possibly be at this point. Sandy's friend parked at the end of Alpine Meadows Road, by the deli, and Sandy walked down to the roadblock that was set up near the water district. There was a young deputy from the sheriff's office working the checkpoint. She pointed out the location of her house to him on his map, and the deputy seemed sincerely sorry to tell her that the area was still closed off. Defeated, Sandy thanked him and turned to go. She was already a few yards away when the young man apparently decided to take a shot at cheering her up. In a tone clearly meant to indicate good news, he passed along the latest search-and-rescue information.

"Oh, wait," he said. "Did you hear they found the girl?"

There was a beat, a long one, before Sandy turned back to him, leveled her voice, and asked, *"What* girl?"

For Sandy, the next little while was a dreamlike blur of desperately calling hospitals on the deli pay phone in an attempt to confirm the report. The emotions of her day had already been stretched to a near fracture point when, at the hospital, she passed through a surge of cameras and reporters to finally reunite with her roommate.

Anna's condition was actually much more serious than she, her family, or her doctors ever let on to the media covering the story around the world. Early on, a near-fatal concern was that toxins had leaked out of the cells in her feet and circulated in her blood to her kidneys. After about a week and a half, her kidneys and liver came close to failing.

Around the same time, one of Anna's IVs split open in the middle of the night, almost causing her to bleed to death. She was being given a variety of medications intravenously, some of them in an attempt to dissolve clots in her system and save her legs. At one point she had seven different IVs and pumps connected all over her body, including her hands and her femoral arteries. Even after more than a week, her doctors still had serious concerns about her dehydration, and she had a central venous catheter in her jugular vein to pump fluids and medicine into her system. When that line ruptured one night, she awoke to the feeling of liquid from her neck flowing out all over her body, her gown getting wetter by the second, her bedclothes soaked with warm venous blood. There was no question that she was bleeding out as she reached for the call button. The nurse walked into a horror show, with Anna drenched in fluids and bright red blood.

Anna recovered from the blood loss, but about a week after that, she had an apnea problem and simply stopped breathing one night. Her body continued to react against the poisons from gangrene, and once again her life was in jeopardy.

After about three weeks Anna was finally stabilized, and then the amputations began, a few toes at a time.

Upon her arrival at the hospital, Anna's feet were swollen to twice their normal size and all of her toes were shriveled and black. Her feet were always tented in her hospital bed so she couldn't see them, but a stream of friends who visited, including Sandy, weren't shy about cheerfully commenting on her "raisin toes."

When the rescuers found Anna, she had been wearing a ski boot on her right foot and a just wool sock on her left. Unbeknownst to Anna, having the boot off actually allowed better circulation, and may well have saved her left leg. Her right foot, which had been confined in the boot, wasn't healing as well.

Anna's doctors worked for almost two months to improve the circulation in her frostbitten feet. In her first surgery, all the toes on her right foot were taken off, as well as a couple on the left foot. The surgeons tried to cut back just far enough to find healthy bone, but she didn't have any. Another surgery took the anklebone of her right leg, destroyed from lack of blood flow.

In May, Anna lost all the toes on her left foot when it was amputated above the ball of the foot. Her doctors finally determined that the tissue in her right leg was dead and they couldn't save it. In the end, her right leg was amputated about seven inches below her knee.

Anna was released from the hospital in early June, 1982, in time to walk, with crutches, across the stage at UC Davis to accept her college diploma. She received a standing ovation. In the same graduation ceremony, Frank Yeatman was awarded his diploma posthumously, with the highest honors in his class.

Anna was back on skis, with a specially designed sports prosthesis on her right leg, by Christmastime of 1982. She returned to Alpine Meadows a year after the avalanche to support a handicapped ski race, where she skied down one of the slopes that had avalanched.

Since Anna's confinement under the snow, her voice has never been the same. In the hospital she almost completely lost the ability to speak, at times barely able to talk above a whisper. It came back to some extent, but due to some combination of the cold, or her screams, or overall trauma, her voice is forever huskier than it was before the avalanche.

The losses Anna suffered in 1982 affect her every day of her life, but she has resolved that the avalanche should never win, and she celebrates that she is alive. She is 48 now, married with two teenage children, Keith and Carissa. She lives in Mammoth Lakes, California, where she works as the host manager at Mammoth Mountain ski resort and still skis frequently.

Bridget's discovery of Anna resulted in a long-overdue awareness of dogs as invaluable search aids in an emergency, avalanche or otherwise, and significantly impacted the future of rescue-dog programs in the United States, in terms of funding as well as growth. New rescue groups started to develop around the country, and vulnerable ski resorts, including Alpine Meadows, began to keep rescue dogs on-site. Roberta Huber went on her last search with Bridget in 1984, just before Bridget died, at age 12. Roberta retired from searching when Bridget did.

Jeff Skover, who survived another near-death experience in a surfing accident in '99, was back skiing at Alpine Meadows within a few weeks of the avalanche. Married with three teenage daughters, he is now a sergeant/inspector for the San Francisco Police Department.

Frank Yeatman's parents have long retired and relocated from California to Florida. Initially Frank's father found it too painful to be around Anna, but he has come to accept that his son's death was not her fault. Frank's special connection to hawks has always stayed with his mom, now close to age 90. Whenever Marie Yeatman sees a hawk, she believes it is a sign from Frank, that he is sending it to remind her of him.

Beth Morrow's dad, John, couldn't bear to look at the mountains after he lost his daughter, especially when they were covered with snow. Two years later, he decided to face, and honor, her death by skiing downhill for the first time. He found that he shared Beth's love of the sport so much that he became a part-time ski instructor. John Morrow has frequently visited the scene of the tragedy at Alpine Meadows. As the Bell Tree where Beth (and Bernie) was found is now gone, when he arrives at the resort he first touches the monument memorializing the resort's employees at the top of Roundhouse lift, where Beth wrote much of her poetry. The plaque bears the Latin inscription *"Si monumentum eorum requiris, circumspice"* ("If you seek their monument, look around you"). Wherever Beth's dad is skiing, he always tries to be at the top of the mountain at 3:45 in the afternoon, and he thinks of his daughter as he skies down.

The National Ski Patrol set up an educational fund for Bernie's daughter, Kris, which was supplemented by donations from the Alpine Meadows ski patrol, the local and national avalanche community, and many other generous people associated with Alpine Meadows. She used the fund to help with both college and veterinary school costs. Kris works now as a veterinarian, a career rooted in the experience of her dad helping her nurse an injured bird back to health when she was a child.

After three years of paperwork, petitions, and public hearings, Jake Smith's brother, Dennis, convinced the U.S. Board on Geographic Names in Washington, D.C., to officially name a mountain after Jake above Lake Tahoe's Emerald Bay. Jake's Peak is a 9,187-foot mountain about a mile south of Rubicon Peak near Bliss State Park. Jake and Dennis had summited that mountain several times together, and it is close to the avalanche that occurred in January 1982 that had so deeply affected Jake. The peak lies in a wilderness area overlooking Lake Tahoe, the perfect location and the ideal tribute to a true mountain man.

Every day for a year and a half after Jake's death, Zach traveled from his home to Alpine Meadows looking for him. Finally out of kindness to Jake's loyal dog, Pam found a home for him farther away from his memories of his master. Each year since the avalanche, Pam returns to the bridge on Ginzton Road (now called Chalet Road) on March 31 to leave red roses for Jake.

To Dave Hahn's daughters, their dad's strength will always be frozen at age 46. Linda and Stephanie have each grown up to have two daughters of their own, and Dave lives on in the grandchildren he never survived to see. Dave's technological wizardry was so ahead of its time that without him in the world, it took decades for his invention—which can best be described as a prototype of the iPod—to be realized. For over a quarter century, Jeanne has kept the coins her husband had in his pocket the day he died.

Just as Katy Nelson was arriving home in Eureka after the avalanche, out of the car window she glimpsed a double rainbow, Laura's favorite, and she knew that it was Laura and Bud saying hello to her. To this day, every time a double rainbow appears, she thinks of the daughter and husband she lost.

Laura was buried on April 6, 1982, in the Gunne Sax–style dress her mom made for her eleventh birthday. Afterward, Laura's Girl Scout leader stopped over to bring Katy a ceramic egg that Laura had been making for her as an Easter present. On the lid Laura had painted "Mom," with a black line above the word and a rainbow arcing over the top. To Katy, it looks like a painting of Mom remaining down on earth while Laura, in the form of a rainbow, is up in the sky.

Katy still lives in the same house she shared with Bud and Laura, and each spring she sees the perpetually reseeding forget-me-nots that Laura planted with her so many years ago. Every year they come back to bloom in the gardens and fill in all the empty spaces, just like Laura's love does in her mother's heart.

When Katy and Eric first returned home from Alpine Meadows, Eric, just six years old, turned to his mom and said, "That wasn't a very good vacation, was it?" In the midst of her crippling grief, Katy realized at that moment that she had to be strong for her son. As he grew up, every so often she would see Bud in one of Eric's facial expressions or mannerisms. Now in his thirties, Laura's little student has conducted cholera research in Bangladesh and is currently enrolled in an MD/PhD program just like his dad.

The lawsuit filed against Alpine Meadows by the Nelson and Hahn families, alleging that the resort should have foreseen the magnitude of the avalanche and taken better safety precautions, went to trial in 1985. After a five-month trial at which most of the avalanche experts in the world testified for one side or the other—virtually resulting in a graduate-level class on avalanche prediction and safety—the jury, which deliberated for two and a half weeks, ultimately determined that Alpine Meadows was not liable for the tragedy.

Since the avalanche, the resort now makes attempts to close the parking lot in times of extreme avalanche danger, posting signs and putting up gates to warn the public. Over the years the ski area has tried many different kinds of signs and fences, but in the midst of a blizzard, they inevitably become hopelessly buried, blown over, or destroyed. The most effective method of keeping people out seems to be for the groomers to create huge snow berms to physically block the entrance.

The avalanche prompted other safety measures as well. The ski patrol now shoots the deeply entrenched snow on the slopes with more powerful artillery than it did in 1982. The Plan E avalanche control designation that was added after March 31, 1982, entails not merely closure, but a total evacuation of the resort. To date, it has never been put into play.

It is the nature of the avalanche control program for the patrollers to believe that they are taming the beast throughout the storm. The hope going forward is that their dedication and their bravery will not prevent them from recognizing—and admitting—when there is a threat that they are not able to control, a danger so extreme that it cannot be conquered.

The snowfall total for that ten-day storm in 1982 was over 14 feet, close to half of the average snowfall for an entire winter in the Sierra Nevada. Once it melted, when all of the millions of tons of snow were gone, somehow the whole thing seemed unreal, as if it had never happened. Looking back at the aftermath of the avalanche with the distance of even a few months, it seemed impossible that there had ever been such a deep snow and so many people dead beneath it.

In the end, the avalanche was responsible for smothering more lives than just those it took on March 31. Afterward, there was guilt and blame and depression and loss. Many people who had been on top of the avalanche trying to save those underneath ended up psychologically maimed for life. Whether or not they would have accepted help, in those days the rescuers weren't given the option. There was no counseling offered to them for post-traumatic stress, no therapy sessions to discuss survivor's guilt.

Many of the people involved in the search and rescue, primarily young men who had previously been searching only for themselves, were forced to grow up overnight. They had thought they were immortal, but nature battered them with proof that they were not. Others simply withdrew, their emotional growth forever stunted. Several of them brandished their self-destructiveness with drinking problems, drug abuse, and failed marriages.

To varying degrees, the tragedy touched everyone in the area. The mountain, while never predictable in the past, now began to seem almost sinister in its capriciousness. People felt a little more raw, a little less safe. The more romantic locals refer to the avalanche as "the day the mountain cried." Others are still haunted by images of that storm, tortured by visions of a snowfall that never stops.

Bob Blair and Jim Plehn returned to Alpine Meadows the following winter, but both of them had left the resort by the end of that season. They have both remained in the area.

Larry Heywood stayed at Alpine Meadows for the rest of his career, stepping into the void left by Bernie's death and Bob's departure. Larry became the patrol director, a position he held for 17 years, and was ultimately promoted to director of mountain operations. He retired in 2004 but still works as a snow and ski safety consultant and continues to lecture around the world as an expert on avalanche safety.

Tom Kimbrough and Lanny Johnson moved out of California to Salt Lake City, Utah, and Jackson Hole, Wyoming, respectively. Igor

O'Toole is living in San Francisco. Casey Jones continues to work as a ski patrolman at Alpine Meadows, as does Gary Murphy, the current avalanche forecaster.

Alpine Meadows itself seems to have survived the tragedy relatively unscathed. During the time of the rescue and the subsequent cleanup, nearby ski areas Squaw Valley, Heavenly Valley, Soda Springs, Boreal Ridge, and Northstar graciously honored Alpine Meadows' season passes. Incredibly, the resort reopened for its legendary spring skiing that year on April 10, the day before Easter, just ten days after the avalanche. The ski area was open for only half a day, in the pouring rain, so that the employees could attend Bernie's funeral, also in the pouring rain, that afternoon.

Bernie's memorial service ended up being moved from Christ the King Lutheran Church on Dollar Hill to the North Tahoe High School auditorium to accommodate more people. At Bernie's wake, a poem was read about his spirit still dancing on the ridgetop. The poet was anonymous, but the sentiment transcendent, comparing Bernie's incredible relationship with the mountain to a dance they shared, his death merely the result of the mountain bumping into him during one of the steps.

After the reopening, the public did not seem frightened off by the avalanche, and business was especially good at Alpine Meadows for the remaining weeks of that 1982 season. The mild spring weather, combined with all the fresh powder from the storm, drew in lots of skiers. There was also a certain contingent of people curious to see the scene of the devastation for themselves, as the debris from the Summit Terminal Building had not yet been removed from the site but merely pushed into a pile and fenced off.

It was just after the resort had reopened that spring that Larry, patrolling Wolverine Bowl early one morning, noticed a dark speck in the middle of the run. It was near the very top of the mountain, almost 8,000 feet high. He doubled back and skied over to examine the object that had caught his eye. It was a dead Saw-whet owl, perfectly preserved in the snow.

ACKNOWLEDGMENTS

My first thank-you goes to Fro, aka Robert Frohlich, who gave me this book in so many ways—the idea, the initial contacts, and the support along the way when I questioned the enormity of researching a decades-old event with so many sensitive issues and conflicting memories involved.

I am also deeply indebted to Larry Heywood, who was perpetually willing to get together with me to review the more technical aspects of the book and engage in long discussions about, for example, gelatin dynamite. My sincere gratitude as well to Jim Plehn, who taught me, among hundreds of other things, the difference between a snowflake and a pure stellar crystal and, over the course of many meetings in his cozy cabin in the mountains, forced me to become a tiny bit of the snow expert that he is. Should there be a misstatement of fact in the book concerning avalanche forecasting or control, the fault is mine alone and certainly not due to the efforts of my ever-patient consultants.

To the other heroic ski patrollers, rangers, rescue personnel, and Alpine Meadows employees I met with and spoke to over the course of my research, especially Bob Blair, Casey Jones, Igor O'Toole, Lanny Johnson, Tom Kimbrough, Gary Murphy, Mike Alves, Ray Overholt, Billy Patterson, Jeff Skover, Don Huber, Bob Moore, Werner Schuster, Sandy (Harris) Horn, Karen Strohmaier, Mary ellen Benier, Thom Orsi, Bernard (Coudurier) Savoy, Bob Blount, and Roberta (Huber) Ward—I am deeply appreciative of your cooperation not only in opening up to me about such a traumatic episode in your lives, but also in allowing me to continuously probe your memories of the details and timelines in order to get the story straight.

To the dozens of other people I interviewed who added invaluable perspectives to the story, most notably Tim Fitzpatrick, Kate and Wendell Ulberg, Larry Guinney, Barbara (Guinney) Schlumberger, Joan and Gene Conrad, and Kathy Heywood, and to the community of Alpine Meadows in general, thank you for letting me in.

Thank you to the many people who loved Jake—among them Bettigene, Dennis, Kathe, Pam, and Billy Davis—for sharing so many vivid stories and memories with me. To Beth's family, Frank's mom, and Bernie's daughter, thank you for granting me access to what special and extraordinary people your loved ones were. And to Jeanne and Katy, who have always viewed themselves as outsiders in the Alpine Meadows community even though their husbands and daughter lost their lives beneath its snow, I am more grateful than you will ever know. Through your willingness to welcome me into your homes and endure the anguish of reliving this most personal of tragedies, Dave, Bud, and especially Laura have become real to me, and hopefully to everyone who reads about them as well. From enduring endless follow-up questions to giving me extra fabric from the dress Laura was buried in, Katy in particular simply could not have done more to bring her family to life in these pages.

In addition, I owe an enormous thank-you to Anna, who described the pain of her ordeal, both under the snow and afterward, with a grace and poise that gave me a glimpse of the strength she called upon to survive.

I am also grateful to my agent, Scott Hoffman, not just for believing in the story but for never doubting my ability to tell it, and to my editor, Nick Simonds, for his insistence on making this a better book.

My final thanks goes to my family—my young children, Tess, Griffin, and Owen, who inspired me throughout the process with their constant desire to tell strangers how proud they were of their mom for writing her "snow book," and my husband, Miles. The contribution my husband made to this book cannot be summed up by simply calling him a sounding board or an editor—he was both of those things and more, and in the final few months of writing he was a partner willing to tolerate my inability to engage in a conversation that didn't somehow circle back to this disaster. For the past three years he lived through my insistence on sharing the obsession I developed with the various life-changing quirks of fate that occurred on the day of the avalanche. He read the pages as I wrote them, and then again and again, tirelessly providing detailed feedback, until one time he just said, "It's beautiful," and I knew then that he was either exhausted or that I had gotten it right. To everyone touched by the tragedy of March 31, 1982, and beyond, I sincerely hope that it is the latter.

ABOUT THE AUTHOR

Jennifer Woodlief has worked as a reporter for *Sports Illustrated* as well as an assistant district attorney and a CIA case officer with a top-secret clearance. Her first book, *Ski to Die: The Bill Johnson Story,* was published in 2005 and optioned by Warner Bros. for a movie. She lives in Tiburon, California, with her husband and three children.